Joseph Morris and the Saga of the Morrisites

(revisited)

C. LeRoy Anderson

2010
Utah State University Press

Logan, Utah 84322-7800

Some of the material contained in Part IV was originally published in *Montana, the Magazine of Western History* 26 (October 1976).

Library of Congress Cataloging-in-Publication Data

Anderson, C. LeRoy.
Joseph Morris and the saga of the Morrisites, revisited / C. LeRoy Anderson.
p. cm.
Includes bibliographical references (p.) and index.
ISBN 978-0-87421-787-2 (pbk. : alk. paper) – ISBN 978-0-87421-788-9
1. Church of the First Born (Morrisites)–History. 2. Mormon Church–History. 3. Morris, Joseph, 1824-1862. 4. Church of the First Born (Morrisites)–Biography. 5. Mormons–Biography. 6. Morrisite War, 1862. I. Title.
BX8680.M64A83 2010
289.3'3–dc22

2010013163

To Jody, Elaine, and Cathy

Contents

Preface

Nineteenth-century America witnessed a great revival of interest, at times fervent, in Christ's Second Advent. Although the Christian movement had been built on millennial eschatology, many Christian sects developed a wide variety of specific expectations about the nature, time, and place of the Second Advent. Dozens, if not hundreds, of sects announced their own particular version of that great event. The premillennialists believed that Christ would appear prior to the time that a perfect society existed, while the post-millennialists preached that a perfect society must be established before the Second Coming. Thousands tried to set their lives in order so that they might personally share in the rapture. Some abandoned their professions, some gave all their possessions to the poor, and still others gave up friends and family to travel great distances and join the millennial throng.

Among the most colorful and enduring of the nineteenth-century millennial sects was the Mormon church. Mormons expected to build a great temple in the City of Zion as a fitting abode for the resurrected Jesus, but their abrupt expulsion from Missouri and Illinois removed them from the designated land of Zion and placed the seeming imminence of the Second Advent into the indefinite future. Their expulsion and migration to the Rocky Mountains disillusioned many adherents, who refused to take the long and problematic journey under the leadership of Brigham Young. They either joined with other dissidents who stayed behind and developed their own version of Mormonism or simply dropped out of the Mormon movement entirely.

In 1857, ten years after the first Mormons came into the Great Salt Lake Valley, Joseph Morris began writing a series of letters to Brigham Young announcing his own prophetic calling and proposing that Young retain the presidency of the church, but relinquish the role of prophet, seer, and revelator to God's *true* prophet, Morris himself. Extensive quotations from Morris's letters to Brigham Young are included in this volume. They are essential to gaining greater insight into the mind of Morris as well as to helping us understand the rather one-sided exchange.

This work chronicles the life and death of Joseph Morris and traces the movement he initiated from its inception in 1857 to its ultimate demise nearly one hundred years later. Although Joseph Morris was originally a devout Mormon, his premillennialist views, fertile imagination, and penchant for claiming to communicate frequently with supernatural beings soon placed him at odds with local and regional Mormon leaders and eventually with Brigham Young himself.

Although the Morrisites were victimized on many occasions, they often contributed to their own victimization. They not only fell victim to the pervasive religious fanaticism in Utah Territory during the latter half of the nineteenth century but were victimized by both Mormon and Morrisite leaders. One might conclude that they were also victimized by the federal government, which appeared to be more interested in protecting the interests of outsiders than those of either Mormons or Mormon dissidents.

Yet, in all fairness we must remember that the Mormon-Morrisite conflict occurred while the Civil War was going badly for the Union, and the federal government had few resources that could be spared. Furthermore, the Mormons were still struggling to develop their own unique place in the American religious scene, and three decades of severe persecution had rendered them intolerant of either outside interference or internal dissent. Besides, religious extremism was not unusual at that time, either in Utah territory or in most places throughout the United States.

In that sense, the story of the Morrisites illustrates the profound truth that a people, to a great extent, are victims of the preoccupations of their entire culture. Perhaps we may learn something from the nineteenth-century preoccupation with religion that will help us better understand twentieth-century social problems.

The first edition of this book was published in 1981. A second, slightly enlarged edition was published in 1988. Since that time, some additional sources related to the Morrisites have come to my attention, and some of that material is incorporated in this third edition. These materials include a photograph of Joseph Morris which I had not previously seen and a copy of the handwritten "Life History of George Morris," brother of Joseph Morris. These are presented courtesy of LaRee Hill Pehrson of Magna, Utah, great-granddaughter of George Morris. In addition, Val Holley, of Washington, D.C., sent me a copy of a letter written by a participant in the Morrisite War that was published in the *Brooklyn Eagle* on February 6, 1863. Neal Chase of Missoula, Montana, also gave me a copy of a newspaper account of the Morrisite War, which appeared in the June 19, 1892, *San Francisco Chronicle.*

Since then I have received two published scholarly articles, written by Professor Robert Balch and several of his students, about a messianic sect, based in Missoula, Montana, claiming a direct connection between their organization and the Morrisite movement. I also obtained copies of three sizable pamphlets, written by leaders of the same sect. Dr. Leland Jensen,

Neal Chase, and John Aardent authored them. The latter five sources constitute the principal materials from which I derived the penultimate chapter of this edition. As I completed this work, Eric Rogers provided valuable insights and facilitated the acquisition of important photos. I also acknowledge and thank my wife, Joanne ("Jody") Rhoads Anderson for her continual support and indispensable assistance in electronic preparation of this manuscript.

In view of this recent messianic movement that claimed a debt to the Morrisites and the insights provided by the "Life History of George Morris," I am profoundly grateful that Utah State University Press is publishing this enlarged and enriched edition of the Morrisite story. I wish to thank Executive Editor John Alley for his efforts in this behalf.

The story of the Morrisites is fascinating in its own right. It is a small slice of Americana that deserves to be preserved. To enhance this preservation, my earlier research collection on the Morrisites is housed in the Merrill-Cazier Library's Special Collections Department at Utah State University. I am pleased that this material, much of which is available nowhere else, is available to anyone seriously interested in the Morrisites. Perhaps this collection is already being put to use, for at least ten presentations, papers, journal articles, and books referring all or in part to the Morrisite movement have appeared within the past two decades.

C. LeRoy Anderson
Missoula, Montana
March 2010

Introduction In Prospect

Who Were the Morrisites?

In his classic novel, *Nineteen Eighty-Four,* George Orwell describes an anti-utopian society called Oceania.[1] One of the most important divisions within the government of Oceania is the Ministry of Truth, and in the Ministry of Truth is the Records Department. It is the business of the Records Department to see that reports of events are properly edited so as to appear congruent with governmental policy at any given time. Since Oceania's governmental policy is anything but consistent, the Records Department is primarily occupied with deleting, adding, rewriting, or otherwise manipulating its documents. The department's control over government records and the media is so complete that with impunity it can manufacture history to suit the needs of government. Or it can literally erase all records of persons or events so that nothing of them remains—so that they have no history and consequently (for all practical purposes) no existence whatsoever.

Perhaps only in fiction could such complete manipulation of history be carried out. Yet the disturbing fact remains that persons, events, or even entire societies may be lost to history and might just as well have never existed if no written recollections, artifacts, or other records about them are known.

Although not quite such an extreme case, the Morrisites came very close to real as well as historical extinction during the hundred years following their organization. Whether by design, ignorance, or oversight, histories of times, places, and events of which the Morrisites were a part completely overlooked them or afforded them little more than a footnote. Yet the Morrisite movement was, in fact, a matter of some concern to the nineteenth-century Mormons and did have its own impact on the history of the West.

The Morrisite movement acquired its name from that of its principal leader, Joseph Morris, an English convert to Mormonism who migrated to

1 George Orwell, *Nineteen Eighty-Four* (New York: Harcourt, Brace and Company, 1949).

Utah in 1853. By 1857 he had gained something of a reputation in the Provo area as a fanatic ne'er-do-well who was openly critical of certain Mormon doctrines and local church leaders. The leaders, in turn, censured him and removed him from the office of teacher in the church.

Soon Morris became convinced that God had spoken to him and had selected him to be a prophet. Before long he was preaching that it was his destiny to supersede Brigham Young—to become prophet, seer, and revelator of the Church of Jesus Christ of Latter-day Saints.

In this respect Joseph Morris was not entirely unique, for numerous contenders had emerged from time to time among the Mormons intent upon wresting the church leadership for themselves or establishing a following of the disaffected. This had been especially true around the time of the death of Joseph Smith, the first Mormon prophet, in Illinois in 1844, when no fewer than six factions developed.[2] Brigham Young assumed presidency of the largest faction in 1847 and was chiefly responsible for establishing the Mormons in the Rocky Mountains.

Brigham Young's success at colonization and attracting converts so overshadowed the efforts of the other contending leaders that he became regarded by most Mormons and non-Mormons alike as *the* leader of Mormondom. Yet he never was able to bring *all* Mormons into his fold. And even in the Great Basin, where his rule was virtually supreme, his leadership was occasionally questioned even before the appearance of Joseph Morris. Nevertheless, Morris began his campaign for spiritual leadership at a time when the Brighamite Mormons were experiencing numerous political and spiritual crises that at the very least made Young's leadership less absolute than it had been at any time since arriving in the Rocky Mountains ten years earlier.

By 1857 the Mormons were established in much of the Great Basin, and their influence was felt from St. Louis on the east to San Bernardino, California, on the west and from the Salmon River country of Idaho to the lightly watered valleys of Arizona. The Brighamite Mormons had literally retreated to the mountains from the more populous East and Midwest, where they had endured numerous acts of persecution and forced expulsion. In the West they hoped to escape persecution, develop their own way

2 In addition to the followers of Brigham Young, factions developed under the leadership of Lyman Wight, Charles B. Thompson, Samuel Brannan, James J. Strang, and Sidney Rigdon. From these and other factions emerged an organization some years later called the Reorganized Church of Jesus Christ of Latter Day Saints. Its leader was the son of the original prophet, Joseph Smith. Also known as Josephites, this second largest faction is headquartered in Independence, Missouri. In 2001 its official name was changed to the Community of Christ.

of life, and gain both temporal and spiritual salvation. Above all else they believed they were the children of God, a chosen people whose destiny it was to soon return to Missouri where they would build a great city with a magnificent temple, thus opening the way for establishing the Kingdom of God on earth. As a devout Mormon, Joseph Morris shared this belief, and he came to believe that his personal role in ushering in the Kingdom of God was unique and far superior to that of Brigham Young.

The characteristic setting the Morrisite movement apart from most of the other Mormon schisms was that Morris tried, with some success, to establish his following in the very heart of Brighamite territory. By 1862 he had organized a communal settlement of several hundred followers on the banks of the Weber River within thirty miles of Salt Lake City and was preaching in open defiance of Brigham Young. Furthermore, he became more and more disdainful of compliance with civil law. In June 1862 the Morrisites were drawn into armed conflict with a territorial posse comprised entirely of Mormons, and because the attention of the rest of the nation was riveted upon the war between the Union and the Confederacy, the conflict ran its course with no immediate attention or intervention from outside Utah Territory. Since the Morrisites were outnumbered in the territory by some forty to one, and since they possessed few military resources, the outcome was never in doubt. After three days of resistance, the Morrisite settlement was overrun, Morris and several of his followers were killed, and the remainder were soon scattered to the winds.

The Morrisite males who had forcefully engaged in the Mormon Morrisite conflict were indicted for resistance or more serious crimes, stood trial, and several were convicted. They were pardoned by Stephen S. Harding, the new territorial governor, in 1863, only three days after the trial. The trial and pardoning gained more national attention than the conflict itself had. It ultimately led to the dismissal of the federal judge who had heard the case, the replacement of the governor, and the exodus of the Morrisites from Utah.

For all practical purposes the Morrisites were without effective or unified leadership following the Weber River conflict. In the late summer of 1862, however, George Williams of Salt Lake City came forward as the first serious candidate seeking to fill the vacancy created by Morris. He claimed to be the Prophet Cainan and that God had told him to assume the Morrisite leadership. Williams met with some success between 1863 and 1883, but he was opposed by William Davies in Montana, John Livingstone and John Parson in Nevada, and George Dove in California, all of whom had been closely associated with Joseph Morris. George Williams probably attracted the greatest following of any of the Morrisite contenders, but neither he nor any other would-be prophets was ever able to unify the movement as it had been under Joseph Morris. The movement remained factional, but it survived more than ninety years after the death of Morris. The last official Morrisite leader was George Johnson of Deer Lodge, Montana, who died in 1954.

The Significance of the Morrisite Movement

Perhaps the most important reason for studying the Morrisites is because they were active participants in nineteenth-century America's great millennial dream. Like so many others of that time, they believed that America was a land chosen of God and that it was chosen above all other lands. They expected the imminent Second Advent of Christ to take place in their midst and that He would cleanse the earth of evil and set up a perfect society that would enjoy peace and prosperity for a thousand years. The Morrisites expected to play a leading part in that society, and they tried diligently to prepare themselves to be worthy participants.

Secondly, the Morrisites were relatively few in number, yet they lived in a sparsely settled region where even a few might make a difference. In 1862 and 1863 they severely disrupted Utah politics, and echoes of the Mormon-Morrisite conflict reached the nation's capital. Because of the Morrisites and their conflict with the Mormons, a governor and federal judge were expelled. Furthermore, the election of Utah's representative to Congress in 1863 was the direct result of his role in the Mormon-Morrisite conflict. And from time to time over the next seventeen years, law suits and criminal trials associated with the Morrisite affair were processed through the Utah courts. One prominent Mormon participant was indicted for murder, stood trial, and was ultimately acquitted.

Brigham H. Roberts, prominent Mormon historian, concluded that the Morrisite incident allowed anti-Mormon malice the opportunity to make of it an occasion of "rank offending" on the part of the Mormon leaders. Furthermore, he noted that the pardoning by Governor Harding had the effect of linking that affair "with the series of events which constantly kept the Latter-day Saints in a state of irritation against the United States federal officers in the territory."[3]

Thirdly, the Morrisites were among the earliest settlers in parts of Idaho, Nevada, and Montana, and many of their descendants remain there still. Theirs is a heritage worth preserving.

Fourthly, until recently few serious or objective scholars have given much attention to the Morrisites. Most accounts are either presented by committed adherents or by equally committed opponents. It is time that a fair description and scholarly analysis of the movement be presented.

---

3 Brigham H. Roberts, *A Comprehensive History of the Church of Jesus Christ of Latter-day Saints,* 6 vols. (Salt Lake City, Utah: Church Deseret News Press, 1930), 5:39.

Fifthly, Americans in general and scholars in particular have usually been far more interested in winners than losers. We often root for the underdog, but if the underdog fails to triumph, our support soon flags. Yet in order to understand success, it is of some importance to also understand failure. In many respects the Morrisite movement paralleled the development of the Mormons. Yet the Mormons grew and flourished; the Morrisites withered and died. By juxtaposing and comparing these two historical case studies we might gain greater insight into the processes that constitute successful social movements.

In any case, this study faithfully traces the developmental history of the Morrisite movement from its beginning to its end. Such tracing is not common in the literature.

Sixthly, although many millennial dreams were built and shattered in the nineteenth century, they did not cease at that time. Many Americans still believe in the ultimate triumph of good over evil and in the creation of a perfect society. As we enter the third millennium after Jesus, Christian eschatology suggests to many that the end is near, that the time of rapture is at hand, that Christ has or soon will return in His glory. The Mormons believe we are living in the last days; so did the Bo and Peep Flying Saucer People; so do the Adventists and the Jehovah Witnesses. And the Guyana Colony of Jim Jones grimly reminds us that those who prophesy the end may indeed be instrumental in bringing it about.

The Morrisite movement commenced over a century and one-half ago and was characteristic of the times. Movements very much like it are not uncharacteristic today.

Finally, the Morrisite saga is filled with idealism, drama, and pathos. It is a story worth telling.

Emergence from Oblivion

Sometimes luck, chance, fate, or some unanticipated juxtaposition of circumstances opens up an entirely new vista. This was how I was introduced to the Morrisites. Although for many years I had been something of a student of Mormon history, prior to the late 1960s my only knowledge of the Morrisites was a short episode portrayed in Vardis Fisher's work of fiction, *Children of God*, where Brigham Young was visited by a shaggy, dirty, fanatic Joseph Morris who babbled about his prophetic calling and exhorted Young to repentance. Young summarily dismissed him, and Fisher did likewise.[4] My curiosity was not excited.

However, in 1967 Robert Johnson, one of my graduate students in sociology, remarked one day that he had acquired some old religious books

4 Vardis Fisher, *The Children of God* (New York: Vanguard Press, 1939)

and papers while seeking antiques in an attic in Deer Lodge, Montana. He asked if I would be interested in them, since they were of no interest to him. I replied I would be, and he soon brought to me two sizable cardboard boxes filled with an assortment of letters, pamphlets, books, and ledgers. Initially I had little curiosity about the contents, but after some time I began to sort through the materials and soon found my interest growing. Among other things, I found a copy of *The Spirit Prevails,*[5] Joseph Morris's massive book of revelations; *Gems of Inspiration,*[6] a pamphlet compiled by John R. Eardley containing selected writings of the prophets Joseph Morris and George Williams; some copies of letters written from George Williams to the Saints in Montana; and some ledgers referring to the Morrisite organization in Montana.

Both *Gems of Inspiration* and *The Spirit Prevails* contain short histories of the Morrisites that excited my interest and stirred my imagination considerably. Consequently, I asked Robert Johnson to give me the name of someone in Deer Lodge who might know more about the Morrisites. Following his lead I contacted Raymond Johnson of Deer Lodge who directed me to Mrs. George (Julia) Staffensen. She had no documentary material, but knew a great deal about the Morrisites in Montana, inasmuch as her father, Andrew Hendrikson, had been one of the last Morrisite leaders in Deer Lodge.[7] She also directed me to her brother, Henry Hendrikson, then in his nineties, who lived in Missoula. Upon interviewing Henry Hendrikson, I found that he had retained a box of Morrisite materials belonging to his father. He consented to let me photocopy the material and gave me permission to publish it. The largest proportion of documentary data about the Montana Morrisites came from that source, since it contained several ledger books filled with copies of letters from the Prophet George Williams, two books of minutes from the Race Track Morrisite congregation, and organizational records from Omaha and Council Bluffs dating back to 1869.

From my interviews with Henry Hendrikson and Mrs. Staffensen, I was led to numerous knowledgeable persons in Missoula, Deer Lodge, Anaconda, and Butte. In Butte I interviewed Spencer Tripp, grandson of John R. Eardley, who graciously supplied me with information about his grandfather. I also received important information from Mrs. Harvey (Helen)

5 Joseph Morris, *The Spirit Prevails: Containing the Revelations, Articles, and Letters Written by Joseph Morris* (San Francisco: George S. Dove and Company, 1886).

6 John R. Eardley, *Gems of Inspiration: A Collection of Sublime Thoughts by Modern Prophets* (San Francisco: Joseph A. Dove, printer, 1899).

7 A native of Jyland, Denmark, Andrew Henrikson was born in July 1843. He migrated to America about 1861 and later changed his name to Hendrikson. For consistency, the spelling will be Hendrikson, except in quotes where the original spelling is retained.

Eliason of Deer Lodge who directed me to acquaintances in Soda Springs, Idaho. Mrs. Lula Barnard of Soda Springs provided me with several photographs and information about the Morrisite settlement in Soda Springs.

In 1969 Larry Halford, one of my Ph.D. students, became interested in the Morrisites and eventually wrote his dissertation about them. He and I collaborated in archival research and in writing two articles. I did research numerous times on the Morrisites in the L.D.S. archives in Salt Lake City and received excellent cooperation there. The county clerk and recorder at Walla Walla, Washington, was most helpful in providing information about William Davies. During my sabbatical leave in 1977 I obtained valuable information from the Bancroft Library at the University of California, Berkeley, and once more at the L.D.S. archives in Salt Lake City.

One of my most delightful interviews was in 1975 with Agnes Just Reid, author and poet. In her pioneer home near Blackfoot, Idaho, she told me of her grandfather, George Thompson, a close associate of and successor to the Prophet George Williams. She also allowed me to copy several Morrisite-related materials and put me in contact with Everett L. Cooley at the University of Utah. Professor Cooley provided me with photographs of George Thompson, George Williams, and John R. Eardley and granted me access to other valuable Morrisite materials.

From two nondescript cardboard boxes emerged the beginning of the Morrisite saga. I tried for over a decade to track down every bit of data available. This work represents a distillation of that data, and a large portion of it is based upon sources that heretofore have been unavailable and/or unknown. Since many of the sources referred to in this work are not readily available to the reader, I have at times quoted extensively to preserve the substance as well as the flavor of the material. In this regard a special note should be made concerning the letters of Joseph Morris to Brigham Young. Many of the originals are in the archives of the L.D.S. Church Historical Department in Salt Lake City. I would have preferred to quote them verbatim; unfortunately, their complete lack of punctuation, erratic capitalizations, and unique spellings render them almost unintelligible without careful editing. Therefore, I have edited all quotations from those letters and have given careful attention to make them readable without changing their content or meaning. The following are examples of unedited excerpts from one of the letters dated "Aprel the 20, 1860":

> behold verily verily i say unto you prepare yourself to go fourth to deliver my people for the set time as now Come for i have heard the prayers and the gronings of mine aflicted people and i will now Come hout of my hiding place to there defence and i will give them the victery over their henemies i have sent a warning voice unto the Chief shepherds of my flock and...

The letter continues for about 400 words without any punctuation or paragraphing. On the fourth handwritten page it continues:

> thou hart moses the Leagal hare to use it and no per son on the hearth shall use it but they self behold i am the eternal father and i testify unt those whome this revelation may Concern that i have sent my son Jesus Christ to make theese things known unto my servant Joseph i now had no more i am he that houlds in mine hands the keys of death and hell even Jesus Christ even so amen and amen

Despite the peculiarities of Joseph Morris's letters, they are logically consistent and understandable when carefully studied. Whether or not Brigham Young bothered to scrutinize them carefully enough to understand them is unknown. More than likely he found them too difficult to read and dismissed them without ever knowing fully what they contained. At any rate, they seem not to have interested him much.

In addition to Morris's letters, I have tried to bring together the many disparate parts of the Morrisite saga and to present the entire story thoroughly and fairly. And I have taken into account recent contributions of others. In this pursuit, I discovered that the influence of the Morrisites extended much closer to the present day than I had previously anticipated. Chapter 16, "The Deer Lodge Jesus," gives a brief account of a Montana millennial sect that seized upon the prophecy of George Williams, aka Cainan, designating Deer Lodge as the site of the Second Advent. A century after that prophecy was made, this sect claimed that their leader was the reincarnated Jesus and that he fulfilled to the letter the words of Williams. The case for their connection to the Morrisites was laid out in three of their major pamphlets and in several news releases. Although the connection to the Morrisites is more tenuous than they have asserted, their alleged attachment to the Morrisite story is an example of how, under certain circumstances, a myth may in a short time become standard, institutional doctrine.

The contents of two brown boxes started me on this research odyssey more than four decades ago. The results have been as unexpected as enlightening. I hope the reader will also find a measure of enlightenment in the story of the Morrisites.

I *The Making of a Prophet*

1 Letters from Obscurity

In 1857, the tenth anniversary of the arrival of the Latter-day Saints (Mormons) in the Rocky Mountains, a series of events was about to unfold that would ultimately change the destiny of the church, the territory, and the Mormon people.

The great Mormon "reformation" begun the year before had continued into the summer. And every Saint was expected to repent of his sins, be rebaptized, and renew his covenants to uphold and sustain the church and its leaders—to consecrate himself to the work and glory of the Kingdom of God.

The Saints in the territory now numbered upwards of 40,000, and, despite the specter of polygamy, the possibility of statehood was being actively explored. Yet strong and bitter feelings existed toward non-Mormons and certain federal officials. Open conflict had occurred from time to time, the most serious of which was a shocking tragedy in September that left over 120 members of a wagon train dead at Mountain Meadows in west-central Utah.

Much of the tension and hostility that produced the Mountain Meadows affair was fostered by the presence on the Wyoming plains of a large military force authorized by the United States government to enforce "obedience" from the Mormon people. In order to resist this military force, the Mormons called home their foreign missionaries, abandoned many of their outlying colonies, and greatly restricted immigration to "Zion." During the late summer and autumn of 1857, the Mormons prepared their defenses.

To further complicate matters, Alfred Cumming, recently of St. Louis and a former mayor of Augusta, Georgia, had been appointed governor on July 30 to succeed Brigham Young. However, Young, president of the Mormon church, refused to acknowledge him, and by late November the Utah Territory found itself with two governors—an unofficial one in Salt Lake City recognized by the territorial citizenry and an official one at Camp Scott with no local constituency.

Amidst these critical circumstances it is hardly surprising that a curious letter dated December 7, 1857, addressed "to si exelency Governor young" and signed by an obscure territorial citizen named Joseph Morris, received scant attention from the church leader. There is no evidence that Brigham Young answered this letter, but neither did he entirely ignore it. For penciled boldly on the letter's margin are three cryptic words: "He's weak minded."[1]

Although Joseph Morris received no reply from Governor Young, he was undeterred. Over the following three years he addressed more than a dozen letters to Young, yet apparently not one received an answer. Young did not take the letters seriously, for he frequently made disparaging remarks on their margins. Nonetheless, the letters were remarkable. They were couched in a grandiose style, yet were so ungrammatical and poorly spelled as to make them almost unintelligible. At first glance they could be quite justifiably dismissed as the incoherent mutterings of someone with even less mental than literary ability. Yet when taken together, the letters display a certain coherence, unity, and creativity that belies their unceremonious dismissal by Brigham Young. Although Young did not take Morris seriously in 1857, within a few short years Morris produced hundreds of pages of revelations, founded a church in the very center of Mormondom, and attracted hundreds of followers who accepted him (at Young's expense) as prophet, seer, and revelator of the Mormon church.

Joseph Morris was deeply troubled by his own domestic and religious problems in 1857, but his near illiteracy made it difficult for him to communicate these problems to Brigham Young. The letter of December 7 fervently begged Young to consider Morris's complaints against certain church authorities, most specifically James C. Snow, president of the Provo Stake of the L.D.S. church, who Morris believed had wronged him. Although not entirely clear, the letter also alluded to Morris's appointment as a prophet. He wrote: "Dear sir, according to my impressions the time of my deliverance has come and as I have born the sins of those men for almost eleven months, I think that it is only right that I should appear before the public as I am, and that they should appear as they are."[2]

---

1 Since Brigham Young had one or more secretaries who might have read the letters of Joseph Morris and since others might have had access to them over the years, there is no definitive proof that marginal comments such as "He's weak minded" or "Balderdash" were actually written by Young. However, lacking counterevidence, and inasmuch as the letters were addressed to Young, I am accepting him as the author of the marginal comments. In any case, the comments are more interesting than crucial to the analysis.

2 The letters of Joseph Morris are almost entirely written in lower case, including the personal pronoun "I." They are also devoid of punctuation. Misspellings are frequent, and many words are run together or broken into peculiar segments. For the purpose of clarity I have edited most quotations in the text to conform reasonably well to standard English usage, although many of the

Accompanying Morris's letter to Brigham Young was a copy of a lengthy letter addressed to James C. Snow also dated December 7, 1857. Although the ending of that letter is missing, the extant part details the wrongs Morris believed he had suffered at the hands of the church authorities, wrongs that left him discredited and impoverished. The letter to Snow also sought to establish Morris's own steadfastness and propriety. Taken out of historical context, it appears very much like the ramblings of someone psychologically disturbed. However, given the temper of the times and especially the spirit of the Mormon "reformation," which had been at its height only months before, the letter to Snow might be viewed as a desperate attempt on Morris's part to clear his name of the many allegations raised against him. Clearly Morris was a religious man, and he wanted to do what he felt was right. He was especially resentful that he had been cut off from the Mormon church without the benefit of a trial and that his several attempts at matrimony had failed—primarily as a result of intervention from church authorities. To bolster his claims to righteousness, he went through the long list of questions asked of those in the reformation, all of which he answered properly, at least to his own satisfaction.

Morris's detailed account of two of his attempts at matrimony are of considerable interest and explain in part his growing resentment toward the Mormon hierarchy.

> I moved from American Fork to Provo with Thomas Smart. Soon after I came to that place I fell in company with Bishop Duke, [and] after having a little conversation with him he advised me to get married.
>
> I felt resolved to take his counsel [and] shortly afterward I fell in company with a young lady named Fanney Nash who came one evening along with her father and mother to Mr. Fisher's. Having taken a fancy to her I went out the next morning and spoke to her father concerning the matter. [I] told him that I had been making some preparations for getting married and that I had taken a fancy to his daughter and that I should like to become fully acquainted with her. He then spoke to me and said that he was going to move to a house a little ways off and . . . that I was at liberty to come and see them.
>
> Accordingly I did so. I then gave him a short history of my proceedings in domestic life. He appeared quite satisfied with my course [of action] and gave me a good recommendation to his daughter, saying that I had never varied in my statements when they were made several times over. He then felt desirous for me to speak to his daughter on the subject . . . .
>
> Accordingly I did so and she was satisfied and [became] engaged with me. I then told her that I was ready to be married forthwith, but she

misspellings have been retained. Bracketed material is added for editorial clarification. The originals may be found in the Archives, Historical Department, Church of Jesus Christ of Latter-day Saints, Salt Lake City, Utah.

desired for us to wait for a few days longer—until they had moved into another house. . . . she said that I need not fear for she would never give her word to another man.

I then . . . purchased bedding and wheat and other articles suitable for the circumstance and brought them to her father's house expecting every day to get married. . . . [But] Deminicus Carter came into the house and lead her away and tried to destroy my character to her or lessen me in her estimation.

I went to him with a written [contract of] engagement that was between her and myself and read it to him and asked him to leave her alone. But I suppose it mattered not to him whether she was engaged or not or who she belonged to. David-like he saw her and he must be with her.

After that I was counseled again by Bishop Duke and very much urged . . . to get married. . . . being a Block Teacher, on my travels I visited . . . [the] house [of a man named] Thomas. He told me that there was a fresh family that had come into his house which consisted of an old lady, two sons and one daughter. He also told me that there was trouble in the family in consequence of the daughter being determined to go to the city.

Being apprised of this trouble, I considered that I had a right to find out the reason [for] it, and settle it if possible. . . . I went in and saw the old lady and she appeared down spirited in consequence of her husband [having died] on the plains and her daughter wishing to leave her. . . . [I asked] her to send for her [daughter] in [order] that I might know the reason why she was determined to leave her mother.

I asked her the reason why she wished to go to the city. She said that she [was] engaged to go and assist John Hokeley to teach school. I then asked her if that . . . [was the only reason]. She said, partly. I then asked her if she had made a covenant for courtship or marriage; and she said that she had not.

...Both of them... [gave] me the impression that she .. . [had become] engaged to assist this person to teach school without the consent of her mother. . I considered that according to the order of this Church . . . no young lady, with living parents, has a right to enter into any [agreement] with any man . . . without first getting their consent. I counseled her under these considerations to remain with her mother.

I, myself being so [much] urged upon to get married, and being satisfied, according to her... words, that she had no engagement, I considered that I had a right to form an acquaintance with her...I did so, and... [later] I found out her feelings toward me, I asked her mother for her. She said, "yes, she could please herself."

I then considered that I had full liberty to court and marry her, having [gained] proper consent from all quarters. Accordingly I did so.

About three days after our marriage hell broke out. . . . James Snow and his associates made her believe that I had married her against her

> will. Allick Williams and another man [named] Windsor went to her and gave her counsel against me, which caused her to leave me.
>
> Nothing would satisfy her after that but a bill [of divorcement]. She then went and filed an affidavit against me, stating that I had unlawfully obtained her to be my wife by using an influence from the devil. This affidavit was brought to me by Allick Williams. . . . and a number of others.
>
> Shortly afterward I spoke to Deminicus Carter and asked him to step out of doors with me for I wanted to speak to him. . . . He did so. I then said to him that the girl [had no reason] to leave me, for you have never tried me nor proved anything against me. I then pleaded with him to give me a trial before a Bishop's Court, but he would not. He then counseled me to give her a bill, threatening . . . that if I would not, it would be the worse for me.
>
> I saw that they were determined to take her away from me, so I had to let her go.

Obviously Morris felt persecuted by his immediate church leaders; that smoldering resentment was directed in part against Young as the ultimate temporal ecclesiastical authority. Morris's sense of persecution and his lengthy personal defense did not convince Young and indeed were probably unpalatable to the church leader. Not surprisingly, given the tone and contents of that first letter, Brigham Young thought that Morris was "weak minded." To take him and his charges seriously would mean recognizing weaknesses in the hierarchy and in the church itself.

2 Prophets of Pentecost

The spring of 1857 was one of great spiritual excitement in Zion. Although rumors of warlike preparations against Mormons in Utah had been heard as early as February, the threat was not imminent enough to cool the fire of the great reformation begun the previous year. In fact, the knowledge of growing anti-Mormon sentiment in the States and local difficulties with certain Gentile officials may well have served to fan the revivalistic flame, increasing the resolve of the Mormon people to separate the righteous from the unrighteous in preparation for the expected conflict. Earlier experiences in Ohio, Missouri, and Illinois had taught them that anti-Mormon sentiment could quickly grow beyond inflammatory rhetoric to open hostility and conflict. At such times loyalty to the church and its leaders could not be taken for granted—it needed to be openly demonstrated.

The first decade in the mountains had required that great attention be directed toward settlement, foreign missionary work, and development of industries to take care of the material needs of the people. Although spiritual matters were not neglected, they could not be given the priority that Mormon leaders believed they deserved. Now, however, they believed the time was ripe for a thorough revival and reformation—for rededication to the church, to its principles, and to its leaders. Some church members were considered to be too friendly to outsiders, were dissatisfied with hard living conditions, or were engaged in sexual immorality, gambling, and drunkenness. Furthermore, some were openly questioning the practice of polygamy.[1]

On September 13, 1856, Jedediah Grant, second counselor to Brigham Young, delivered a fiery speech concerning the state of virtue of the Mormon people. This date has been generally considered the beginning of the reformation, but more appropriately it might be regarded as the date when the general church authorities gave public approval to it. Grant was simply giving official sanction to a revival movement that had been underway at least

---

1 Nels Anderson, *Desert Saints: The Mormon Frontier in Utah* (Chicago: University of Chicago Press, 1942), pp. 151–52.

since early spring.[2] Brigham Young had called on the people as early as 1854 to begin consecrating their property to the church, and historian Juanita Brooks reports that in April 1856 members of the church in southern Utah were confessing their sins and being rebaptized. That they were already in a revivalistic fervor is clearly illustrated in the account taken from the minutes of a meeting on April 26 recorded by Rachel Lee, a plural wife of John D. Lee.

Rachel Lee recorded that several men reported slothfulness and neglect of duty. Then Isaac C. Haight, stake president, baptized (that is, rebaptized) several men, including Rachel's husband, John D. Lee.

> All those that were [re]Baptized spoke their feelings and resolution to be better men henceforth—when Bro. Roundy spoke he felt truly pentinent before the Lord and floods of tears gushed from every eye. I do here bear witness that never since Harmony has been settled has their been such feelings of penitence and contrition and joy and thankfulness to God for his mercies and loving kindness toward us through all our wickedness, and hardness of heart that have existed in this place one toward another. Yea every one melted down in a flood of tears with thankful to their God and Savior for giving us a chance before it was gone too late for us to repent, of our ways, etc.
>
> Many of the brethren spoke and all rejoiced together. Priest Haight and council rejoiced exceedingly and spoke their satisfaction to see the true penitence of the Brethren in *the course of the reformation* [emphasis added] and said that this was not a revival like had been sometimes of short duration but it would continue until the dividing line should be drawn between the righteous and wicked and the great struggle would commence between the two Kingdoms.[3]

In addition to rebaptism, all Saints over the age of sixteen were encouraged to go to Salt Lake City to receive their endowments.[4] Before being

---

2 The Mormon religious reawakening of 1856–57, called the Reformation of 1856, has also been called a *revival.* Numerous references to it use the terms *reformation* and *revival* synonymously. The term *revival* might be preferable, for although individuals were expected to reform or repent, there was little effort to reform (i.e., remake) existing church doctrines or practices. Among other things, emphasis was given by church leaders to the reaffirmation of polygamy and the Law of Consecration, but these were both extant principles. Although I prefer the term *revival,* I have generally used the term *reformation* in this work to be consistent with other references to that episode. For an extensive treatise on the relationship between American revivalism and social reform see Timothy L. Smith, *Revivalism and Social Reform: American Protestantism on the Eve of the Civil War* (New York: Harper and Row, 1965).

3 Quoted in Juanita Brooks, *John Doyle Lee: Zealot, Pioneer Builder, Scapegoat* (Glendale, California: Arthur H. Clark Company, 1961), p. 187.

4 Endowments are special ordinances or blessings conferred upon worthy members of the L.D.S. church. The term literally refers to being endowed

rebaptized or receiving endowments, all were privately questioned, or catechized, by church authorities. Each member was expected to satisfactorily answer all of the following questions:

> Have you committed murder by shedding innocent blood—or consenting thereto?
>
> Have you betrayed your brethren or sisters in anything?
>
> Have you ever committed adultery by having connection with a woman that was not your wife or a man that was not your husband?
>
> Do you pay your tithing promptly?
>
> Have you spoken against any principle contained in the Bible, Book of Mormon, Doctrine and Covenants, or any principle revealed through Joseph the Prophet or the authorities of the Church?
>
> Do you wash your bodies and have your family do so as often as cleanliness requires or circumstances permit?
>
> Do you teach your families the Gospel of Salvation?
>
> Do you preside over your family as a servant of God and is your family subject to you?
>
> Do you fulfill your promises, do you pay your debts, or do you run into debt without prospect of paying?
>
> Have you taken anything that did not belong to you without the owner's knowing it, or giving consent?
>
> Have you found lost property and not returned it to the owner or used all diligence to do so?
>
> Have you lied about or maliciously misrepresented any person or thing?
>
> Have you branded any animal that you did not know to be your own?
>
> Have you taken up strays and converted to your own use without accounting to the proper authorities?
>
> Do you work 6 days and go to the house of worship on the 7th?
>
> Have you taken the name of the Deity in Vain? Have you been intoxicated by strong drink?[5]

Although many of these questions were highly specific, others were extremely general and subject to a wide variety of interpretations. Therefore, it is not surprising that the reformation produced numerous misunderstandings, overzealousness, and excesses of various kinds. Most Mormons seem to have joined eagerly in the reformation and took whatever steps were required to demonstrate their faith and steadfastness. For some, however, the requirements were simply too stringent. Many of these became

---

with powers from On High. The endowment ceremony may be performed only in Mormon temples or in buildings especially dedicated to that purpose e.g., the Salt Lake Endowment House prior to the completion of the Salt Lake Temple.

5 Brooks, *John D. Lee,* pp. 193–94.

virtual outcasts, and several left the territory. Others were simply repelled by the whole experience and lost, rather than gained, faith.[6]

Many of the requirements of the reformation were relatively benign, but one feature was truly frightening: the idea of "blood atonement." The gist of this concept was that such sins as adultery, killing of innocent children, and apostasy were so serious that they could not be forgiven by the sacrifice of Jesus but required that the blood of the offender must be shed to purchase redemption. On September 26, 1856, Brigham Young declared that: "There are sins that men commit for which they cannot receive forgiveness in this world or in that which is to come, and if they had their eyes open to see their true condition, they would be perfectly willing to have their blood spilt upon the ground, that the smoke thereof might ascend to heaven as an offering for their sins."[7]

Blood atonement is mentioned briefly by Walker, Turley, and Leonard[8] and is treated at some length by Bigler, who notes that this doctrine was not intended to punish sinners.[9] It was intended to ensure their salvation. Although the concept of blood atonement was generally attributed to Brigham Young, it had actually been announced by Joseph Smith in 1843. However, its most vocal advocate was Jedediah M. Grant, Young's second counselor and former mayor of Salt Lake City. Grant traveled among the Saints and caused great excitement wherever he preached.

Bigler affirms that most Mormons were content to keep the blood atonement simply at the preaching level, but he does document several cases where over-zealous adherents shed the blood of unfortunate sinners or dissidents. He also emphasizes that none of the perpetrators were ever brought to court, even though their identity was widely known. Walker, Turley, and Leonard suggest that the inflammatory rhetoric and apparent sanction of violent vigilante justice may have helped set the stage for the tragic Mountain Meadows Massacre.[10] Perhaps it also helped justify the use of excessive force against the Morrisites. Although he did not believe his brother Joseph was worthy of death, George Morris in 1876 used blood atonement as a successful argument with Brigham Young, allowing George to serve as proxy to perform temple ordinances for Joseph.

---

6 Brooks, *John D. Lee,* pp. 193–94.

7 Brigham Young, et al., *Journal of Discourses,* 26 vols. (London: Church of Jesus Christ of Latter-day Saints, 1853–86), 4:52–54.

8 Ronald Walker, Richard E. Turley and Glen M. Leonard, *Massacre At Mountain Meadows* New York: Oxford University Press, 2008), pp. 24–27).

9 David L. Bigler, *Forgotten Kingdom, The Mormon Theocracy In the American West* (Logan, UT: Utah State University Press, 1998), pp. 121–33.

10 Walker, Turley, and Leonard, *Massacre at Mountain Meadows,* pp. 25–26.

The actual overt practice of blood atonement seems to have been very rare and limited to a narrow time frame. But remnants of that concept endured for more than 150 years in Utah's law, allowing those receiving a death penalty to chose death by firing squad, – which would, of course, shed their blood.

One of the persons who claimed to have actually helped perform blood atonement was Bill Hickman, a one-time close associate of Brigham Young. Although the authenticity of Hickman's confessions has been strongly questioned by some Mormons and historians, it should be noted that he confessed to involvement in at least ten murders, a majority of which were ordered by church leaders, including some by Brigham Young himself. Several of these Hickman linked directly or by implication to the doctrine of blood atonement. Whether or not these killings occurred in the manner Hickman asserted, his confessions were widely read and were accepted by many as authentic. They served at the time to fuel anti-Mormon sentiment and color perceptions of life in Utah Territory in the late 1870s.[11]

The reformation of 1856–57 was undoubtedly the most intense and far-reaching that the Saints had witnessed since coming to the Great Basin, but it was not unique. The practice of rebaptism and renewal of covenants dated back to 1847, when Brigham Young, the apostles, and all members of the pioneer company were rebaptized less than two weeks after arriving in Salt Lake Valley.[12] In addition, Rachel Lee's previously quoted minutes indicate that brief revivals were not unusual among the Mormons during their first years in the mountains.

The revival of 1856–57 had many features unique to Mormonism, yet the intense emotionalism and much of the colorful rhetoric were characteristic of more general American revivalism dating back to the eighteenth century. Although the first six decades of the nineteenth century saw revivalism in American Christianity ebb and flow, revivalism was never completely absent from the rural scene, particularly on the frontier. The camp meeting revival was part and parcel of the American religious experience and was of central importance to the birth of Mormonism.

Joseph Smith, the founder of Mormonism, came from a family touched by the spirit of revivalism, which was evident in the "burnt over" district of western New York State where the Smiths lived.

Historian Fawn M. Brodie describes the emotional intensity of the repeated revivals in the state and their cumulative impact:

---

11 Bill Hickman, *Brigham's Destroying Angel: Life Confessions, and Startling Disclosures* (Salt Lake City: Shepard Book Company, 1904)..

12 Joseph Fielding Smith, *Essentials in Church History,* 13th edition (Salt Lake City, Utah: Deseret News Press, 1953), pp. 455–56.

> Palmyra [Smith's home town] was the center of what the circuit riders later called the "burnt over" district. One revival after another was sweeping through the area, leaving behind a people scattered and peeled, for religious enthusiasm was literally being burnt out of them. There are no detailed descriptions of the revivals in Palmyra and Manchester between 1824 and 1827, when they were at their wildest;
>
> The revivals by their very excesses deadened a normal antipathy toward religious eccentricity. And these pentecostal years, which coincided with Joseph Smith's adolescence and early manhood, were the most fertile in America's history for the sprouting of prophets.[13]

Although Smith reported that he had deep religious interests during his childhood, he did not demonstrate any propensity for prophethood until he was confronted by an intense religious revival about 1820. He wrote:

> Some time in the second year after our removal to Manchester, there was in the place where we lived an unusual excitement on the subject of religion. It commenced with the Methodists, but soon became general among all the sects in that region of country. Indeed, the whole district of country seemed affected by it, and great multitudes united themselves to the different religious parties, which created no small stir and division amongst the people, some crying, "Lo, here!" and others, "Lo, there!" . . . .
>
> In the midst of this war of words and tumult of opinions, I often said to myself, What is to be done? . . . While I was laboring under the extreme difficulties caused by the contests of these parties of religionists, I was one day reading the Epistle of James, first chapter, and fifth verse, which reads: *If any of you lack wisdom, let him ask of God; that giveth to all men liberally, and upbraideth not; and it shall be given him.*
>
> Never did any passage of scripture come with more power to the heart of man than this did at this time to mine. . . . I at length came to the determination to "ask of God," concluding that if he gave wisdom to them that lacked wisdom, and would give liberally and not upbraid, I might venture. So, in accordance with this my determination to ask of God, I retired to the woods to make the attempt.[14]

Joseph Smith then explained that in answer to earnest prayer he was rewarded by a personal visitation from God the Father and Jesus Christ, who told him that all of the extant churches were wrong and that he should join none. He reported that he was later visited by other heavenly messengers who instructed him and ordained him to his prophetic calling—to restore the true church of God upon earth.

---

13 Fawn M. Brodie, *No man knows my history: The Life of Joseph Smith,* 2d ed. Rev. And enl. (New York: Alfred A. Knopf, 1971), pp. 14–15.

14 Joseph Fielding Smith, *Essentials in Church History,* pp. 41–43.

According to Smith he told a revivalist minister of his experience a few days after the first heavenly interview. To his surprise the minister treated him with contempt and said: "It was all of the devil."

> I soon found, however, that my telling the story had excited a great deal of prejudice against me among professors of religion, and was the cause of great persecution, which continued to increase; and though I was an obscure boy only between fourteen and fifteen years of age, and my circumstances in life such as to make a boy of no consequence in the world, yet men of high standing would take notice sufficient to excite the public mind against me, and create a bitter persecution; and this was common among all the sects—all united to persecute me.
>
> It caused me serious reflection then, and often has since, how very strange it was that an obscure boy, a little over fourteen years of age and one, too, who was doomed to the necessity of obtaining a scanty maintenance by his daily labor, should be thought a character of sufficient importance to attract the attention of the great ones of the most popular sects of the day, and in a manner to create in them a spirit of the most bitter persecution and reviling.[15]

The circumstances, substance, and early public reaction to Joseph Smith's own reports of his early life have been questioned by a number of his critics as well as by serious scholars.[16] Neither the veracity and accuracy of Smith's statements nor the ensuing religious and scholarly controversy, however, is of prime importance here. What is significant for our purposes is that Smith's personal account was and remains the official one endorsed by the Church of Jesus Christ of Latter-day Saints and the one adhered to by faithful Mormons everywhere. It was the account preached by missionaries, and it must have been a prime factor in converting Joseph Morris to Mormonism in England in 1848.[17] That same year it had sustained Morris in his journey to America with his bride, Mary Thorpe, and it had seen him through trials and sickness while working as a fireman on a riverboat out of St. Louis. Later Morris lived in Pittsburgh, but his faith in Joseph Smith's story led him and his wife to leave there in 1853 and journey overland to Salt Lake City, arriving in the fall. Significantly, despite Morris's many disputes with Brigham Young and other Mormon authorities, Morris never lost faith in Joseph Smith. There can be no doubt that Morris accepted Joseph Smith's account of his prophetic calling at face value and that it served as a model for his own emergence as a prophet of God.[18]

---

15 Joseph Fielding Smith, *Essentials in Church History,* pp. 45–46.

16 Brodie, *No man knows my history,* pp. 21–27.

17 Eardley, *Gems of Inspiration,* p. 7

18 On 1 September 1859, Morris wrote to Brigham Young: "As concerning Joseph Smith, I love him as I do my own heart's blood, and I swear by the Gods

Whether the great Mormon "revival" of 1856–57 grew spontaneously and entirely out of the needs and circumstances of the Latter-day Saints is difficult to determine. But there is reason to believe that the revivalistic fervor concurrently developing across the United States, which culminated in great urban revivals in 1858, was no mere coincidence.

Timothy Smith, a leading authority on American nineteenth-century revivalism, writes:

> There can be no doubt that the popularity of revival men and methods surged forward in the major segments of American religion between 1840 and 1860.
>
> It is difficult but necessary for modern students to realize, moreover, that in the nineteenth century revival measures, . . . usually went hand in hand with progressive theology and humanitarian concern. Only thus could they have won the support of so many, both in and outside the churches, who wished Christianity to become a dynamic force for the reformation of human society.
>
> Finally, on the practical level revivals meant many things to many people. Those blessed with a wide social vision thought of them as a chief means of converting human institutions to Christian principles. Individual converts, in many cases, sought only fulfillment of the aspiration for forgiveness and personal union with the Savior. Pastors saw church problems melt away and financial surpluses appear. . . . The substantial fruits of fervor thus became an authoritative object lesson to pragmatic Americans. . . .
>
> The awakening of 1858 . . . was both the climax of long trends and the result of united efforts by urban churchmen of many denominations. In the two years immediately preceding it hundreds of them had labored to precipitate a national Pentecost which they hoped would baptize America with the Holy Spirit and in some mystic manner destroy the evils of slavery, poverty, and greed.[19]

Timothy Smith might also have added polygamy to this list, for by the mid-1850s it too was gaining national prominence as a political, social, and religious issue.

Despite their geographic isolation, the Mormons were neither culturally isolated nor markedly provincial in the mid-nineteenth century. Church leaders and missionaries were continually crisscrossing not only the United States but much of western Europe as well. They were tuned into the times even though they rejected much of the Gentile world, and certainly the Mormons were not ignorant of the revivalistic methods and the evangelical fervor so characteristic of Protestant America at that time.

---

of eternity that I will avenge his blood upon the United States."

19 Timothy L. Smith, *Revivalism and Social Reform*, pp. 59–62.

Whether the Mormon leaders purposefully borrowed techniques from other revivalists in promoting their own revival or whether the two revivals developed coincidentally is perhaps less important than the fact that both were occurring at the same time. The fervor and excesses of the Mormon reformation provided evidence to the American citizenry and government that the Mormons were overzealous fanatics who should be brought into line, while the swelling revivalistic fervor in the States provided a fertile climate for the mobilization of a military expedition to put the Mormons in their place.

The revival in the States ran its full course and culminated in 1858. However, the military expedition cut the Mormon reformation short so that it reached its zenith in the early months of 1857. Brigham Young officially announced the existence of the hostile military force on July 24, 1857, and called upon the people to turn all of their efforts toward resisting its advance. That date might properly be regarded as the practical and official end of the Mormon reformation. The heightened zeal of the people was directed thenceforth toward a more pressing need.[20]

Nevertheless, at least one Mormon was not yet ready to accept the reformation as complete. Joseph Morris believed that he had much more than just a personal stake in the reformation—he was convinced that significant changes should be made in the leadership and authority structure of the Mormon church.

One of Morris's followers and a later apologist, John R. Eardley, made light of the Mormon reformation and cynically wrote:

> . . . history shows that it was a "reformation" in name only, as she [the Church] still persisted in disobeying the laws of the land, in the practice of polygamy [sic], and "other corrupt doctrines," and in rebellion against the Government of the United States. It was rather an attempting on the part of the leaders of the Church to strengthen their hold upon the confidence, faith and obedience of the saints, and to overawe them with a sense of their importance and greatness as "servants of God."
>
> . . . [Morris] was appointed to the office of ward teacher—a very important office in the system of espionage practiced in Utah—an individual who is authorized to enter the abodes of the saints, and learn of their disaffections and signs of apostacy, and make reports to the bishop and his council, for their consideration and action; in reality an official spy among the saints.
>
> . . . Joseph Morris was not such a success in this office as they desired. He would teach the saints the pure principles of truth, and impress upon them their allegiance and duties to their divine Savior; but he abhorred

20 Joseph Fielding Smith, *Essentials in Church History*, pp. 499–500, and Nels Anderson, *Desert Saints*, pp. 168–69.

> man-worship; he held that the president was as duty bound to observe the counsels of the Almighty as much as the most humble saint, and that only while doing so was he entitled to the respect of the saints. . . . He also taught them many of the principles revealed to him, and which condemned many of the teachings and practices among the saints, and it was found necessary by the bishop to curtail his opportunities of mixing with the saints, and he was finally prohibited from speaking to them.
>
> It was here that he received the appellation of "Praying Joe," from his regular custom of repairing to some sheltered spot in the bushes, twice or thrice each day to pray; for this exercise was the source of much joy and comfort to him; but it seemed to exasperate his persecutors, and they were not content without besmearing the spot where he was wont to kneel and pour forth his soul in agonizing prayer and supplication for his enemies. But he never resented these insults, but bore them meekly and patiently, hoping some day that their hearts would be touched by the same mellowing influences which had pervaded his soul since he first gave his heart to God and His services.
>
> During these times it was difficult for him to get employment, and he consequently was compelled to dress in a manner that was humiliating to him, and which tended to encourage the disrespect and ridicule of his enforced associates, forgetting that the Master himself, whom they professed to serve, "had no where to lay His head." It was one of these days, when he was almost overwhelmed with grief at the circumstances which seemed to circumvent him, that he wrote his first official revelation.[21]

Regardless of Eardley's cynicism concerning the reformation, there can be no doubt that Morris took the reformation seriously, joined enthusiastically, and was gravely disappointed when he was no longer allowed to preach. He was literally "carried away" by the spirit and fervor of the times and was branded as a fanatic because he insisted on preaching and practicing a piety that went considerably beyond the expectations of the Mormon leaders.

Regardless of how peculiar it seems today, Morris's claim to direct revelation was not out of character with the spiritual gifts many Mormons believed they possessed at that time. Morris made stronger claims than most, but his claims were only a matter of degree, not kind. Of course, when he claimed to receive revelations affecting the entire church, he incurred the displeasure of the Mormon authorities, but that was to be expected. Their disbelief and persecution only served to confirm Morris's belief that he was fulfilling the proper role of prophet.

Although Morris later claimed he had received numerous spiritual manifestations before arriving in Utah, and these continued thereafter, it was not until the spring of 1857 that he recorded his first official revelation. It served

21 Eardley, *Gems of Inspiration*, pp. 9–10.

as the basis for establishing his prophetic calling and, of course, placed him at odds with the Mormon establishment. George Dove, a devoted disciple of Morris, agreed with Eardley in reporting that this revelation came at a time when Morris was in the depths of disillusionment and despair, "when he was the most utterly cast down."[22] No doubt that was true, but it is significant that the revelation came when the revivalistic fervor in Utah was at its height and Morris had been officially excluded from it. The revelation stated:

> Verily, verily, verily, thus saith the spirit unto thee, my servant Joseph: I the Lord, have beheld thy afflictions, and know the intentions of thy heart. And because thou art pure before me, I will give unto thee power over thine enemies; and thou shalt know that I am the Lord, and that I regard not the persons of men only in their obedience to me. And, now, I say unto thee, let thy heart be comforted, and know that I am with thee, and will be with thee, through thy faithfulness, unto the end.
>
> And I say unto thee, my servant, that I have chosen thee from the foundation of the world to be a mighty man, yea, to be a prophet in Israel; and thou shalt prophesy, to many nations, and peoples, and kings, and tongues. Yea, I say unto thee, that the mountains shall tremble at the uttering of thy voice; and men shall seek thy life from place to place, and thirst after thy blood as an ox thirsteth after water; but they shall not have power to take it before thy work is finished.
>
> Thou shalt be betrayed by friends and relatives, and even by thy own flesh and blood.
>
> And I say unto thee, that I have chosen my servant Brigham Young, and also mine apostles to lead my people in Israel; and that power shall not be taken out of their hands only through transgression.[23]

This was the first of over 300 revelations recorded by Joseph Morris—destined to make him the most prolific of all Mormon revelators and anathema among the followers of Brigham Young.[24]

22 Joseph Morris, *The Spirit Prevails,* p. 3.

23 Joseph Morris, *The Spirit Prevails,* p. 9.

24 The designation of Joseph Morris as the most prolific of Mormon revelators refers to recorded revelations presented as special messages from God. However, if the Book of Mormon and other works of Joseph Smith, purported to have been translated by heavenly inspiration, are also classified as revelations, Smith would be the more productive.

3 The Seventh Angel Speaks

Joseph Morris waited ten months before writing a second letter to Brigham Young. It was dated October 11, 1858. By this time many of the serious differences between the Saints and the United States government had been largely settled. The "invading" troops were stationed at Camp Floyd, south of Salt Lake, and Brigham Young had relinquished the governorship to Alfred Cumming. Young was still the most potent religious and political force in Utah, but the sovereign power of the United States had been reaffirmed, and except for a brief time in 1862 the autonomy and independence of the Mormons were gone forever. The times were changing, and Joseph Morris took the opportunity to propose a dramatic change in the Mormon church.

To Brigham Young he wrote:

> . . . thus saith the Lord unto you, that I the Lord chose you to be the Chief Shepherd of my flock and I delivered them into your hands. And you have given your mind to trading and to speculating and you have increased in riches. In abundance you have added house to house and barn to barn and land to land, and you have thrust my poor away from me and you have given the adversary the advantage over the remainder to lead them to idolatry by running them too fast. They saw the progress that you were making in wealth and they thought that they must follow your example and become wealthy. Also no matter which way their wealth came their eyes were filled with greediness and their hearts were set upon their cattle and their horses and their houses and their lands, their wives and their children and not upon me saith the Lord. They have oppressed the poor and needy and turned them away from their rights and forced away those that were better than they. But I will gather them together again and they shall no more be scattered, saith the Lord.
>
> Surely the Smiths Family are now satisfied now they have thrown down the authority of the Church and [have] brought all the people under the power of the devil—they may rest satisfied. They have always thought that the presidency of the Church belonged to their family and Lucifer, the devil, has deceived them and being influenced by the devil they have run an undercurrent against you [Brigham Young] until they have accomplished their desire.

I will now satisfy you concerning Joseph Smith. The Lord commanded him to leave Nauvoo and start for this place and he did so and returned back again from following the Lord, and the Lord had no more use for him on the earth. . . . The Lord then permitted him to be slain that he might . . . be saved. And in consequence of this his seed was cut off from the reigns of government . . . .

It is true that Joseph Smith laid the foundation of a great and mighty work on the earth and he laid the foundation also to throw it down again, and that brings him on a level with an ordinary man. He laid the foundation to make thousands of devils, and if the Lord had not provided a redeemer, this people must have remained devils to all eternity. Dear sir, you might think it hard that the Almighty has dealt so hard with you, but I will now appeal to your judgment. Were you not the first person that the Lord manifested the true situation of his people to? Yes you were. And you saw that the devil had got possession of the Church and you made an effort to gain your power back and forced the influence back again until you came in open contact with the devil and then you could go no further and, there you stopped. . . . Then the devil tried his hand to see what he could do and he forced the influence back upon you and the people were worse than ever. Now what can you do? Was the Lord justified in raising up a deliverer to deliver you and this people or not? If he was, I should think that you would not think it hard to take his counsel. I, therefore, counsel you to seal no more people; for you have continued to seal people off and on ever since I first wrote to you and you have hurt my feelings grievously. Ye, you have grieved the Holy Ghost. This has not been a time to marry wives.

And as I [Morris] have by the help of my Heavenly Father broke the grasp of the devil and redeemed this people, the Lord has made a promise to me that I shall have the power to deliver them.

I now wish to address myself to you and the rest of the Apostles. Inasmuch as you received ordinations to the Apostleship under the the hands of Joseph Smith and that authority is no more, inasmuch as you are willing to become one with me in the great work of the last days and willing to take my counsel, I am ready and willing to reinstate you into your former offices with all my heart. It is not my object to interfere with the apostleship in anything that can be avoided. The Lord has called me to be a prophet and to hold the keys of the last dispensation. I shall expect President Young to hold the Presidency of the Church as he has done before, for it is not a prophet's place to preside but to dictate him that presides.

. . . I now counsel you to call meetings throughout the territory forthwith, and call a meeting in the tabernacle, also, and do not linger. If there is anything in the way move it out, for the people are perishing under the influence of the devil. The devil is wide awake and, if we are not [also awake] we shall be behind. Yea all earth and hell is on the move to overthrow the Kingdom of God. And all heaven and the gods of eternity is

> on the move. Also, when the Lord presses me I am obliged to press you. And if you do not move the fear of the Almighty will consume you. I shall therefore come forward the first meeting that you hold in the tabernacle to destroy the power of the Devil, for I shall be hard on evil spirits.
>
> And now dear sir, come out of your hiding place and do your duty and no weapons shall prosper against you.
>
> I am stopping now in the First Ward at Joseph Mosse's and I am waiting for your move. Life and death [are] set before you. Choose you which you will. I would like to see you as soon as I can, for I have made known to you my destitute condition. I am in this situation for the Gospel's sake.
>
> And now I will leave this matter with you. I can be found at the place before mentioned. I keep myself as secret as possible.
>
> So no more from your affectionate friend and brother in the bonds of the covenant. Joseph Morris

Apparently this letter met with no more favor from Brigham Young than the first one. A brief note was penciled on its margin: "Balderdash."

Although Brigham Young again ignored Joseph Morris, undoubtedly considering him to be no more than a crank, this letter was an important one because it contained certain elements Morris used later in his assaults upon the Mormon leadership. First, it declared that the authority of the present Mormon leaders was null and void and could only be reinstated by Morris, God's new prophet. Second, it proposed that there be a separation of prophetic and administrative authority within the church. Third, it condemned excessive materialism. Fourth, it attacked the present practice of plural marriage. Fifth, it identified Morris as the deliverer of the Mormon people who was to dictate policy to the administrative leaders.

It is also significant that although this letter had certain elements associated with a restoration, it basically cast Morris in the role of reformer and deliverer, not rebel or apostate. Morris consistently maintained this stance until he became convinced some two years later that reform within the Mormon establishment was impossible.

The next correspondence Brigham Young received form Joseph Morris was dated January 26, 1859. Probably Morris was still living in Salt Lake City, having arrived there the year before from American Fork. Morris presented his letter as "a revelation from Jesus Christ concerning the reorganization of the holy priesthood." The revelation commanded:

> Verily I say unto you my servant Joseph, inasmuch as I have chosen you to stand at the head of my Church as the prophet, seer, and revelator of the same, you shall take my servant Brigham to be your first Counselor and place upon him the presidency of My Church—under your direction and inasmuch as he will give ear to your counsel and stand by you, I will greatly multiply blessings upon his head.

> As concerning my servant Heber [C. Kimball], I the Lord am not well pleased with him for he has commited a grievous sin against me, and if he humbleth not himself before me he shall be destroyed.
>
> . . . I the Lord have ordained that another shall act in his place in the first quorum of My Church—even my servant John Banks.

On February 18, 1859, Morris enlightened Brigham Young on the significance of a brilliant comet appearing recently in the sky. He explained:

> . . . the seventh star that John speaks of in the Book of Revelation, representing the seventh angel that has come forth, and the tail that was attached to it is a representation of the Army of Heaven that was to follow the seventh angel represented by the four horses that John saw at the head of the Army of Heaven and their riders are the captains of the Lord's host.
>
> Behold, I am Jesus Christ and I testify unto all men upon the earth that I have sent forth the seventh angel to preside over My Church upon the earth and all nations and kingdoms on the earth shall feel his power and this world shall know that I am the Lord.

The foregoing theme was continued and expanded in the next letter Morris directed to Brigham Young on April 21, 1859. It was a "revelation from Jesus Christ giving an explanation of the rod of Moses." In this revelation Morris began to develop some distinctive doctrines concerning the plurality of gods, the organization and number of earths they had created, these earths' evolutionary stages, and their ultimate destiny. The role Morris was to play in this earth's destiny was also made more explicit.

> . . .the Rod of Moses . . . is a rod [scepter] and proceeded forth from the first God of all. And it is as endurable as Himself and he placed his superscription upon it and . . . is sworn to sustain that man which is called to use it. And it cannot be used by any person but the Seventh Angel and those that he shall appoint, for the Seventh Angel is always the president over that world in which he dwells, and it is always his place to preside over the dispensation of the fullness of times. And thus the Seventh Angel is sustained by all the gods of eternity which number millions from the first god downward. And to every quorum of god there is a world like unto this passing through a state of mortality, and thus there is no end to the creation of the Great King of Kings and Lord of Lords. And behold I say unto you my servant Joseph, I the Lord have called you to use that rod for thou art the Seventh Angel, and I will place it in thy hand, for thou art worthy.
>
> Behold I am Jesus Christ, and I testify unto [all] mankind that dwell upon the face of the earth that I have opened the last seal by the Seventh Angel. And I will give him power in a rod and he shall rule the nations of the earth.

Joseph Morris seemed particularly fascinated with the temporal and spiritual power symbolized by the Rod of Moses; he maintained that he received several later revelations dealing with the scepter. Morris believed that the rod would be personally delivered to him by Jesus Christ in a great public ceremony that would officially usher in the millennium. He also believed that the rod would be more than a symbol of power. It would actually contain supernatural powers that would make all manner of miracles possible.[1]

During this time Morris tarried in the vicinity of Salt Lake City expecting (or at least hoping) that Brigham Young would grant him an audience so that he might personally explain his calling from God. He also hoped that Young would provide him with food, clothing, and shelter. Two years later, while comfortably situated in South Weber, Morris described his discouraging and impoverished circumstances in earlier times.

> For two years and a half I wrote to and labored with President Young in the most faithful manner, *revealing to none but to him and his immediate associates* [emphasis added] the designs and purposes of the Almighty. During this time, I suffered trials and privations of various kinds, and often prayed the Lord to remove from me a burden that I seemed scarcely able to bear. My mind was wholly occupied with the things that the Lord had revealed to me, so much so, that I had no pleasure in conversation that did not relate to God and Godliness. I was a cipher among the People. If I was silent, I was looked upon and ridiculed as dull and stupid; if I spake, I spake that which occupied my whole attention, and was derided as a fanatic, stigmatized as crazy, or treated as an imposter. Under such circumstances, with which I had to cope, from the date of my first visitation from the Lord to the time that I arrived in this place [South Weber], I had no less than twenty-eight different homes, or rather stopping places, for I had no place of residence worthy the sacred name of home before I came here.[2]

It seems clear that Morris's difficulties, as well as his spiritual manifestations, had not just begun with his recorded revelations, but in fact had been with him from the time he migrated from England, if not earlier.

Morris was born December 15, 1824, in Burwardsley, Chester-shire, near the city of Chester, England. According to the *The Spirit Prevails*, he was the fifth in a family of eight children. John R. Eardley, one of his later disciples, reported that he was of "poor and respectable parents and was under the necessity of laboring for a living from his early youth, and therefore had few privileges of obtaining an education. He was religiously inclined, and the spirit of God seemed to attend him and pervade his whole being while he grew up to manhood."[3] As a youth Morris, who had worked as a

1 Morris, *The Spirit Prevails,* pp. 25, 68–70, 183–84, 205, 546, 549.

2 Morris, *The Spirit Prevails,* pp. 670–74.

3 Eardley, *Gems of Inspiration,* p. 7.

farm laborer and coal miner in England, suffered an accident that left him severely burned. His brother George believed that the shock of this accident and a later illness in St. Louis affected his mental balance.[4]

In his "Life History," George Morris, Joseph Morris's brother, stated that his parents, Joseph and Elizabeth Morris, had six children: George, Mary Ann, William, Joseph, Fanny, and Matthew. This would have made Joseph the fourth born, with three brothers and two sisters. Since George Morris knew his family history firsthand, his account is probably more accurate than that of George Dove, who compiled and published *The Spirit Prevails*.[5]

Very few details are known of the early years of Joseph Morris's life, although some might be inferred from the account of his brother. George reports that their father was a journeyman shoemaker who earned between five and six schillings a week. This meager income required that the boys of the family gain employment at an extremely early age. George was forced to go to work for local farmers at the age of seven, when his few months of formal schooling came to an end. Given Joseph's literary weakness, it is likely that his time of formal education was also extremely brief. The life of these young brothers was extremely hard. George worked in the fields from six in the morning until six in the evening, frightening away birds or driving plow horses. He was required to arise at four in the morning and had to work in the horse barn for two hours after returning from the fields—a sixteen-hour day for a seven-year-old boy. George worked for farmers until age fourteen, then worked a year as a servant and ostler in an inn, and moved on to gardening, boiler-making, and eventually coal mining. He worked in the mines for four years, until he was severely injured by a roof cave-in that left him with a damaged back and knee that never fully recovered. After that George took up shoemaking, presumably with his father, at about age twenty-one. Eventually, George met Mormon missionaries and was converted and baptized. He emigrated to The United States in 1842 after a voyage of nine weeks.[6]

Although his early years probably did not exactly parallel those of his elder brother, it seems more than coincidental that Joseph began very early to work for local farmers and that he was also severely injured in a mining accident. Eventually, he became a mason's helper. Clearly, both brothers had minimal education and worked at a variety of hard, often dangerous manual-labor jobs. Such labor was also typical after they reached the United

4 Roberts, *Comprehensive History,* 5:39.

5 "A Short Sketch of the Genealogy and History of George Morris," Historical Department, Church of Jesus Christ of Latter-day Saints, p. 1. See also Morris, *The Spirit Prevails* p. 2.

6 "History of George Morris," pp. 1–24.

States. However, George reported that Joseph tried with some success to avoid much manual labor after arriving in the Salt Lake Valley.[7]

The "Life History of George Morris" is the most complete account of Joseph Morris's adult life and provides the best insights into his character and personality. The following is George's verbatim narrative, which begins with Joseph's death and then provides a chronological recounting of Joseph's early life, his baptism into the Mormon Church, his marriage, his emigration to the United States, his time along the Mississippi River, his migration west, and his activities after arriving in Utah Territory. This account was probably written in the late summer or early fall of 1862. Joseph is treated as a loved, but prodigal brother.

> I have now come to a subject that is painful to think about. Namely to give a short account of some portion of the life and also the death of my brother, Joseph who was killed with John Banks up at East Weber, Utah Territory on June 15, 1862, in the 38th year of his age—But how to represent the matter in the best manner possible I hardly know—but I will begin by saying that after he was baptized into the Church, he became very zealous and received the Gift of Tongues—to a very great degree but was unwise in the use of them and after some time he had given offense in the branch to which he belonged and was suspended for a time until he made reconciliation.
>
> Sometime afterward he was very severely burnt by the fire damp in the coal mines and suffered great torture while recovering which affected his mind very much and he began to feel very self-righteous and that he was in very high estimation with the Lord. He got married. His wife's name was Mary Thorp.
>
> They emigrated soon after for America. He arrived in St Louis, Missouri and there remained for several years. He ran the river on a steamboat for some time—finally he was taken sick and had a very severe spell of sickness and became very flighty and visionary in his mind—his mind running chiefly to religious matters—dreaming wonderful dreams, seeing visions and getting revelations about his being one of the hundred and forty-four thousand spoken of in the scriptures—and about the heirship of the priesthood and so forth—reading and studying the scriptures and praying continually—that the Lord would qualify him to stand in the Great Place and Station which he had pictured out for himself at the head of his father's family—thus his prayers were offered up in a vain, self-righteous manner—instead of bowing before the Lord in humility and meekness and asking him in the name of Jesus to help him with wisdom and his holy spirit that he might be qualified to become a useful instrument in helping to build up his Kingdom in the Lord's own way.

7 "History of George Morris," p. 119.

When he had so far recovered as to be able to travel—he started for Pittsburgh, Pennsylvania to preach to an older brother named James Silverthorn, the firstborn of my mother by a former marriage. While there he began to preach around considerably in a small branch of the Church that had been established there and came in contact with the Presiding Elder and succeeded in establishing himself as President of the Branch as he said it was the wish of the Branch that he should preside over them having studied the scriptures a great deal and having an excellent memory to retain them—he had become quite a scriptorian and spoke with great earnestness and fluency and being strongly prompted by that aspiring spirit which had accompanied him all his life. He continued on from step to step until it finally brought him to an untimely end.

Shortly after he left that part of the country and returned to St. Louis—I received a letter from England informing me of the death of my brother James and oldest son called Enoch whom Joseph went to visit (before emigrating) and preach to caused by the explosion of the Gafs [?] or as it is generally called by the coal miners' fire damp—which burned them to death. His wife's name was Elizabeth Higginbotham and was sister to my first wife.

Shortly after Joseph returned to St. Louey he obtained means and emigrated to the valleys of the mountains—when he arrived in the fall of 1853 with his wife and one child. I took them in and made a home for them as long as they chose to stay. About the third day after they came my brother was sitting at the stove in a deep study with his head down. After a while he raised up his head and began to talk in the following manner—Well says he when I was back in the old country and in St. Louis if I could only get to the valleys of the mountains to where our George was that he would be able to sit down and tell me all about the Mysteries of the Kingdom and things that I never then (thought?) about—But now I have got here I find that I am ahead of him. I find that I know more than he does—this came out rather unexpected to me—I looked at him and wondered what could be the matter with him but made him no reply at that time—he continued on talking from time to time generally to my family when I was absent—about how much more he knew than I did—and that the Priesthood never descended down from the father to the oldest son according to heirship but that the Lord generally passed by the oldest and made choice of some younger member of the family to bestow his choicest blessings on—and place them at the head and it would be so in his case the Lord designed to place him at the head of his father's family.

When I thought he had gone far enough I checked him and talked very plain to him at which he took offense and his wife persuaded him to leave me and take her down south where she had a brother and some other friends who would make them a better home than I did.

I told him that if he went he would lose everything that he had—but he went and in the course of 2 months he returned with nothing but the clothes that he had on his back. His wife had left him and claimed whatever things they had. He stayed around from place to place in the city and after a while he married again to a widow by the name of Elizabeth Mills but in a short time they parted.

The next trouble he got into was down at Provo. While living there they made a Teacher of him and as usual he wanted to be the biggest man—but there were others there who were very strenuous on that point so he got the worst of it there—while acting a Teacher there he became acquainted with a young woman by the name of Elize Jones—courted and married her. Immediately after that was done there were those in authority who raised objections to it and went to work to separate them—which they accomplished—and he returned to me again feeling very bad having lost all confidence in everybody with whom he had anything to do so he sat himself to work in good earnest to bring about that great work which he said the Lord had called him to perform—by reading and study and labored with his hands but very little—and while he lived with me he was always praying—and would as soon have thought of going without his breakfast as to have missed going up into a ravine on the side of the mountain to pray—but he continued to pray that the Lord would help him to carry out his own wishes—So he began to receive very great revelations preparatory to starting an organization so he came to me and wished a private interview with me—He had a revelation that he wanted to read to me—He said the Lord told him to revisit to me and no one else—and if I would receive it I was a rightful heir to the Apostleship—I heard him through and when he had read his revelation and emptied his "Bugyet" [?]—I told him that he was laboring under the influence of delusive spirits and that his revelations were from the Devil—and that if he continued on in the course he was then going that he would run against a snag before long—He went on and gathered around him quite a number of old apostles who had been prominent Elders in the Church—and ordained Counselors—Apostles, High Priests and so forth.

They had also a military organization—they numbered altogether men, women and children about eight hundred and lived together on what is called the Common Stock Principle throwing in their property into one pile—and receiving their flour from the same bin. They raised no crops for 2 years considering that they had property enough to last them to live upon until the Lord should cut off the people called Latter Day Saints which he had revealed to them should soon be done on account of their great wickedness that they were committing before him—and when that was done—that they would be blessed with the enjoyment of all their property which they left behind—but in this they were disappointed for trouble arose amongst themselves.

Several of their members wishing to apostatize from their faith and have them (their property)—but they would not permit them to leave so they took them and bound them and kept them as prisoners—complaints

> were made to Judge Kinney who was then Presiding Judge of the Territory of Utah—who issued a process for their liberation as they were confined contrary to law and justice—but it was not heeded—so he issued another to bring the offenders to justice living or dead.
>
> A strong armed posse was sent up but they were resisted and the consequence was they brought down the dead bodies of Joesph Morris and John Banks the two principle ones—there were also two young men belonging to the posse killed whose names were Peter Waldin and Jarad Smith—and here ends the cares of a poor weak deluded mortal who was hurried on through a short and troublesome life to a premature grave—by an over ambitious deluded fanatical religious zeal—it has been asserted since his death by some that he was corrupt and unvirtuous in his intercourse with the other sex—but this I believe to be incorrect for I have never been able to learn either from himself or anyone else that knew of him taking an unlawful course with any female outside of the marriage circle—but he has done [?] a great many foolish things and his blood has been shed to atone for his sins and he has never had his endowments nor entered into the house of the Lord to make any covenants before him—therefore he is in the hands of a merciful Jehovah who will reward all men according to their works and the honesty of their motives before him.[8]

Little is known about Morris's activities and circumstances during his two-year sojourn in St. Louis, but there can be little doubt that firing a wood-powered steamboat was a dirty, backbreaking, unrewarding means of gaining a livelihood. It was probably as close to the fires of hell as Morris wanted to get, and it is not surprising that he began directing his attention toward more ethereal affairs. George Dove wrote that while Morris was in St. Louis he "had remarkable visions and spiritual impressions about the heirship of the priesthood."[9] Eardley concurred with this assessment: "While thus engaged, he received many visions and spiritual inspirations concerning the great principles which afterward became incorporated in the science of the Fullness of the Gospel of our Lord Jesus Christ, as revealed through him in the 'Rounds of Eternity.'"[10]

The above statements make it clear that at least some of Morris's theological ideas were formulated while he was in St. Louis seven or eight years before he penned his first letter to Brigham Young. The variety and detail of these earlier ideas must remain matters of conjecture, but two of them—the

8 "History of George Morris," pp.114–22. The above excerpt from George Morris' "A Short Sketch of the Genealogy and History of George Morris." has been edited for some spellings, punctuation, and paragraphing, but his words are verbatim.

9 Morris, *The Spirit Prevails*, p. 2.

10 Eardley, *Gems of Inspiration*, p. 7.

"Keys of the Priesthood" and the "Rounds of Eternity"—took very definite form and were central to his theology by 1859 or 1860.[11]

Morris's basic cosmology was contained in a diagrammatic chart and explanation called the "Rounds of Eternity." It is of special interest because its sophistication, variety, and detail contrast so sharply with his illiteracy in letters. The "Rounds of Eternity" explained in some detail the order of creation of the universe. According to Morris the universe evolved from the first celestial planet where the first god of all and his family resided. "The celestial sun revolved around it (the first celestial planet) once in one thousand years, and all celestial planets that surrounded it, were governed by it; that is the reason why the Almighty declares that, 'one day with Him is as a thousand years' with the children of men."[12] These celestial planets had already passed through their mortal existence. Each one was presided over by a god and each of these was subject to the first god of all. God the Eternal Father and His son Jesus Christ resided on the most recently exalted of these celestial planets, and they in turn presided over the earth and 144,000 additional planets, which were in various stages of spiritual and mortal development. Presumably each of the gods who presided over the other celestial planets also presided over 144,000 planets that were in various stages of spiritual and mortal development. According to Morris, all of these planets were small in the beginning and grew many times their original size. When created, the earth was less than one-hundredth its present size. It has since increased in size 144,000 times and has been growing ever since. Morris taught that this world was created 1,008 million years ago and that it was the abode of spirits until about 6,000 years ago, when it evolved to its present position and passed from its spiritual to its mortal condition. He believed that the millennium was at hand and that at the end of 1,000 years the earth would be purified to inherit celestial glory. It would then ascend into a celestial atmosphere and become numbered with the other celestialized planets.[13]

The "Keys of the Priesthood" contained the concept of reincarnation, or more technically, transmigration of spirits that was most certainly suggested to Morris in St. Louis. Although transmigration has no counterpart in orthodox Mormon theology, it was central to the teachings of Charles B. Thompson, a Mormon who withdrew from the leadership of Brigham Young when he moved west. No direct evidence has been found that Morris was in contact with Charles B. Thompson while in St. Louis, although both were in that city at the same time. Thompson had published a tract as early as 1848,

11 Eardley, *Gems of Inspiration,* pp. 34–43.

12 Eardley, *Gems of Inspiration,* p. 40.

13 Eardley, *Gems of Inspiration,* pp. 40–42.

explaining, through the voice of "Baneemy" (an alter-ego or separate identity of Thompson's), that the Mormon church had been rejected by the Lord on the day that Joseph Smith and his brother were martyred and the church had become partially disorganized. The church no longer held the keys of the priesthood and so became filled with darkness. On December 27, 1847, Thompson (Baneemy) had prayed to the Lord and had been given the key words of authority and instructions to organize and cleanse the priesthood. He was also commanded to organize "schools of Preparation, for the Order of the Priesthood of Regeneration and Restitution."[14]

Thompson's explanation of the impact of Joseph Smith's death upon the church and the subsequent need to redeem it from the powers of darkness was almost identical to the explanation given by Morris in his previously cited letter to Brigham Young on October 11, 1858.

In January 1849 Thompson began issuing a periodical entitled *Zion's Harbinger and Baneemy's Organ,* which was published in St. Louis until he left there for Minona County, Iowa, in August 1853.[15]

On April 15, 1850, Thompson received a revelation that explicitly contained the principle of "regeneration" (transmigration of spirits). "And now behold I send unto you my servant Charles B. Thompson, in whom is regenerated my dear son Ephraim, my first-born, with the voice of Baneemy."

Exactly two years later the Lord again spoke to Thompson by the voice of Baneemy, reiterating his dual identity: "Because in thee is regenerated Ephraim, my first-born, of the seed of Joseph, to whom the birth-right of Israel was given by my servant Jacob."[16]

Morris combined the principle of spirit transmigration with his evolutionary cosmology. Its basic tenet was that a spirit must enter a variety of states or manlike bodies at different points in evolutionary development in order that all eternal laws might be obeyed and the spirit might gain sufficient knowledge to become perfected "in order that they might continue to pass on from one stage of progression to another, and, ultimately, become Gods like unto the Eternal Father."[17] Morris illustrated this process by giving an account of the various stages that God had passed through and that all faithful men might emulate.

14 Dale L. Morgan, III, "A Bibliography of the Church of the Dispersion," *Western Humanities Review* 7 (Summer 1953):255–66.

15 Morgan, "Bibliography," pp. 147–49.

16 Charles B. Thompson, *The Laws and Covenants of Israel Written to Ephraim from Jehovah, the Mighty God of Jacob. Also Ephraim and Baneemy's Proclamations* (Preparation, Iowa: Zion's Presbytery, 1857), 19:506, 23:596. (The numbers that follow *Ephraim and Baneenzy's Proclamations* stand for section and verse numbers, as in biblical citations.)

17 Morris, *The Spirit Prevails,* p. 10.

> How many progressive estates did the Eternal Father pass through before he became a God? Ten. What were they? His First was a spiritual estate, his Second, a probation in the flesh; his Third, a resurrected or celestial estate. In his Fourth estate he went forth upon a mortal earth, received a body, died upon a cross, and was raised again from the dead. In his Fifth estate he sat at the right hand of his Father, and was a Mediator, and contended against and conquered death, hell, and the grave. In the Sixth estate he took mortal bodies upon many mortal earths, and officiated in the office of a high priest, a prophet and a president.

His mission to each of the last five of these earths, was to preside over a dispensation of a thousand years on each earth; on the first of the five he presided over the first thousand years, on the second of the five, over the second thousand years, and so on, unto and including the fifth. In the Seventh estate he was a prophet, and held the keys of the sixth dispensation. In his Eighth estate he was a prophet, Redeemer, lawgiver and president of [the] seventh dispensation holding the keys of the holy priesthood. In his Ninth estate he went forth upon his own earth to commence mortality, and having completed his mission, he died. He afterwards returned to his own earth and commenced the resurrection of his own posterity, and after its last great change he ascended his throne, and this was his Tenth estate.[18]

Joseph Morris's own multiple identities and prophetic destiny were further revealed in "An Article on the Order of Sevens," appearing in *The Spirit Prevails.*

> The Earth continues in mortality during a period of seven thousand years, which period is divided into seven equal parts, called dispensations. There are also seven high priests who are appointed to preside over the several dispensations. These high priests are called in the Scriptures the seven angels of the seven churches. Their names are Seth, Enos, Cainan, Mahalaleel, Jared, Enoch and Methuselah. . . . Methuselah, though the last one born, is the first angel, and presides over the first thousand years. Enoch, the second; Jared, the third; Mahalaleel, the fourth; Cainan, the fifth; Enos, the sixth; and Seth, the seventh. The seventh is the senior and presides over the other six. The seven angels in connection with Jesus Christ, open the seven seals when they go forth to fill their respective missions.

The seven angels are subject to each other, and succeed each other in presiding. Two of them, Enos and Seth, the sixth and the seventh angels, are obligated by law to fill three missions on the earth. Enos filled his second mission to this earth in the person of Elijah, and his third in the person of Joseph Smith. Seth filled his second mission in the person of Moses, and

18 Eardley, *Gems of Inspiration*, p. 34.

is filling his third in the person of Joseph Morris. He is the president of the high priesthood, and, as such, will continue to preside over the church and kingdom of God till the close of the seventh thousand years.[19]

This revelation clearly identified Joseph Morris as a central figure in God's eternal plan. Not only was Morris the Seventh Angel, but also he had previously served two probationary estates upon the earth—first as Seth and then as the greatest of law-givers, Moses.

The extent of Morris's debt to the ideas of Charles B. Thompson remains a matter of inference, but it seems unlikely that Morris's metaphysics would have taken quite the form it did if he had not been in St. Louis during the early 1850s.

From St. Louis Morris and his wife moved to Pittsburgh, Pennsylvania. Eardley reported that Morris:

> . . . became identified with the Church in that city, and as the spirit continued to manifest itself to him in visions and revelations, he made known to the saints some of its workings with him, which caused distrust and doubt to arise as to the source from which they sprang. But as they were fully supported by the Doctrine and Covenants and the Scriptures, many of the saints accepted them as divine truth, and he was finally induced to accept the presidency of the Branch.[20]

Dove also concurred with Eardley's report, but went on to note that "owing to some dissatisfaction he [Morris] resigned."[21] After resigning, Morris took his wife and child (apparently born that year) and moved to Utah.

These brief statements are about all the records tell us of Morris's stay in Pittsburgh. Unfortunately, they raised more questions than they answer. First of all, what was the nature of his teachings that led a number of Saints to oppose his appointment as branch president and later created enough opposition to force his resignation from the position? Secondly, what was the nature of the Mormon congregation over which he presided? Did it consist of "Brighamites," or was its membership made up largely of those who opposed Brigham Young? The L.D.S. Historical Department has no records of a Pittsburgh branch of the Utah church during the time Joseph Morris lived there. The absence of such records does not, of course, prove that no "Brighamite" branch existed in Pittsburgh at that time, but perhaps Joseph Morris actually presided over a group of Mormons opposed to Brigham Young. Certainly there was a sizable number of disaffected Mormons scattered throughout the Ohio, Mississippi, and Missouri valleys at that time. Although he had already departed for south-central Pennsylvania during

19 Morris, *The Spirit Prevails,* pp. 644–45.
20 Eardley, *Gems of Inspiration,* pp. 7–8.
21 Morris, *The Spirit Prevails,* p. 2.

Morris's sojourn, Sidney Rigdon had lived in Pittsburgh during 1844 and 1845.[22] Some of his followers or members of other dissident groups may well have been in Pittsburgh in 1852–53. In any event, it is likely that Morris encountered considerable anti-Brigham Young sentiment in both Pittsburgh and St. Louis, and this may well have colored his vision of the Utah church very early in his career.

If Morris did actually preside over the non-"Brighamites" in Pittsburgh, his hasty departure for Utah makes sense. He may well have felt that inasmuch as the non-"Brighamite" Mormons were unreceptive to his new principles and doctrines, he would go west to try them out on the followers of Brigham Young. Besides, Morris already had a brother living in Utah who would undoubtedly welcome him with open arms.

Upon arriving in Utah, Morris and his family were, indeed, welcomed by his brother George. They lived with him in Salt Lake City until the spring of 1854, when they moved south to Ephraim—again lodging with relatives, this time with Mary's brother. Almost immediately Joseph Morris seems to have aroused the suspicion and enmity of the church authorities. Eardley explained:

> . . . here again he began to declare the wonderful principles and to denounce the errors and corruptions which were destroying the spiritual life of the Church. His reputation as an opposer of the Church, a fault-finder, a religious fanatic, spread more and more, and the bishop attempted to close his mouth, but failing to do so, began to persecute and denounce him, and finally set his wife against him, causing her to cast him off. He returned to Salt Lake City destitute of all his earthly possessions, and of his family, wounded in spirit, and disheartened from the ever-increasing abuse and calumny which was heaped upon him.[23]

Dove reported that Morris then married Elizabeth Mills, a widow, in 1855, but that she left him in about six months. "Then he went from place to place, endeavoring to find employment. He succeeded in getting work, but was not as successful in obtaining his pay; in fact, he was baffled in all his temporal pursuits."[24]

As previously noted, Morris moved to Provo in 1857 and married once again, this time to Elizabeth Jones, the wife he had failed to identify by name in his letters to Brigham Young and James C. Snow in December of that same year.

22 F. Mark McKiernan, *The Voice of One Crying in the Wilderness: Sidney Rigdon, Religious Reformer, 1793–1876* (Lawrence, Kansas: Coronado Press, 1971), pp. 133–42.

23 Eardley, *Gems of Inspiration,* p. 8.

24 Morris, *The Spirit Prevails,* p. 2.

By this time the prophetic pattern was firmly established. Morris had suffered greatly both physically and spiritually. Destitute of friends, family, and worldly possessions, his real or imagined persecutions for the sake of God made him virtually an outcast in the wilderness. It is hardly surprising that at this low point in his career he not only turned to God, but also sought redress from the most powerful mortal in the territory—Brigham Young.

4 Threats in Desperation

On June 15, 1859, Joseph Morris wrote to Brigham Young describing a visit he had recently made to Salt Lake City with the intention of visiting him. Apparently, this was by invitation or supposed invitation based upon some reference Brigham Young had made to Morris in the Deseret News, the local newspaper. Morris interpreted the article as an acknowledgment of his role as a prophet, although the reference was undoubtedly facetious. Whatever the case, Morris did not receive an audience with Young, and his subsequent letter contained sharp words of rebuke. The letter ended on a militant note: "a Commandment I give unto you that you call my servant Joseph [Morris] up to the head of my Church forthwith and linger not, or you will be cut off; for my time has come."

Following this letter, Joseph Morris began more and more to stress the imminence of the Second Advent of Christ and the beginning of the millennium. On September 1, 1859, Morris wrote:

> To President Brigham Young: Dear Sir, I am happy to inform you that I am still alive and in the discharge of my duty . . . .
>
> It is true that the full keys of the Priesthood is now given and it will make a material difference in the organization of the Church when it is reorganized again. But a perfect organization cannot take place at present until Jesus comes and brings with him those hundred and forty and four thousand that John speaks of clothed upon with their resurrected bodies and they shall bring their wives with them. And at their appearance upon this earth a certain portion of it will undergo a change and be prepared for their reception and they will commence the resurrection.
>
> It is now turned two years since I was first call[ed] of the Lord and from that time to the present I have fought the Devil and everything else that came in contact with me, without a person on the earth that I could tell my afflictions to. And now I am compelled to fight feelings with you and the twelve. This I never expected.
>
> I have written nothing to you, only that which the Lord dictated me and if you do not know it now, you will know it hither to your salvation or damnation. I have never had a feeling in my heart to lessen your influence in the estimation of the saints; but my feeling has always been to raise

you up and to bless you all the day long. It is not in my heart to hinder you from enjoying any blessing that the Lord has laid out for you. I have pleaded before the Lord for you in your affliction that he might bear you up and that you might do your duty. I wish you to become one with me in the great work of the Lord, and let us work together in union, that we may bring about the purposes of the Lord.

As concerning Joseph Smith, I love him as I do my own heart's blood, and I will swear by the Gods of eternity that I will avenge his blood upon the United States. I do not only love Joseph, but I love you and the twelve, those of them that are faithful, and I could lay my life down for you if it were necessary, if you would only become one with me. But if you set your heart against me to hinder me from coming to the head of the Church rest assured that the Lord will accomplish his own purposes. Israel will be delivered and the Kingdom of God will triumph. And Jesus will come to reign and Adam's posterity will be saved and this world will be glorified whether you give us your hand or not.

The purposes of the Almighty cannot be frustrated by mortal man, and if you do not give us your hand, it will be your own loss and if you value your own standing as the President of the Church, you will take the counsel that I am about to give unto you.

I wish to come up to the head of the Church for I have some business to attend to before a public meeting is called. [It is] business of importance, and as soon as you have read this letter I want you to send for me [to come] up to the head of the Church so I can do that which the Lord requires at my hands.

I came once and you drove me away and now I expect that you will send for me. This I require at your hands: I am destitute of a place to live. I travel about from one place to another. . . . Hell follows after me or else it goes before me and I have about worked-up all of my parading ground. And if you do not take my counsel and send for me, I shall conclude in my mind that you want to use me up and that you are an enemy to God and I will call for the destroying angels of the Lord . . . and I will deliver Israel. . . .

. . . Let your whole attention be upon the deliverance of Israel and open the way for me so that I can soon come up to the head of the Church. . . . I long to have the privilege of meeting with you where I can have the opportunity to speak face to face with you, for I have never had the opportunity to make known much unto you. As yet I have only, as it were, hinted to you, . . . but when I come up to the head of the Church I will make known unto you all things that is necessary for you to know.

I now close my letter.

So no more from your never failing friend and brother, Prophet, Seer and Revelator of the Church of Jesus Christ of Latter-day Saints, Joseph Morris.

Although this letter was filled with meekness, humility, and conciliation, it threatened dire consequences if Morris's advice was not taken. For the next several months Morris's letters reflected an increasingly militant and demanding note, but by late autumn the threats and demands virtually faded away.

On New Year's Day, 1860, Joseph Morris wrote a blistering letter to Brigham Young. Although dated January 1, 1859, there can be little doubt from the text that it succeeded the letter of September 1, 1859. Morris began with his sharpest rebuke yet.

> It seems a small thing to you to disregard and trample under your feet the counsel of the greatest prophet that ever lived upon this earth. Verily, verily, thus saith the Lord unto you: When you was small I took you and raised you up and I watched over you by night and by day. And when you was afflicted I rose you up again and I guarded you. as a father and you was unto me the apple of mine eye. . . . I multiplied your substance, your cattle and your horses, your houses, and your lands, your gold and your silver until you have waxed great. And when I rose up a prophet to deliver my people Israel and sent him unto you, you drove him away when he was destitute of food to eat or a place to lay his head. And I say unto you, my wrath and my indignation is kindled against you for you have both insulted me and my Father and you have committed a grievous sin against my servant by rejecting him when I sent him up to the head of my Church to do the work that I appointed him. Yea, I say unto you, if you had not done this wicked thing, I would have established both you and your seed upon the throne of Israel forever. But now I will deliver you into the hands of my servant Joseph and he shall deal with you as seemeth him good, and what he does I will sanction; for I will be with him and his words shall never fail.

At this point, the letter began to describe certain features of the millennium, the nature of the resurrection, and the eventual deification of Adam. However, the last page or pages are missing.

The next letter Brigham Young received from Joseph Morris was dated April 20, 1860. It was presented as a revelation to Morris for the purpose of instructing him in his ministry. Apparently it was sent to Young as a point of information and as a warning.

> Behold verily, verily I say unto you [Joseph Morris] prepare yourself to go forth to deliver my people; for the set time has now come. For I have heard the prayers and the groanings of mine afflicted people and I will now come out of my hiding place to their defense and I will give them the victory over their enemies.
>
> I have sent a warning voice unto the chief shepherds of my flock and they have hardened their hearts and stiffened their necks against it, and trampled my words under their feet as a thing of naught. And now they shall know that I am the Lord and that I can deliver my people and do my own work without their assistance. I am Jesus Christ and I have done my duty to them. And when I have most needed them they have left me alone.

> But, although they have left me when I needed their assistance the most, yet I am not with[out] friends in the world—and that they shall see. And now I say unto you my servant, Joseph, place yourself in readiness for that which is coming upon you. For, behold, I give unto you a commandment that you shall go forth with all your power and warn this people of the destruction that is coming upon them. You shall open your mouth both long and loud and proclaim against the abominations of this people. For they have departed from me altogether and I have rejected them as they are. And I say unto you that you shall gather together all those that will harken unto me, and I will preserve their lives and supply their needs, and I will be their true shepherd and I will leave them no more; but I will feed them in a fat pasture and I will be their God, and they shall be my people.
>
> And I say unto you that you shall not regard those shepherds which I placed over my flock which are now mine enemies; for tears of sorrow shall roll down their cheeks. Now I have done all in my power to save them, but it is all in vain. And they shall be the first to feel my withering hand and all those that will not gather themselves together according to your command I will cut them off. If it needs be . . . I will cut off the whole community, for I will establish the full keys of the Holy Priesthood upon the earth.
>
> And inasmuch as you have desired a greater manifestation of my power than . . . you have previously had, I will grant it unto you. And when you are called to deliver my people I will place the rod in your hand. Therefore, prepare yourself to receive it for I will speedily send an holy messenger with it and he shall place it in your hand with all the power that accompanied it in the days that it was upon the earth. For thou art Moses, the legal heir to use it and no person on the earth shall use it but thyself.
>
> Behold, I am the Eternal Father, and I testify unto those whom this revelation may concern, that I have sent my son Jesus Christ to make these things known unto my servant, Joseph.
>
> I now have no more. I am he that holds in mine hands the keys of death and hell even Jesus Christ, even so Amen and Amen.

This eloquent revelation not only served to inform and warn Young, but it contained several ideas that carried Morris far beyond previous commitments. First, it emphasized that the leaders of the Mormon church had failed to heed God's advice and were now rejected. Second, the time for deliverance at the hands of Joseph Morris was nigh. Third, Morris should now turn his attention to preaching among the people. Fourth, the righteous should gather together with Morris in an undisclosed location. This letter contained the first hint that Morris contemplated a separatist movement rather than a reformation.

Despite the stern note of this revelation and the specific charges given to Morris, Brigham Young remained unimpressed. On the margin was boldly penciled: "Twaddle."

Although the revelation of April 20, 1860, contained a clear note of rejection and finality, apparently it was really intended to intimidate Brigham Young in the hope that he would still call Morris to the head of the church. At any rate, Morris's next letter, dated June 24, 1860, gave Young and the apostles another chance.

> Gentlemen, I have waited with great patience . . . fully expecting that you would open a way for me that I might come up to the head of the Church in a pleasant manner—to do the work which the Lord has called me to do. But, I have waited in vain. I am therefore now compelled to come up whether there is a door open or not.
>
> I have visited the homes of a few of the twelve and conversed with them and I acknowledge that I have never been satisfied with the spirit which they have manifested towards me. They have treated me with coolness. . . . if I had been some great lawyer or doctor and could have drawn a large train of people after me by flattery, I should be better received by some people. But as it is, I am so small that some people can hardly see me at all . . . .
>
> . . . Oh ye Chief Shepherds of Israel, hear . . . the word of the Lord and obey it that it may be well with you . . . .
>
> I am Joseph Morris, Prophet, Seer and Revelator of the Church of Jesus Christ of Latter-day Saints.

The latter part of the letter consisted of a brief revelation given by "The Eternal Father," and Morris included it for the Mormon leaders' edification.

> I speak unto you oh ye Chief Shepherds of my flock through mine only begotten son. And I say unto you that mercy has had its claim upon you and justice will now take place. I have pleaded with you and advised you and rebuked you for your sins. . . . I have now sent my servant Joseph to you for the last time and if you open the way for him it will be well with you, but if you do not, I will forthwith cut you . . . and your seed off from the earth. . . . I will open the way for him myself, for I am the Lord and I do despise those that are rebellious, but I delight in those that are humble.

The note of warning and finality is unmistakable in this letter, but it was apparently still unheeded by the Mormon leaders. Nevertheless, Morris must have been granted an audience with Brigham Young some time during the summer or early fall of 1860, for his next letter (dated November 20, 1860) referred to such a visit. Apparently, Morris was rebuffed, but the audience itself must have renewed his hope that his mission might yet be acknowledged by the church hierarchy. More than likely this letter was written as much in a spirit of desperation as conciliation, for Morris had already used threats to no avail and had once more been driven out of house and home. He wrote:

To President Brigham Young, Dear Sir, I feel a deep realizing sense of my obligations to you and this people having been called of the Lord. . . . It is now expected that you will do your duty. The Lord holds you responsible for all the innocent blood which may be shed on your account. Therefore, prepare yourself for the task. . . . the decree of the Lord has gone forth, and he will never stay his hand until he has accomplished his purposes upon the earth. And if you are in the way you will be consumed, for wrath has gone out from the presence of the Almighty. I am now standing between you [and God] and I am holding . . . [his wrath] off you. Therefore, if you wish to save your lives and the lives of this people, you will rise up and do your duty. And do not think that the time has not yet come, for it has. I cannot hold the wrath of God off you any longer, for he says that he will destroy you all in one day. He will not suffer that the destroyer [devil] shall hold his people in bondage any longer.

Excuse me for being so plain, [but] remember that the rebuke of a friend is better than the kisses of an enemy. I have often thought that the men who ought to be my best friends have been my greatest opposers. All that I ever asked of them was to open my way that I could come up, but that was too much.

I have traveled about for years and never had a sure abiding place to lay my head. I may ask, what do you require at my hands? Am I worthy of a home? What think ye about it? If ye can do without me, I can do without you. I have seen the day that I have had a home, but I have lost it for your sake. I have often thought that you are not worthy to have the full keys of the Holy Priesthood in your midst. You have never learned how to treat a servant of the Lord. I have often pleaded with the Lord to take me out of your midst for my burden is greater than I can bear. Do you not think that I ought to have a home as well as you, seeing that I must remain with you? If a home adds comfort to your mortal existence, do you not think that it does to mine? Why should you seek to deprive me of the blessing which you enjoy? If you love pleasure, why should you strive to hinder me from enjoying the same? Have I not a claim with you of a livelihood? If this is all true, then let us act like a band of brethren towards each other and lay aside all selfishness.

I do not wish to trample upon your rights. You have rights as well as me and your rights will be respected by me. Why then won't you try to meet me upon equal ground?

It is true that I have been very severe with you betimes, but the Lord has done it himself and as far as being illnatured is concerned, that was never a failing of mine. I am persuaded that you know very little about me. When you have conversed with me you will form other ideas of me. But there are times when it is necessary to be severe with those that will not do their duty. But if you wish me to be good-natured, you will do right.

. . . I do not wish you to be destroyed. I will do anything for you that lies in my power to save you. What do you desire of me? Tell me and I will

> grant it unto you. . . . I do not like to break up the feelings of my fellow creatures when it can be avoided. Then rest assured that I am your never failing friend and if you are destroyed you will do it [to] yourselves.
>
> Since my last visit to you I have written a number of revelations which you have not seen . . . which I should like you to see. There is many things contained in them that has been hid from you . . . and if you open the way for me you can see them. The Lord has now sent me up to the head of the Church to commence the work—having now placed all power in my hands . . . He says that I shall meet with no disappointment as I have done hitherto for, for he says that he will consume everything that stands in my way, so I never expect to be disappointed any more.
>
> Chancy West has driven me away from the place which I was staying at and now I have no place to go . . . but to you. Therefore, prepare for me. . . . I am Joseph Morris, Prophet, Seer and Revelator of the Church of Jesus Christ of Latter-day Saints.

It seems clear from the above letter that Morris was greatly discouraged. It was not so much a matter of patience as endurance. It is curious, though perhaps characteristic, that he held Brigham Young responsible for his own sad state of material affairs. From the very beginning of his ministry, Morris had been destitute, but he always blamed others for this misfortune. He expected the church in general and Brigham Young in particular to provide him with a comfortable house, respectable clothing, and abundant food. Actually he was not asking for more than most ministers (to say nothing of prophets) might reasonably expect. The Brighamites did not believe in a paid ministry. They believed, much like the Puritans, that a man's material possessions were a manifestation of God's favor. If a man could not provide handsomely for himself and family, there was little likelihood that he was highly favored of God. Certainly he would not be likely to manage the affairs of the church judiciously if his own were in disarray. Morris lacked both family and material substance—evident signs to the Mormons of God's disfavor.

Furthermore, Morris had several times spoken out against what he thought was the excessive materialism of Brigham Young. Undoubtedly, Morris's basic inconsistency in condemning wealth on the one hand, yet wishing to share Young's material substance on the other, caught Brigham's notice. In all likelihood, Morris's pleading of poverty not only failed to arouse Young's sympathy as intended but stirred feelings of disdain and contempt. Thus, it is not surprising to once more find a terse response penciled on the letter's margin: "Bosh!"

Hoping against hope that he would finally be listened to, Morris addressed a letter to Brigham Young the following day (November 21, 1860). It is the last of Morris's letters found in Young's papers. Morris personally delivered both letters to Young at the same time, but apparently he did not obtain an audience. A copy of the second letter is also contained in *The Spirit Prevails.* There it has been subjected to considerable editing, but the two letters are the same in substance until near the end of the final paragraph. At this point significant discrepancies emerge, which will be detailed momentarily.

The letter begins with a review of Morris's theory of reincarnation or transmigration of spirits. Then it becomes not only conciliatory but pleading in tone—begging Brigham Young to take Morris in and minister to his needs. In many ways, this letter shows Morris at his lowest point. Devoid of threats, it lacks Morris's customary touch of bravado. Morris appears here as a prophet completely without honor—a touching and pathetic creature lost in a friendless wilderness and one who does not even call upon God to intimidate his hoped-for benefactor.

> Oh, how I feel the responsibility of my office. Do not add to my burden, I entreat you; for if you do, you will run my cup over. I want you to open my way without causing me any trouble. Why should you pack [burden] me when I am now weighted down? If you won't . . . [burden] me, I won't . . . [burden] you anymore than I can help. Why should we be a burden to each other? I wish you to consider my situation. I am constantly sick. Therefore, what you do, do it quickly for I cannot wait. I have no place to stop at, and if you are my friend, prove it now for this is the time that I need help. You have promised to be faithful to me, and now show it. Oh, what a burden it would remove off my shoulders if I could only feel that any way was open that I could come up without any trouble. For, if you stand against me, I know the consequences that will arise from it. I have suffered everything that a man could suffer to save this people, and I do not want to see them destroyed. Now, therefore, if you love your fellow creatures, you will open my way at once. I have heard your pleadings and I have willingly granted your request. And now what is there in the way? I am willing to meet with you and converse with you and hear your complaints and minister all the comfort to you that lies in my power. And if I have ever written anything to you that you do not understand, I am perfectly willing to explain it to your understanding. I will remove everything out of your way that I can. [I hope] you will excuse my imperfections. I am with you.

At this point Morris's original letter diverges from the version found in The Spirit Prevails. The latter version concludes: ". . you will excuse my imperfections in writing and spelling, for I have had to write under very unfavorable circumstances. I am not above being taught by a child that can teach me anything. I am willing both to teach and to be taught. I hope to live and to learn, for I do not know all things yet. I now add no more, but remain, Yours etc. [Signed] Joseph Morris.[1]

1 Morris, The Spirit Prevails, p. 666.

The conclusion of the original letter not only departs strikingly from the one above, it is one of the most perplexing bits of Morris's writings. If it is taken literally, it sounds very much like a lovelorn letter to "Sarad" (whoever that was) from Morris, her erstwhile admirer. On the other hand, if taken allegorically (which seems more reasonable) , "Sarad" may well be symbolic of the Mormon church or of Brigham Young as the representative of the church. Whatever the case, this ending represents a dramatic change of pace and style from the earlier part of the letter, and it has some stylistic counterpart in the Old Testament "Songs of Solomon."

> I long to behold the face of my dearest Sarad, for she lies near my heart. I have thought that she was preparing a place for me and I want to go where she is. Let that be where it may, for I claim her as mine own. And when I see her, it will be a happy meeting. She has pleaded with me to be gentle, and I have granted her request. She should not be afraid to meet me for I will speak words of comfort unto her and hear her tales; for she has my confidence. I have not had the privilege to converse with her much yet, but I know her. My dearest, open the way for me and I will come to you, for you have given yourself to me and why should you be afraid of your own? My heart is with you. Therefore, prepare for me. I am yours. I have no more.

Despite the fact that this letter shows Morris demoralized, discouraged, and even desperate, it also may be seen as the darkness just before the dawn. Help was on the way, but not from the object of his petitions. On the way to deliver the letters to Brigham Young, Morris had a most providential encounter with a man who was to provide the means to his temporal salvation.

Sometime in the spring of 1860 Joseph Morris had moved to Slaterville, forty miles north of Salt Lake City, where he remained until fall. According to George Dove, he had attracted only one disciple, a Father Jones, but Mother Jones and others opposed him. "At last, notice was given him by some of the leading men of the place that he must leave in so many hours."[2]

Although Dove gives this time as October, it seems more likely that it was actually November and that it provided the impetus for Morris's two desperate letters to Brigham Young. Whatever the case, Morris wrote:

> In the fall of 1860, as I was going to Salt Lake City, to deliver two letters to addresses that I had written to President Young, I met Brother John Cook [of South Weber] near the Warm Springs. We entered into conversation, in which I told him who and what I was, and what the Lord was about to do. He invited me to his house, which invitation I accepted after transacting my business in the City, and it has ever since been a home where I have been well cared for.[3]

2 Morris, The Spirit Prevails, p. 3.
3 Morris, The Spirit Prevails, pp. 671–72.

Clearly, this was the turning point in Morris's career. He continued:

> On my arrival here [at South Weber] I was introduced to John Cook's brother, Richard, who was at that time bishop of this ward, to whom I unfolded the great and precious things which the Lord had revealed to me.
>
> After a few days spent in the careful and prayerful examination of the revelations I had received, and the doctrines embodied therein, he came to the conclusion that they were from heaven. Others began to investigate also, and their investigations likewise resulted in a conviction of the truth and divinity of my mission, and of the revelations which God had been pleased to give through me.[4]

Morris's new sense of temporal security and the attachment of a few disciples did wonders for his sagging spirit. His courage and fervor returned, and he again spoke boldly to Brigham Young. On December 21, 1860, Morris penned his last stinging rebuke:

> I must acknowledge that I am astonished when I think of the willful blindness and rebellion of men who profess to be the servants of the Lord. But when I trace the Bible and Book of Mormon and see how men acted who were kings and judges, there were very few cases wherein they have not destroyed themselves in the flesh. Oh, what a shame it is that men on whom the Lord has placed a little authority should destroy themselves therewith. What is the cause of this? It is rebellion. When they commence to go astray, they will not stop, but continue to go on until the Lord is obliged to cut both them and their seed off from the earth. Oh, how my heart pains me when I think of the situation of this people. They are going like a lamb to the slaughter. Their shepherds have been warned, but they have not warned the flock, and destruction will come upon them in one day. . . . If you do not wish to be subject to the man who holds the keys of the kingdom, you can take your own course. I have never been an enemy to you, and you will find that out hereafter. You have always treated me as an enemy, but you will find out that you have chosen the weakest side and that you cannot stay the hand of the Almighty. You may set yourselves against [Him] as strongly as you please, but you will go down. You shall know that the Lord Omnipotent reigneth, and raiseth up at his pleasure, and he will not ask you who he shall call to rule his kingdom. . . . I have striven with all my power to penetrate your hard hearts; but it appears to be in vain. . . . You have shut your ears and hearts against the truth, determined to take your own course; but can you maintain your ground against the god who sent you here? . . . I have done my duty to you whether you think so or not. My skirts are clean of your blood. . . .
>
> I have now said and done all that I could do for you, except you will humble yourselves and comply with the Lord's request. If you will do this, I will be with you with all my heart, and you shall prove that I am a

4 Morris, The Spirit Prevails, p. 672.

> never-failing friend; but as long as you go on sustaining the power of the devil upon me and upon this people, you keep my feelings worked up against you. There are but two ways before you. You must take either one or the other of them; the one leads to death, and the other leads to life. I must now leave the matter with you; do as you please.[5]

This letter was Morris's last real attempt to call Brigham Young and the apostles to repentance. For all practical purposes Morris gave up on them at this point and thereafter directed his attention toward promoting his own ministry among the people. Morris continued to mention Young in his revelations, but more and more he perceived the church president as an enemy rather than as a friend.

The die was now cast. Joseph Morris was a prophet emerging from the wilderness. From this point forward he considered both the Mormon church and its leaders to be lost, and he set about the business of preparing to establish his own church rather than attempting to lead the "Brighamites." More and more Morris took on the characteristics of a doomsday prophet, predicting the sudden destruction of those who would not follow him. Increasingly he preached the gathering together of the righteous to await the imminent appearance of Jesus Christ, who would deliver them from worldly cares and usher in the Kingdom of Heaven upon earth.

5 Morris, The Spirit Prevails, pp. 667–69.

5 The Millennial Hope

The number of groups that have held millennial expectations in America, or that have tried to usher in some form of collective utopia with millennial overtones is absolutely astounding. Donald Pitzer compiled a list of such organizations formed during and after the colonial period until 1965. This comprehensive list includes such well-known groups as the Shakers, the Harmony Society, New Harmony, the Oneida Perfectionists, the Bishop Hill Colony, the Hutterites, the Icarians, and hundreds of less-known groups. The total list exceeds fifteen hundred.[1] Arrington and his coauthors stated that communalism in America experienced a remarkable re-birth between 1965 and 1970 with more than two thousand secular communities being founded in many parts of the United States.[2] Pitzer puts the number as high as ten thousand. He also notes that after the death of Joseph Smith, Mormon schismatics founded numerous communities based on the United Order. These included eleven in Mexico, two in Arizona, two in Iowa, two in Kansas, one in Missouri, one in Texas, and four in Utah—including the Morrisites.[3]

Quinn asserts that half of the L.D.S. membership in 1844 refused to follow Brigham Young to Utah.[4] Steven F. Shields has identified at least four hundred churches that trace their routes to the church founded by Joseph Smith in 1830. Many of these no longer exist but a large number still do, and they are still proliferating.[5]

Of the hundreds of millennial or communal groups in America, only a few seemed to have experienced violent opposition to the extent Mormons

1 Donald E. Pitzer, ed. *American Communal Utopias* (Chapel Hill: The University of North Carolina Press, 1997). pp. 441–92.

2 Leonard J. Arrington, Feramorz Y. Fox, and Dean L. May, *Building the City of God: Community and Cooperation Among the Mormons* (Salt Lake City: Deseret Book Company, 1976), p. 12.

3 Pitzer, *American Communal Utopias.* pp. 12, 441–92.

4 D. Michael Quinn. "To Whom Shall we Go? Historical Patterns Of Restoration Believers With Serious Doubts." *Sunstone,* May 2005, p. 33.

5 Newell G. Bringhurst and John C. Hamer, eds., *Scattering of the Saints Schisms in Mormonism* (Independence, Missouri: John Whitmer Books, 2007), p. ix.

and Mormon schismatics did. Joseph Smith, the founder of Mormonism, was killed by a mob in 1844 at age thirty-nine. Joseph Morris was killed by a posse of Mormons in 1862 at age thirty-seven. James J. Strang, who established a colony on Beaver Island in Lake Michigan, was killed by a mob in 1856 at age forty-three. And the Gladdonites, an anti-polygamy schism, were threatened with dire consequences if they did not cease open opposition to plural marriage.[6]

It has been said that Americans are obsessed and most entertained by two things: sex and violence. No doubt the fact that these were such pronounced elements in early Mormon history accounts for much of the interest and fascination that so many non-Mormons have had with things Mormon. The popularity of recent books such as Krakauer's *Under the Banner of Heaven*, Beck's *Leaving the Saints*, Foster's *Religion and Sexuality*, and Walker, Turley, and Leonard's *Massacre At Mountain Meadows* provide persuasive evidence of this fascination. Of course, earlier exposés such as *Brigham's Destroying Angel* by Hickman and *Mormonism Unveiled* by John D. Lee also exploited similar themes. And if it had not been for the Morrisite War, the Morrisites probably would have attracted hardly any notice in western history.[7]

This is not to imply that Mormons, Mormon schismatics, or their serious detractors acted as they did because they regarded sex and violence as entertaining. On the contrary, they took plural marriage, civil disobedience, and other aspects of confrontation seriously— sometimes with lethal consequences. It should be recognized that the meanings and implications of plural marriage were very different from the standpoints of Mormons and their detractors. Gentiles (as Mormons referred to non-Mormons) saw sexuality, lustfulness, and exploitation of women in polygamy. Mormons saw polygamy as a fulfillment of God's will for building God's kingdom, increasing one's own posterity, and preparing for eternal exaltation. These divergent views are still extant in the conflict between Fundamentalist Mormons who still practice polygamy and the broader American society. To a considerable extent, even mainstream Mormons now view the polygamist practices of the Fundamentalists in much the same light as other Americans do. This is almost a complete reversal of nineteenth-century Mormon attitudes.

---

6 See Nels Anderson, *Desert Saints,* p. 223.

7 John Krakauer, *Under the Banner of Heaven: A Story of Violent Faith* (New York: Doubleday, 2003); Martha Beck, *Leaving the Saints,* (New York: Crown Publishers, 2005); Lawrence Foster. *Religion and Sexuality: The Shakers, The Mormons and the Oneida Community* (Urbana: University of Illinois Press, 1984); Walker, Turley, and Leonard, *Massacre at Mountain Meadows*; Hickman, *Brigham's Destroying Angel*; John D. Lee. *Mormonism Unveiled,* reprint of 1877 edition (Albuquerque: Fierra Blanca Publications, 2001).

Although Joseph Morris was aware of various schismatic Mormon groups, he generally had little or nothing to say about them. As noted earlier, he probably had contact with some of them while living in St. Louis and Pittsburgh, but that cannot be verified. One faction, however, caught his attention sufficiently that an entire chapter, given as a revelation, in *The Spirit Prevails* is devoted to it. That was the church headed by Joseph Smith III, founded just one year before the Morrisite church. It was known as the Reorganized Church of Jesus Christ of Latter Day Saints (RLDS, now known as Community of Christ). The revelation was dated May 4, 1861. Part of it declares:

> You (Joseph Morris) have heard of a new sect rising up calling themselves the 'True Latter Day Saints' headed by the son of my servant Joseph Smith, and you wish to know whether I have anything to do with them or not. I answer that I have. I am using them to be a scourge to those false shepherds of my flock that through them, I will turn them another way. I have given unto them a portion of my holy spirit to prepare them for the work which I have called them to do.
>
> Therefore, I am using them to assist you, and in the end, I will bring them up to you, and many of them will obey the fullness of the gospel and become one with you.
>
> ...I have not, as yet, called my servant, Joseph Smith to be a prophet...
>
> ...*When I call my servant Joseph Smith to be a prophet I shall call him through you.* (Emphasis added)[8]

This revelation answers the conundrum posed by Rogers in his prize-winning article in 2001. Rogers wrote that Mark Forscutt reported that prior to Morris's death (no date given) he, Forscutt, presented Morris with an article appearing in the *The True Saints Herald,* the official publication of the RLDS Church. This article warned against false prophets including Morris.

According to Forscutt, "Mr. Morris listened and instead of denouncing the attack, quietly smiled and withdrew. In a short time he returned and handed me a revelation in which Joseph Smith, the leader of the Reorganization was declared to be a prophet of God and rightful heir to the presidency of the church." Rogers then raises the question, "Why did Morris persist in his prophetic role if it had been revealed to him that Joseph Smith III was the rightful heir to the presidency of the church?"[9]

Although no corroborating evidence of this incident has been found in Morrisite records, there is no reason to doubt that it occurred as Forscutt reported. The answer to the first part of Rogers's question may be found in Morris's May 4, 1861, revelation. That revelation made clear that Joseph Smith III was not a prophet in May 1861, but that at a future time he

8 Morris, *The Spirit Prevails,* p. 90.

9 Eric P. Rogers, "Mark Hill Forscutt: Mormon Missionary, Morrisite Apostle, RLDS Minister," *John Whitmer Association Journal* 21 (2001): 74.

would be made a prophet with the approval of Joseph Morris. Assuming the exchange and revelation reported by Forscutt occurred sometime after that 1861 revelation, it was the fulfillment of that first revelation. The 1861 revelation also made it clear that there would be many prophets but that only Joseph Morris held the ultimate keys of authority. Numerous other passages in *The Spirit Prevails* assert that Morris held the supreme Keys of the Kingdom. And there is no doubt that he presented himself as the supreme representative of God on earth right up to his death.

The question of the legitimate presidency of the church can also be readily addressed. Earlier, Morris had organized the Church of Jesus Christ of Saints of the Most High. When he said that Joseph Smith III was the rightful heir of the presidency of the church, he was probably referring to the Mormon church organized by the first prophet and president, Joseph Smith Jr. Two sects—the Utah-based Church of Jesus Christ of Latter-day Saints and Smith III's Reorganized Church of Jesus Christ of Latter Day Saints—were then the principal contestants for the mantle of the original church. Morris had already written off Brigham Young and several other authorities in the Utah church. He was simply affirming that Joseph Smith III had the legitimate claim to the presidency of all factions of the L.D.S. Church other than the Church of the Most High; Brigham Young had defaulted on his claim. Morris believed that *his* church was distinct from all other L.D.S. factions and superior to them. Thus he could acknowledge the presidency of Joseph Smith III without in any way relinquishing his own exalted position. Joseph Morris revered Joseph Smith Jr.. He also was very accepting of anyone who also revered Joseph Smith Jr., providing they followed his teachings and had not led others astray.

From the very beginning of his ministry Joseph Morris preached that he would play a central role in ushering in God's Kingdom upon the earth. Without doubt he had seen the great revival of 1856 and 1857 as the beginning of the final cleansing of the church prior to the dawning of the millennial day. For that reason he was gravely disappointed when the reformation was cut short by the Utah War and never again strongly promoted by the church hierarchy. Brigham Young's insistence upon gaining economic self-sufficiency and in promoting the material welfare of his people seemed to Morris to be out of keeping with the urgency of preparing spiritually for the Second Coming, which might occur at any hour. Morris believed that the church now more than ever before needed direct revelations from God to school the people for that great event, and only he was capable of truly fulfilling that urgent need.

By February 1861 Morris had already produced over forty written revelations, which he could compare with only one for Brigham Young. The fact that many, if not most, of Young's followers took Brigham's instructions as divinely inspired hardly impressed Morris. To him a prophet, seer, and revelator was one who confidently intoned: "Thus saith the Lord" and who produced written scriptures. On December 21, 1860, Morris arrogantly challenged Young: "Now select the most clever man among you, and let him use his own faculties and write as I have done; let him write revelation after revelation, and give the Keys of the Holy Priesthood that have never before been given by man. If you can do this, you are clear and can go on as you are doing; but if you cannot do this, you are under condemnation, and your destruction will be just."[10] Brigham Young, however, never took up that challenge, and Morris continued to produce revelations at an ever-increasing rate. The central theme of Morris's revelations was the imminence of the Second Advent, but, of course, his was only a variation on a very old theme. It was the logical extension of the theme preached so eloquently by Joseph Smith three decades earlier and which was so characteristic of American Christianity.[11]

10 Morris, The Spirit Prevails, p. 669

11 Of course, neither the preoccupation with the Second Coming nor the expectation of the transformation of America into a paradise originated with the Mormons. They simply made more specific some already well-developed cultural traditions. Christopher Columbus was certain he had approached paradise upon discovering the New World, for he believed that the fresh water he found in the Gulf of Paria had as its fountain the four rivers of the Garden of Eden. He believed he was fulfilling prophecy through his discovery and that he was opening the way for the end of the world and ultimately the millennium. Eliade, an European historian of religion, writes:

> The colonization of the two Americas began under an eschatological sign: people believed that the time had come to renew the Christian world, and the true renewal was the return to the Earthly Paradise . . . . In the eyes of the English, for example, the colonization of America merely prolonged and perfected a Sacred History begun at the outset of the reformation. Indeed the triumphal push of the pioneers toward the West continued the triumphal march of Wisdom and the True Religion from East to West . . . .
>
> More than any other modern nation the United States was the product of the Protestant Reformation seeking an Earthly Paradise in which the reform of the Church was to be perfected . . . . It is significant that the millenarist theme enjoyed its greatest popularity just prior to the colonization of America and Cromwell's revolution. Hence, it is not surprising to note that the most popular religious doctrine in the Colonies was that America had been chosen among all the nations of the earth as the place of the Second Coming of Christ, and the millennium . . . would be accompanied by a paradisical transformation of the earth, as an outer sign of an inner perfection. As the eminent Puritan, Increase Mather, President of Harvard University from 1685 to 1707, wrote: "When the Kingdom of Christ has filled all the earth, this Earth will be restored to its Paradise state . . . . "

In codifying the Mormon belief concerning the millennium, Joseph Smith had written: "We believe . . . that Zion will be built upon this [the American] continent; that Christ will reign personally upon the earth; and, that, the earth will be renewed and receive its paradisiacal glory."[12]

This belief in the establishment of Zion (The City of God) within the boundaries of the United States was perhaps the most central feature of Mormonism taught by Smith. Most of his other teachings and doctrines were designed to promote this great event. Smith taught that the restoration of God's church was the first step in paving the way for the imminent establishment of the Kingdom of Heaven upon the earth and the ushering in of the millennium. However, for Smith, and especially for Brigham Young, the mere establishment of the church was not sufficient to bring about the Second Advent. They believed that Zion must literally be built by the Saints prior to Christ's appearance. A grand city must be constructed suitable for his presence and a temple built wherein He might dwell. In this regard Joseph Morris either failed to understand the place of materialism in the Mormon plan of salvation or thought that it was misdirected.

As previously noted, the Mormons believed that their materialistic success was a sign of God's favor. However, unlike the Puritans, they did not believe such success was predestined. Rather, they believed that it was a just reward for their temporal and spiritual diligence. Furthermore, they believed that the fruits of their labors should be used primarily for building up God's Kingdom in preparation for Christ's Second Advent. Thus, their emphasis upon hard work and temporal success was closely linked with millennialism. They were convinced that the time of His coming was near and that they must labor with all their might to prepare a place for Him.

On the other hand, Morris taught that Christ would come prior to the building of Zion—the spiritual preparation and proper ceremonial activities

---

> . . . the certainty of the eschatological mission, and especially of attaining once again the perfection of early Christianity and restoring paradise to earth, is not likely to be forgotten easily. It is very probable that the behavior, of the average American today, as well as the political and cultural ideology of the United States, still reflects the consequences of the Puritan certitude of having been called to restore the Earthly Paradise.

Mircea Eliade, "Paradise and Utopia," in Utopias and Utopian Thought (Boston: Beacon Press, 1967), pp. 260–69.

For further discussions of these points see Brodie, *No man knows my history*; Timothy L. Smith, *Revivalism and Social Reform*; and Ernest Lee Tuveson, *Redeemer Nation: The Idea of America's Millennial Role* (Chicago: University of Chicago Press, 1974).

12 James E. Talmage, *Articles of Faith* (Salt Lake City, Utah: Church of Jesus Christ of Latter-day Saints, 1956), p. 2.

were the true prerequisites to His appearance. Furthermore, to relieve the anxiety of his followers concerning their needs for physical necessities, he taught that the homes and buildings of the Brighamites would be made available for their own use after Christ appeared and that God would see that their needs for food and clothing were met. Given these marked differences in conceptualizing the Second Advent, it is hardly surprising that Brigham Young and Joseph Morris never came to a meeting of the minds. The lack of a need for material preparation also allowed Morris, like William Miller, leader of the nineteenth-century Millerites, to set early and specific dates for Christ to make his appearance.[13]

Despite these differences with Young, Morris was orthodox in several other millennial teachings. He believed that there must be a physical gathering together, that all material possessions should be held in common by the Saints, and that Zion ultimately would be built on the site designated by Joseph Smith.

In July 1831 Joseph Smith had declared:

> Harken, O ye elders of my church, saith the Lord your God, who have assembled yourselves together, according to my commandments, in this land, which is the land of Missouri, which is the land which I have appointed and consecrated for the gathering of the saints.
>
> Wherefore, this is the land of promise, and the place for the city of Zion.
>
> And thus saith the Lord your God, if you will receive wisdom here is wisdom. Behold the place which is now called Independence is the center place; and a spot for the temple is lying westward, upon a lot which is not far from the court-house.[14]

On August 3, 1831, Joseph Smith, in company with seven trusted disciples, dedicated the temple site, and in September of the following year he identified the time span within which its construction would occur. "Verily this is the word of the Lord, that the City New Jerusalem shall be built by the gathering of the saints, beginning at this place, even the place of the temple, which temple shall be reared in this generation.

"For verily this generation shall not pass away until a house shall be built unto the Lord."[15]

This clear identification of the place and time of construction of the City of Zion became central to the millennial expectations of the Mormons.

13 Sylvester Bliss, *Memoirs of William Miller*, reprint of 1853 edition (New York: AMS Press, 1971).

14 The Doctrine and Covenants of the Church of Jesus Christ of Latter-day Saints, rev. ed. (Salt Lake City, Utah: Church of Jesus Christ of Latter-day Saints, 1921), 57:1–4.

15 Doctrine and Covenants, 84:4–5.

Time and circumstances quickly modified the temporal expectation, but the location of Zion and its temple remains firmly fixed in Mormon doctrine.

Reluctance to leave the site of the future City of Zion (identified in Joseph Smith's writings as Jackson County, Missouri) had caused some Saints to refuse to follow Brigham Young to the West. They thought that going farther west would effectively constitute the abandonment of the land of Zion. However, those who followed Young had no question but that they would sometime return to redeem Zion. Nevertheless, this sense of deserting the land of Zion must have caused widespread concern, for Brigham Young's one and only revelation contained in the Doctrine and Covenants noted:

> And let my servants that have been appointed go and teach this, my will, to the Saints, that they may be ready to go to a land of peace.
>
> Go thy way and do as I have told you, and fear not thine enemies; for they shall not have power to stop my work. Zion shall be redeemed in mine own due time.
>
> I am he who led the children of Israel out of the land of Egypt; and my arm is stretched out in the last days, to save my people Israel. Fear not thine enemies, for they are in mine hands and I will do my pleasure with them.
>
> My people must be tried in all things, that they may be prepared to receive them, even the glory of Zion; and he that will not bear chastisement is not worthy of my kingdom.
>
> Therefore, marvel not at these things, for ye are not yet pure; ye cannot yet bear my glory; but ye shall behold it if ye are faithful in keeping all my words that I have given you.[16]

Almost from the time the Mormons arrived in Utah they expected to be called to return to Jackson County to begin constructing the City of Zion. Some of them even kept their teams harnessed and supplies on hand, anticipating to be called at a moment's notice. Brigham Young, however, remained convinced that for the time being Zion must be built in the Rocky Mountains, and he directed his energies to achieving that goal. Nevertheless, the expectation of returning to the land of Zion (or more correctly, to the Center Stake of Zion) was kept alive in the hearts of the people. In February 1861, when Joseph Morris was preaching the imminent return of Christ, Apostle Heber C. Kimball delivered an address in the Salt Lake Tabernacle clearly expressing the belief that the return to, Independence was not far distant, but that preparations were still to be made. He said: "Brethern, I shall go back to Jackson County with thousands of this people who will be faithful in their integrity; but we cannot go back until we have built some good houses."[17]

---

16 Doctrine and Covenants, 136:16, 17, 18, 30, 31, 37.

17 Heber C. Kimball, "Gathering of the People of God in the Last Days—.

Joseph Morris shared the belief that the Saints must return to Jackson County to build up the City of Zion and the temple, but he thought that enough material preparations had already been made. On October 24, 1860, he had recorded a revelation designating the location of the gathering place where Christ would appear and where eventually the march to Jackson County would begin:

> For I am about to gather together, unto one place all those that will harken to me:
>
> I have appointed a place for the gathering together of my people, which place is the Public Square in that City called the Great Salt Lake City—even the central point.
>
> And I will there stand side by side with my servant Joseph, and speak to him mouth to mouth; and I will instruct him in those things which will be necessary for him to know at the appointed time.
>
> And I will give unto him power to discern between the sheep and the goats [so called]; and he shall place the sheep on the one side and the goats on the other; for this is the harvest spoken of in the Scripture when the angels were to be sent to gather out the tares from among the wheat, that the wheat might be saved, and that the tares might be destroyed.
>
> And at that time the hosts of heaven shall be there, and I will lead them up to battle, and go before them from conquering to conquer; and I will never again stay my hand until I have laid mine enemies low; for my time is now come to make manifest mine almighty power among the nations and kingdoms of the earth.[18]

Morris was forced by succeeding events to postpone the gathering in the Salt Lake City Square, but he never lost sight of that objective. During the remaining months of his life he confidently expected to participate in that event and laid elaborate plans for the ceremonies that would precede and accompany it.

Upon arriving in South Weber with John Cook, Morris was introduced to Cook's brother Richard, the bishop of the South Weber Ward. Morris told Richard of his prophetic calling, and Cook soon accepted him in that role. Richard Cook was the first Mormon leader to take Morris seriously, and his conversion soon led others to investigate the self-proclaimed prophet and his tenets.

By February Morris had attracted a large enough following to warrant investigation by general church authorities, who appeared in the persons of Wilford Woodruff and John Taylor. Through Richard Cook they called

---

Return to Jackson County, etc.," 17 February 1861, in *Journal of Discourses*, delivered by Brigham Young and other church leaders, 26 vols. (Liverpool, England: 1854–86), 8:348–51.

18 Morris, *The Spirit Prevails*, p. 31.

a meeting for the members of the South Weber Ward on the 11th. George Dove reported:

> They called the people together and demanded to know what folly was going on, and what they were doing there. They said: "We hear it reported that you have a prophet among you, and we cannot accept of any prophet but Brigham Young." Joseph being questioned, replied: "I am by right of my heirship, prophet, seer, and revelator to the Church of the Latter Day Saints." Seventeen of the Weber people said that they accepted him as a prophet; so they were "cut off" from the Church.[19]

Morris later gave an account of this meeting to his friend, George Leslie. He wrote: "This was the first time that I had been publically proclaimed as God's prophet, and W. Woodruff stood up and prophesied that my influence should from that time go down. Since that time, however, the spirit of the Lord has rested upon the people, and they have come from almost all parts of the Territory to inquire after these strange things that have so mysteriously been brought about."[20] The official Mormon record, however, places a somewhat different emphasis on the meeting:

> The hearing was long and great patience was exercised by the two apostles. Morris himself was sent for and given a hearing though it appeared that he was not very forceful in presenting his claims, and he had to be strongly urged before he would make any statement at all. Bishop Cook was commended by Elder Taylor for his frankness in declaring his belief in the order of things set forth in the claims of Morris. An overzealous brother by the name of Watts, opposed to Bishop Cook and everything Morrisite, made harsh accusations against the bishop, charging him with lying, with not abiding the council of President Young, and denouncing him as worthy of destruction. "He made some very unwise statements . . . which were disapproved by Elders Woodruff and Taylor, and Bishop Cook said he was satisfied with their disapproval" [of what Watts had said].
>
> . . . In concluding the meeting Elder John Taylor admonished the brethren who had remained faithful in the South Weber ward "to go to work in the fear of God and work righteousness. Treat those well who cannot believe as you do, they have expressed themselves very candidly, you can afford to treat them well. You that profess the principles of Jesus Christ, show it by your works." All which represents fair and gentle treatment towards the brethren so far lost in error.[21]

John R. Eardley stressed a more ominous note in the meeting. He reported that "the anathemas of the Church were pronounced against any

---

19 Morris, *The Spirit Prevails*, p. 4.

20 Morris, *The Spirit Prevails*, p. 672.

21 Roberts, *Comprehensive History*, 4:41–42.

who should go to see the new prophet."[22] Eardley further noted that the faithful Mormons in attendance were "astonished and confounded" when the seventeen believers, with Bishop Cook at their head, defied the general authorities. This defiance generated an acrimonious and vehement response from at least one church member. "An old man named Watts [a Mormon] arose, and in an inflammatory speech recommended that the adherents of the new prophet should be 'cut off under the chin,' and laid away in the brush, at the same time accompanying his words with a motion of the hand, drawing it across his throat. This, he said, was what ought to be done, according to his understanding of the laws of the Church."[23]

Whether or not this occurred exactly as Eardley reported it is uncertain, but it does serve to illustrate the strong feelings of resentment some Mormons held toward dissenters from the faith. Certainly it was prophetic of the hostility that was to develop between the Mormons and Morrisites—a hostility which would ultimately result in open conflict and death.

Converts began almost immediately to gather around their newfound prophet at South Weber, or Kington Fort, also known variously as Kingston Fort, Morris 'Town, and Weber Camp. The "fort," which formed the nucleus of the community, was located near the mouth of Weber Canyon on a flood plain a few hundred yards south of Weber River.

Immediately east of the fort the foothills rose gently, then abruptly, into the upthrust of the Wasatch Front, which towered thousands of feet overhead. Low, sandy hills overlooked the fort to the south and west, as did similar bluffs across the river to the north. The surrounding bluffs and rolling hills were barren of trees, covered only with grass, sage, and other small plants and shrubs. Willows and cottonwoods formed a green fringe along the Weber River, but most of the river bottom was relatively open, consisting of pastureland and some irrigated fields. Because the fort sat in a bowl surrounded almost completely by hills and mountains, it afforded very limited visibility of the larger valley. Thus, it was remarkably isolated, even though Ogden was only a few miles to the north and smaller Mormon settlements such as Slaterville and Kaysville were nearby. Hardly a fortification, the fort was a fragile collection of log and willow and mud buildings surrounded partially by a low, crumbling adobe wall and a pole corral for livestock and horses. It had been started in 1853, when word had gone out from Mormon headquarters for local communities to construct forts for their protection. The fort was named after James Kington, the local bishop, and enclosed a ten-acre square.[24] It had never been completed and had been abandoned

22 Eardley, *Gems of Inspiration*, p. 17.

23 Eardley, *Gems of Inspiration*, p. 17.

24 G. M. Howard, "Men, Motives, and Misunderstandings: A New Look at the Morrisite War of 1862," *Utah Historical Quarterly* 44 (Spring 1976): 120. Be-

in 1858 when the order came for the Saints to move southward before the advance of Johnston's Army.

When the Morrisites took possession of the fort, a large tent and a bowery were set up for the purpose of holding meetings, but few permanent structures were built. However, the rapid attraction of converts severely taxed the available shelter so that a hodgepodge of tents, wagon boxes, and daub and wattle shelters were soon erected in and around the fort. At no time did Morris regard the fort as a permanent settlement. He expected that the Saints would soon be delivered and would proceed to Salt Lake City where the official gathering would occur.

Although the fort was poorly constructed, it was not a dirty or disorderly place. On the contrary, it was kept in spotless condition. Henry Firth, one of Morris's followers who lived for a time at the fort, reported that "the Morrisites swept the fort daily and kept it in such perfect order that not a straw was out of place. They also whitewashed their little huts at least once a week; and this is all because they expected Christ daily.

Between February and April 1861 Joseph Morris received some ten revelations, including one on April 3 that provided instructions for organizing a church. This revelation named certain persons to hold positions in the new organization. Among these was Richard Cook. He was designated as first counselor to Joseph Morris and was promised that he would one day be made church president under Morris's direction. John Parson was to be appointed president of the apostles, and John Cook, William Kendall, and John Firth were to be ordained high priests.[25]

The revelation of April 3 was not uniformly accepted by the Morrisites and caused some murmurings in the ranks. In response to this, another revelation was received the next day. It began:

> Inasmuch as there has been some dissatisfaction manifested by some concerning the blessing which I have given unto my servants whom I called, I will answer them upon this matter.
>
> They have thought that I am partial to one more than to another, and they have also thought that I have not fulfilled my promises which I have made in those blessings; but they condemn me before I have had an opportunity of fulfilling them. . . . they think that if I do not fulfill my promises immediately after I have made them, that all is over, and that I am false.
>
> It was necessary for me to call these two men [Richard Cook and John Parson], in order to commence an organization; and as soon as I can do so, I will call all the others, and place them in honorable places, also.[26]

---

cause Morris used the name Kingston in *The Spirit Prevails*, the name of the fort appears as Kingston in the first two editions of this book. This edition uses the correct name, Kington.

25 Morris, *The Spirit Prevails*, p. 77.

26 Morris, *The Spirit Prevails*, pp. 78–79.

Apparently this revelation was sufficient to quiet the troubled waters, for on April 6, 1861, the thirty-first anniversary of the founding of the Mormon church, the new church was formally organized with six members—Joseph Morris, John Cook, Richard Cook, John Firth, William Kendall, and Nathan Byrne.[27] The organization was called The Church of Jesus Christ of Saints of the Most High. But this, of course, was soon shortened to Morrisite. Later on it also became known as The Church of the Firstborn, but there is no connection between it and a polygamous Mormon schism that used the name Firstborn many years later. Thirteen other individuals were also baptized and confirmed members on that founding day.

Although many converts had already gathered at South Weber, it was not until May 11, 1861, that Morris received a revelation commanding the scattered believers to assemble at that location. Thereafter the numbers grew rapidly. Eardley reported that three months after the church was organized it had a membership of over 300 souls and that there was a great outpouring of God's spirit upon the believers.

> The prophet scarcely saw a day without writing a revelation on doctrine, and to guide the people in their daily conduct. They were required to lay aside all kinds of labor, except such as was absolutely necessary for their daily conveniences, and to live in common. Every believer was instructed to consecrate all his property to the Church—his surplus clothing, and whatever the Lord had blessed him with, except his wife and children—so that all fared alike in their mode of living. A bishop was appointed to take charge of consecrated property, and from it he supplied the wants of the people.
>
> From the bishop's accounts we learn that there was consecrated to the Church property to the amount of $167,622.54, and private donations to the poor amounted to $7,306.16. Thus the saints were bound together as one family, having made a covenant with the Lord by sacrifice. It was by this consecration that the entire Weber camp were enabled to live until the time of their dispersion came. It was particularly enjoined upon all to become thoroughly acquainted with the principles revealed from day to day, and for this purpose daily meetings were appointed for their study and explanation, as the time would soon come when they would not enjoy this privilege.[28]

A year later the baptized membership of the Morrisite church had reached 507 while another 500 were believers or openly sympathetic.[29]

Surprisingly, the growth of the sect was not the result of vigorous missionary activity, for little if any was done. Neither was there an outpouring

---

27 Richard W. Young, "The Morrisite War," *The Contributor* 11 (June 1890):281.

28 Eardley, *Gems of Inspiration*, pp. 18–19.

29 Richard Young, "The Morrisite War," p. 281.

of tracts or other printed material, for the Morrisites lacked such capability. Interest in seeking out the new prophet seems to have resulted entirely from rumor and a propensity for many Mormons to seek some alternative to their present situation. Eardley noted:

> It was contemplated by the prophet to send out missionaries, but the word of the Lord came: "I do not require any preaching at your hands. I will do the preaching, and I will influence those to come here whom I want," and this was truly, and in a remarkable manner, fulfilled beyond the expectations of the prophet. Scores of people came testifying that a mysterious influence had seized upon them, and they could get no rest, day or night, until they came and investigated for themselves; and it became a household word among the Mormons, "if you go up there, you are sure to be caught."[30]

The first apostles to be ordained were John and Richard Cook, William Kendall, and John Parson. In June 1861 Mark A. Forscutt, John E. Jones, and John Banks were added to that group, and in September the apostolic organization was completed with the addition of John Trolsen, Goodmund Gudmundsen, Neils Jacobsen, James Cowan, James Dove, James Mather, John R. Eardley, and Abraham Taylor.[31]

G. M. Howard has suggested that much of the success of the movement must be attributed to the appearance of the gifted John Banks in the spring of 1861. Undoubtedly Banks was a great asset in this regard, for Forscutt referred to him as one of "the two great leaders, [Morris] the inspirational prophet, and [Banks] the eloquent orator."[32] However, it is evident that despite Morris's fear of public speaking and his need for a latter-day Aaron, he possessed enough personal magnetism to attract a sizable following before Banks appeared on the scene. Perhaps it was more Morris's message than his appearance that gained him converts, for Forscutt described him as an unlikely candidate for prophethood, at least at first glance.

> There was nothing in his quiet manner, or in his appearance to indicate ambition for leadership, or to suggest the part he was destined to play in a religious tragedy, yet many fancied there was something very strange and indefinable about him. He was small in stature probably not more than five and a half feet in height, but he possessed a muscular, well-built and firmly knit frame. He looked far more the meek and submissive mason's help—the hod carrier he had formerly been, than the dignified prophet. Yet, with remarkably clear, white skin, a handsome face with a beard which

30 Eardley, *Gems of Inspiration*, p. 18.

31 Howard, "Men, Motives, and Misunderstandings," p. 120.

32 Mark H. Forscutt Manuscript, "Sketch of Joseph Morris," p. 24, Archives, Historical Department, Church of Jesus Christ of Latter-day Saints, Salt Lake City, Utah.

> he wore uncut and an expanded brow which were surrounded by almost jet black, soft and curling hair hanging in rich, soft, clustering curls, there was a general expression peculiarly spiritual and compassionately tender, one that could not fail to strike the observant as decidedly pleasing.[33]

Henry Firth, a Morrisite who also knew Morris personally, provided a briefer but similar description of Morris. He reported that "Morris was quiet, modest, and unassuming. He spoke seldomly in public meetings, and had but little to say to anyone."[34]

Morris had first become acquainted with John Banks in 1857, when he was living in American Fork. At that time both Morris and Banks considered themselves firm believers in Mormonism, but both were dissatisfied with the church leadership. Banks must have favorably impressed Morris, for, as previously noted, he was designated by revelation in September 1860 to replace Heber C. Kimball as a counselor in the Mormon church presidency.

Although Banks had rendered invaluable missionary service to the Mormon church both in his English homeland and in the eastern states, he had earned the enmity of Brigham Young, which resulted in his excommunication in November 1858. Banks believed he had been promised the office of presiding bishop, but while he was serving on a mission in Ohio, another had taken his place. Upon returning to Salt Lake City to claim the office, he became enraged with Brigham Young, whom he physically assaulted. A few weeks after his excommunication, Banks was readmitted to the church, but he remained a frustrated and disappointed Pleasant Grove

33 Forscutt Manuscript, pp. 7–8. Mark Forscutt was born 19 June 1834, in Godmanchester, England. He was baptized in the Mormon church in 1853, against parental wishes. He served as a missionary from 1855 to 1858. Along with his wife, he emigrated to the United States in 1860, arriving in Salt Lake City in August. Soon after arrival he was appointed secretary to Brigham Young. After a few months he was pressured to enter into polygamy. He refused and joined the Morrisites where he was soon appointed an apostle. He was at Kington Fort during the summer, fall, and winter of 1861 and was present during the Morrisite War. After Joseph Morris's death he remained in Utah for several years. During that period he served in the U.S. military and affiliated with the RLDS Church. He held a variety of leadership positions in the RLDS Church until his death in 1903. Probably in the late 1870s, he wrote the manuscript of fifty-four pages he entitled "Sketch of Joseph Morris." It was acquired by the Historical Department of the L.D.S. Church in 1902. That manuscript was, of course, written by a partisan, but it seems to be a fair and accurate account.

For a more complete treatise on the life of Mark Forscutt, see Rogers. "Mark Hill Forscutt."

34 Banks, "A Document History of the Morrisites in Utah," B.A. thesis, University of Utah, 1909. p. 7.

farmer until hearing of "his" revelation. Still harboring resentment against Brigham Young, he left his children and wife, who refused to accompany him, and joined Joseph Morris at Kington Fort.

In many ways Banks was everything in appearance and experience that Morris was not. He was large and ruggedly built, eloquent in speech, and distinguished in demeanor. He had served in the British Mission presidency prior to coming to Utah, a position that provided him with considerable executive experience. Earlier he had converted scores of people to Mormonism and was regarded as "one of the ablest and most eloquent missionaries" to serve in the British Mission.[35] Above all, despite his frustrations, Banks was ambitious and optimistic. He was used to, and expected, success.

By an interesting coincidence Banks had the credentials of a journeyman stonecutter, which occupation he had pursued prior to leaving England. Morris, his mentor, had once been a mason's helper.[36]

The activities of John Banks during the summer of 1861 are not recorded, but undoubtedly he grew in favor with Joseph Morris, for on September 7 a revelation designated Banks as the official spokesman for Morris. Thereafter, Morris more and more assumed the role of Revelator, leaving the executive affairs of the church and the teaching of his doctrines to his trusted disciples, especially Richard Cook and John Banks—his first and second counselors.[37]

In a recent insightful article focusing primarily on Morrisite residents of Slaterville and Marriott, Weber County, Utah, Val Holley suggests that the motives for Morrisite conversion were more political than religious. His conclusion is based largely upon a letter that was published in several British newspapers and subsequently in the *Brooklyn* (New York) *Eagle*, on February 6, 1863. The letter was probably written by William H. Hill, a former Morrisite resident of Marriott who also participated in the Morrisite War. Hill neglected to mention Morris by name, as did many or most Morrisite residents of those two towns. After being excommunicated from the L.D.S. Church and moving away, they chose not to acknowledge their Morrisite past to their descendants or anyone else. Apparently they were ashamed to be so identified. Hill mentioned that the neighbors had often met to discuss Mormon-caused problems in Utah's government and economy.[38]

---

35 Howard, "Men, Motives, and Misunderstandings," p. 117.

36 Andrew Jenson, *Latter-day Saint Biographical Encyclopedia*, 4 vols. (Salt Lake City, Utah: Andrew Jenson History Company, 1901–36), 2:590; Howard, "Men, Motives, and Misunderstandings," pp. 116–18; Roberts, *Comprehensive History*, 5:42–43; Banks, "A Document History of the Morrisites in Utah."

37 Morris, *The Spirit Prevails*, p. 137.

38 Val Holley. "Slouching Toward Slaterville: Joseph Morris' Wide Swath In

No doubt some persons joined the Morrisites for political reasons. Certainly John Banks had political issues with Brigham Young as did others, including Hill. However, the testimony and behavior of others suggest that motivations for joining were complex, and that faith in Morris as a bona fide prophet was an important reason for seeking membership. For example, as late as 1899, John Eardley, a Morrisite apostle, published *Gems Of Inspiration* which extolled the prophetic calling of Joseph Morris. Mark Forscutt, also a Morrisite apostle, referred to John Banks as "the eloquent speaker" but to Joseph Morris as "the inspirational prophet." Both John Cook and his brother Richard, a Mormon bishop, became Morrisite apostles and acknowledged the authenticity of Morris's prophetic calling. The same was true of James and George Dove, who went to great pains and expense to publish the revelations of Joseph Morris in *The Spirit Prevails* in 1886. James Dove even moved from San Francisco back to South Weber in 1885, expecting that the Morrisites would again gather there. He remained there for several years, hoping to witness the Second Advent in the place designated by Joseph Morris. Perhaps the most telling example of faith in Morris was given by Emma Thompson Just, who witnessed the shooting of Joseph Morris. She reported that, "When Morris was killed, my father sat upon his body and said, 'Now kill me, for I have nothing more to live for.'"[39]

Seth Bryant delivered a paper based on his master's thesis that explores the conflict between the more institutionalized Mormon Church and the more primitivistic Morrisites. He emphasized the ideological differences between the two factions rather than their power struggle or sociological variables.[40]

In a presentation at the 2006 annual meeting of the John Whitmer Historical Association, Eric Rogers emphasized the importance of sociological influences on growth and development of the Morrisite religious schism. These variables were resentment of Brigham Young, conflict with local authorities, poverty, family ties, and immigration networks. Rogers noted an interplay between ideological and sociological factors but concluded that in the case of the Morrisites, sociological influences on the whole outweighed ideological ones in the formation and growth of the group.[41]

I agree that all of the above factors were relevant in the conversion and continued affiliation process, but I am reluctant to assign primacy to one

---

Weber County." *Utah Historical Quarterly*. July 2, 2008. pp. 247–264.

39 John Banks. "A Document History of the Morrisites In Utah," pp. 80–81.

40 Seth L. Bryant, "Reviving the Millennial Kingdom: Mormons, Morrisites and Massacre," The John Whitmer Historical Association Annual Meeting, Voree, Wisconsin, September 26, 2008.

41 Eric Paul Rogers, "The Morrisites and the Sociology of Religious Schism," The John Whitmer Historical Association Annual Meeting, Independence, Missouri, September 30, 2006.

of them. This is because, with the exception of a few leaders such as Banks, Forscutt, and the Doves, we have very little information about the motivations of most persons who joined the Morrisite movement.

Although it is evident that various motivations were involved in attracting converts to the Morrisite movement, the teachings of Morris seem to have been more important than any striking personal characteristics such as physical appearance or rhetorical ability. So what did Morris teach that appealed to so many people? What could induce so many to forsake their relatively secure life among the Mormons and join a group of outcasts in a ramshackle fort? A complete answer to this question might not be possible now, but a number of factors and conditions certainly contributed to Morris's appeal.

First, he preached that a new prophet had arisen among the people, and he produced substantial scriptural evidence to prove it. He was no more hesitant to say "thus saith the Lord" than his model, Joseph Smith, had been. Clearly this style appealed more to some Mormons than the brusque, earthy words of Brigham Young. Second, Morris taught that the Second Coming was nigh. Many Mormons were prepared by long tradition to accept and follow that message. Third, his law of property consecration appealed especially to those who were impoverished, and it was probably no accident that many of his followers were very poor. Fourth, he condemned polygamy, at least as it was then practiced by the Mormons. Beyond doubt this was a delicate issue with many Mormons. It was especially troublesome for foreign converts who may not have been apprised of the practice before reaching Utah. Many of them were completely unprepared to accept spiritual leaders who practiced a form of marriage seeming to be nothing short of immoral. Perhaps the issue of polygamy produced more converts to the Morris faction than any other factor, for a very large proportion of Morris's followers were recently arrived emigrants, especially from the Scandinavian countries.

It is of some importance to note, however, that Morris's opposition to polygamy was not unequivocal. He believed that at the right time and place the Lord had sanctioned that practice and that He would again approve the plurality of wives for the purpose of raising up righteous seed. He taught that polygamy was a correct principle but not a celestial law. That is, a man might have several wives for time but only one for eternity.[42]

Forscutt has provided us with considerable detail concerning the practical way the Morrisites dealt with converts who had plural wives. The solution seems to have been both remarkably just and humanitarian. Certainly numerous converts were made among polygamous families, among the most notable being Richard Cook. Forscutt explained:

42 Morris, *The Spirit Prevails*, pp. 651–53.

> The Morrisite and Reorganized Churches were both antipolygamic, but with this very essential difference. Polygamists were received as members in the Morrisite Church; husbands, wives, and families together. They held this as due the families who otherwise might suffer want. The gospel was designed for the people of the Orient as well as those of the occident. Polygamy was tolerated there. The Church must have a platform broad enough for all. Hence the rule adopted was this: Those who had entered into polygamous relations before entering the church, . . . might be received into the church fellowship, but polygamic relations must not be entered into after joining the church. If polygamists were received, they must be monogamic in life. There must be no sexual commerce between the husband and his polygamous wife or wives after entering the church. The husband was to be held strictly accountable for the maintenance and provisional comforts of all whom he had covenanted by marriage to sustain, and their offspring. From the day of his connection with the church it must be understood that every wife excepting the first was freed from her wifehood, and might contract marriage with another man than the former husband. To admit necessity for divorce, would be to admit the legality of the plural marriage, hence no divorce was allowable. The new husband might or might not assume the care of the children of the wife he took.[43]

In June 1861 Morris received a revelation that was largely misunderstood by both his followers and critics and that subsequently set the stage for ridicule and disappointment concerning the time of Christ's Advent. The revelation declared:

> There are those, also, among these people, who think that I shall not come out of my hiding place to deliver them before their substance is wasted. They fear that I shall lead them into difficulty, and leave them there. . All the revelations which he [Morris] has written, I have given unto him, and all the promises which have been made unto my people through the revelations which I have given, I will fulfill them to the very letter, for I have made them. Therefore, let my people trust in me and I will supply their needs in every respect.
>
> And as touching the reaping of crops, it is necessary that those who are the chief acting officers under the fulness of the holy priesthood, should know my will concerning them upon that matter. When I called them, I called them to preach my gospel, and to do nothing else.[44]

This revelation was interpreted by the people as a promise that their deliverance would occur before or shortly after harvest time and that they should not be concerned about the harvest, for God would provide. On July 20 Morris tried to correct this impression with an explanatory revelation.

43 Forscutt Manuscript, pp. 19–20.

44 Morris, *The Spirit Prevails*, p. 106.

> When I spoke to them concerning the sowing and reaping of their crops, they did not understand me aright. I spoke in the first place, to those men whom I had chosen to hold a place in the apostleship. I called upon them to study the gospel and to do nothing else, but at that time they did not hearken unto me; but sought to do their own will. They had not sufficient confidence in me, and for this I gave unto them a rebuke. I told them that if they sowed, they should not reap. I wished them to leave all of their worldly affairs alone, and devote all their time to the ministry; for when I need their assistance myself, I cannot allow them to dabble with the things of the world . . . .
>
> But those whom I have neither called to the apostleship, nor to fill any other office in my Church, whereby the whole of their time is taken up in my service, I will that they should follow their employments until they are called . . . .
>
> When I spoke about the crops I spoke also unto those of my people who had yielded obedience to the fullness of my gospel, who did not reside in this place; but who were residing in other parts of the territory. I advised them not to plant their land. I told them on this wise: that if they sowed their wheat, and planted their land, they would have to leave it again, and would, consequently, have their trouble for naught.
>
> I also told my people to sell their surplus property, and purchase wheat and other useful provisions; but they have not hearkened unto me in this thing. But they must purchase provisions for they will need them. There are people gathering here from different parts of the Territory, and some of them have not much provisions with them. My people must feed those who are hungry; and if they do as I command them, I will furnish them with fresh means by the time that they require them. But they are afraid that I shall let them perish. They think that winter will overtake them as they are now situated; but they may trust themselves in my care. I can deliver them in one day, and can place everything which they need in their hands. And unto those who are faithful unto me, I will give cities that they never built, and vineyards that they never planted; and, in due time, they shall be the richest of all people upon the earth; for I will deliver all things into their hands.[45]

Unfortunately, despite this strong disclaimer, the latter rather than the earlier parts of the revelation became fixed in the people's minds. His followers increased in the expectation that God would supply their needs and that Christ would make His appearance before the onset of winter. At the same time, his detractors branded him as an impractical visionary who was stuffing the heads of his followers with spiritual nonsense while their stomachs were becoming ever more empty.

Jane Firth, a Morrisite who lived at South Weber during the Morrisite residence, once asserted that "some of the Morrisites went so far as to tramp

45 Morris, *The Spirit Prevails*, p. 116

down their crops of wheat and corn, doubtless to prove . . . that they were certain that Christ would come before the grain would have time to ripen."[46] The fact is that Morris himself believed that the year 1861 would not only witness the organization of God's true church and the gathering together of the righteous, but that Christ would also make His appearance and deliver His people. This expectation had been held since December 21 of the previous year when Morris had received a specific revelation to that effect.

> Behold, verily, verily, thus saith the Lord: It shall come to pass that I will commence a mighty work upon the earth in the year eighteen hundred and sixty-one—commencing in Utah Territory.
>
> I will begin with men who now stand at the head of my Church, and I will cut them off first; and from them I will go to those who are next to them in authority, and I will cut them off also; and so I will continue until I shall have cut off every shepherd in my Church—both large and small—that will not stand by my servant whom I have called.
>
> And I will gather my people together to one place, even to the Great Salt Lake City—the central point in this Territory. And I will be there myself, and stand side by side with my servant Joseph, and speak to him mouth to mouth. And all the hosts of heaven shall be there. I will lead them up to battle, and I will separate the sheep from the goats. . . .
>
> And when I have purged my Church, I will go to that nation called the United States, and I will purge her also; for I will not leave anything alive in that land but the pure in heart; for that nation is ripe for the harvest, and I will cut them down now.
>
> And not many years shall pass away before my people shall return to the land of promise [Missouri]; for I will go before them and fight their battles.
>
> And a temple shall be built in that Land; . . .
>
> And when I shall have taken my people back to that land, I will give unto my servant Joseph power to write a law which shall govern the nations of the earth; and they shall abide it, or be cut off from the earth.[47]

Undoubtedly the specificity and urgency of this revelation provided much of the impetus for impelling the people toward the prophet of South Weber. It also caused them to become more and more excited and expectant as the year 1861 drew to a close. They were both fearful and jubilant. For as autumn gave way to the first signs of snow, they knew they were ill prepared for a rigorous winter. Yet they firmly believed that Christ would come and that He would provide for all.

Food and shelter were not the only things concerning the Morrisites. Their opposition to the Mormon leadership stigmatized them as heretics

---

46 Banks, "A Document History of the Morrisites in Utah," pp. 34–35.

47 Morris, The Spirit Prevails, pp. 40–41.

and apostates. Consequently, their relationships with Brigham Young's followers became more and more strained with every passing day. Before 1861 drew to a close, many of them had come to believe that the Mormons were bent upon their destruction and that an attack could be expected at any time.

II *Prelude to Battle*

6 The Gathering Storm

Although the Mormon church record reports that the apostles Wilford Woodruff and John Taylor had counseled the Mormons living in South Weber to be tolerant of the Morrisites and had rebuked Brother Watts for his extreme verbal attack upon them, it is clear that hostility between the two factions was present from the beginning and grew in intensity as time passed. Perhaps the Mormon apostles felt they could afford to be tolerant when Morris's avowed followers numbered fewer than a score and his influence was expected to rapidly diminish. But they might have spoken less softly if the extraordinary growth of the Morrisite church had been foreseen.

Certainly the climate in Utah had never been friendly toward apostates, and Brigham Young himself had directed some intemperate words toward apostates only a few years before the appearance of the Morrisites. Shortly after plural marriage was officially sanctioned by the church in August 1852, Gladdon Bishop, a Mormon apostate, began an anti-polygamy crusade hoping to capitalize on the Mormons' ambivalence toward that principal. By the spring of 1853, his followers, called "Gladdonites," numbered several score and were fomenting considerable dissension among the Saints. In response to this disruption, Brigham Young delivered a scathing public rebuke in the Tabernacle on March 27. He declared: "I say rather than apostates should flourish here, I will unsheath my Bowie knife, and conquer or die. Now you nasty apostates, clear out, or judgment will be put to the line and righteousness to the plummet . . . . Let us call upon the Lord to assist us in this very good work."[1] Gladdon Bishop did not wait for these threats to be carried out. He fled from Utah never to return.

Although the tone of this statement suggests that Brigham Young was prepared to personally lead an attack against apostates, Mark Forscutt believed Young could accomplish his objectives by threat and suggestion that others would carry out for him. Forscutt wrote: "The spirit of Brigham indicated the temper of the people. He pointed the finger; they went where

1 Brigham Young, "Joseph, a True Prophet—Apostates—Dream," 27 March 1853, *Journal of Discourses*, 1:82–83.

he pointed. He spoke of unsheathing his knife, they unsheathed theirs. He threatened apostates, they murdered who he threatened."[2]

It is hard to tell whether Brigham Young still endorsed such harsh sanctions against apostates a decade after the Gladdonite affair. But there can be no doubt that Forscutt was only echoing the sentiments of Joseph Morris and a large share of his fellow Morrisites who firmly believed that Young would stop at nothing to halt the growing disaffection from his ranks. At least one contemporary Mormon historian, Nels Anderson, has also agreed with this assessment. Anderson concludes that the Mormons did not disturb the Morrisites prior to mid-1861, because "the Army was in Utah and the Gentiles were in control. A few years earlier Morris might have fared as Gladdon Bishop."[3]

Anderson's assessment is certainly worth considering, for it was not until after the U.S. Army was withdrawn from Utah in July 1861 to participate in the Civil War that the Morrisites began to experience serious harassment from their Mormon neighbors. However, it should also be recognized that it was not until about that same time that the size of Morris's following had grown large enough to upset the status quo in the Ogden area or to pose any real threat to the established power structure. Undoubtedly the influx of several hundred people with their herds of livestock requiring many acres of pasture must have severely upset the established grazing patterns in the vicinity of South Weber. It should hardly be surprising, then, to find that some of the earliest and most enduring disputes between the Morrisites and their Mormon neighbors involved livestock.

Eardley reported:

> Among other property consecrated and turned over to the bishop were horses and mulch cows which were daily turned out on the range adjoining the camp, the cows being brought into camp in the evening. Unprincipled scoundrels on horseback, calling themselves saints, were in the habit of riding over the range, and when they saw these horses and cows, would steal them and take them away. These occurrences became so frequent that a watch was placed over them, and one of the thieves was caught in the nefarious business. With a desire to put a stop to this misappropriation of our property, a complaint was made to Bishop Chauncy West who was acting Justice of the Peace for Ogden Township. He very complacently informed the complainants that he could do nothing for them; that "there was no law for apostates." They, therefore, were compelled to return to the camp without justice, and it became necessary to appoint herders to watch the stock and protect it from the grasp of these roving thieves.[4]

2 Forscutt Manuscript, p. 24.

3 Nels Anderson, *Desert Saints*, p. 223.

4 Eardley, *Gems of Inspiration*, pp. 19–20.

The Morrisites soon became convinced that they could not get redress for grievances by turning to the officers of the law, for they were nearly all Mormons and none were Morrisites. Therefore, in July 1861, when several horses were stolen and their absconders located, several Morrisites proposed that a posse be formed to bring them back by force if necessary. However, their prophet received a revelation which strongly advised against it. It said:

> . . . you should be very careful in dealing with mine enemies, for they are prompted by men who are in authority; and those men who prompted them, did so in order that they might have a cause to come up against my people. But I will give them what they are seeking for, and I will fight the battles of my people myself. I do not wish them to fight with their enemies. Let my people guard their property well. I wish to hold mine enemies off for a short time; yet, if my people will do as I command them, they will not be the losers. They must not, in this case, lay violent hands upon mine enemies; but leave them in my hands, and I will settle with them. And in due time, I will restore to my people all that they have lost by their enemies, and I will add a hundred fold to it.[5]

Forscutt reported that the Morrisites subsequently saw the thieves riding their animals, but they were powerless to recover them. The thieves even rode into the camp and brandished their revolvers in an attempt to provoke a fight, but the Morrisites simply looked on in silence.

Because of this harassment, the Morrisites organized themselves like military companies under the leadership of those who had served in European armies. Experienced men went out daily to help watch the herd, and an armed guard accompanied those who went into the mountains to gather wood. Sentries were stationed around the camp at night, and a general sense of anxiety and insecurity permeated the area. This was not only because of the depredations of thieves, but because threats of violence were frequently heard, including three threats to burn the fort.[6]

Richard Young, Mormon apologist for the "Morrisite Affair," also remarked upon the militant preparations made by the Morrisites, but he gave another reason for this development.

> As religious enthusiasm and faith increased among them, they became more aggressive, and, as time rolled on, began to reap the inevitable consequences of their system. Military guards were posted around the fort at nighttime, challenging all who approached; it is said that the main objective of this patrol was to prevent escape of the disaffected. An unbeliever, who, in an unguarded moment in the presence of some of the people of

5 Morris, *The Spirit Prevails*, p. 112.

6 Forscutt Manuscript, pp. 30–31.

> the fort, had ridiculed some feature of the Morrisite faith, was dragged back to the fort as he was returning to his farm nearby and was whipped with willows by women, encouraged and assisted by men. The process of local courts was at times resisted and officers prevented from executing their orders.[7]

It is interesting, that no Morrisite accounts mention this whipping incident, nor on the other hand do any Mormon accounts refer to the harassment of Morrisites.

The Morrisites were subjected to obscenities, humiliating epithets, and disruption of religious services from time to time by local rowdies. Whether or not these rowdies operated under the direction of Mormon authorities is difficult to determine, but there was no question about that in the minds of the Morrisites.

Typical of such harassment was an incident that occurred in November 1861. Half a dozen young rowdies forced their way into the Kington schoolhouse where Alonzo Brown and his wife lived and where they, along with a Mrs. Moss, were eating supper. The toughs began to tussle with Alonzo, all the while spouting vile insults and curses at him and the two women. After pushing him around the room for a few minutes, they suddenly departed, grabbing his hat as they went. The noise of their "little game" had attracted a considerable crowd of Morrisites who were waiting outside the schoolhouse door when they emerged. The crowd pursued the toughs and "persuaded" them to return the hat. The Morrisites then returned triumphantly to the enclosure thinking that the matter was ended. But it was not.[8]

> On December 8, 1861, two of the original group of intruders, Amos Hawkes and George T. Peay, swore out a complaint against Alonzo Brown, James Cook and Peter I. Moss, and eight other Morrisites involved in the fray. Davis County sheriff Lot Smith thereupon issued a warrant "for the apprehension of A. Brown and others." Peter I. Moss was the only one taken into custody. Tried in March 1862, he was convicted of assault and sentenced to imprisonment at hard labor for forty days and fined fifty dollars plus court costs.[9]

The harshness of this verdict could only serve as certain proof to the Morrisites that they could expect no justice in the courts. Certainly it helped set the stage for their later decisions to take justice into their own hands and to ignore official writs issued by constituted authorities.

Shortly after the army departed from Utah a call went out for citizens over the age of twenty-one to report for regular training in the territorial militia.

---

7 Richard Young, "The Morrisite War," p. 348.

8 Forscutt Manuscript, pp. 38–39.

9 Howard, "Men, Motives, and Misunderstandings," p. 122.

This order also became a source of contention between the Morrisites and Mormons, for the militia was, in fact, the Nauvoo Legion, comprised almost entirely of Mormons and, therefore, highly suspect from the Morrisite point of view. The Morrisites believed that this order to train was a plan of the enemy to lay a trap for them. They thought that if they went to train, their strength at the camp would be greatly compromised, for the military commanders could order the men away on the pretext of some emergency and then occupy the fort. On the other hand, if the Morrisites refused to train, they could be arrested for evasion and possibly fined or imprisoned— either way coming under the control of the Mormons.

In the end, the Morrisites refused to train, and subsequently some of them were required to pay fines ranging upwards from fifty dollars. A large number of cattle and horses was legally attached for this purpose, and Eardley reported that the Morrisites began to fear for their food supply. Eventually they refused to pay more fines or to allow their livestock to be confiscated, and the matter was allowed to drop—at least for the time being.

Although the Morrisites sustained more or less continual harassment from their neighbors, they gave little or no thought to the possibility of fleeing the territory. Indeed, they were convinced that such harassment was a necessary prelude to the final showdown between themselves and the Mormons. Whether justified or not, the Morrisites made no distinction between Mormons who were church officials and those who were civil authorities. Indeed, the Mormon public servants usually also held one or more church positions so that making distinctions between church and state seemed futile to the Morrisites. They felt certain that a Mormon's first loyalty was to his church and that a Mormon would not hesitate to use a public office to achieve church goals.

The crystallization of this attitude did not, however, result entirely from unfortunate experiences with Mormon rowdies and prejudiced public servants. It was also clearly affirmed in several of Joseph Morris's revelations. After his excommunication from the Mormon church, Morris regarded all Mormon leaders and faithful church members as servants of the devil and hence enemies of God and the Morrisite people. Since Morris had personally striven so long and hard to gain the approbation of Brigham Young, it is not surprising that Young ultimately became the focal point of Morris's verbal attacks once he gave that cause up for lost. Morris became convinced that Young was the mastermind behind any and all incidents of harassment and that he was seeking an effective plan to destroy Morris and his followers.[10]

---

10 Originally Morris had believed that Young was an honorable but misguided man who was being led astray by his first counselor, George A. Smith. Smith

Morris publicly referred to Young in most uncomplimentary terms. Morris's revelations called Young a "blasphemer," a "deceiver," "an insult to God," and one who justified all his "abominations." One revelation singled out Young as the most vicious and evil man ever to live upon the face of the earth. "He surpasses in wickedness all that have ever lived before him, or that will ever live after him."[11] On several occasions Brigham was designated as the first to die when the Morrisites were delivered.

Since these revelations were publicly read daily in Weber Camp and since non-Morrisites were not excluded from attending such readings, they were soon as well known to the Mormons as to the Morrisites. Given the vulnerable situation of the Morrisites, it might be supposed that Morris would have exercised more restraint when referring to the Mormon leader. Certainly he should have known that such vitriolic denunciations would be offensive to the Mormons and might even be partially responsible for the series of local harassments directed against the Morrisites.

But Morris was not interested in mollifying the Mormons. Indeed, he was striving to produce the opposite effect. He believed that the Second Coming must be accompanied by a direct confrontation between the Mormons and Morrisites—that the Mormons must be incited to attack the Morrisites in order that Christ might be fully justified in destroying them when the Hosts of Heaven came to the Morrisite defense. Although Morris was not anxious to hasten this confrontation, still he believed that the time had arrived. As early as March 1861, this expectation had been elucidated by revelation.

> Verily, I say unto you, my son, that inasmuch as the cloud is now fast gathering, and must shortly burst upon the heads of your enemies to the destruction of many thousands of souls, it is necessary that you should understand my will concerning this matter.
>
> The warning has now reached the ears of almost all of this people. It will not be more than a few more days before it will have reached the ears of all. Your enemies are already setting themselves against you. They are seeking to raise a mob to destroy you, and you need to prepare yourself for it; for although it will not come until I am ready, it will, nevertheless, soon come. I am controlling it. I will make mine enemies do what I wish them to do, and they shall go so far, and no farther. I will raise up a standard against them.
>
> And behold, I say unto you, that the men who now stand at the head of . . . [the Mormon] Church are at the head of this mob, and it will involve all the shepherds who are corrupt before me. As I said unto you

---

was defined by revelation as a fallen angel who had gained control of the church and was leading it, Judas-like, to destruction. Morris, *The Spirit Prevails*, p. 12.

11 Morris, *The Spirit Prevails*, p. 177.

> in a former revelation, so I say unto you again, I will not keep you waiting after the warning has reached the ears of all. And when your enemies come upon you, you must not fear, but stand to your post like a man, and I will fight your battles. I will lay your enemies low before your face. You must place your confidence in me in this case; for I shall require it of you. And it is my will that these people, who are one with you, should also place their confidence in me. They must not fear their enemies, for the great test is near at hand, and those who forsake me through fear and turn traitors to me, as they may suppose to save their lives, shall lose them, for I will cut them off first. But if they stand fast to their integrity, and act honestly towards me, I will be true to them, and not a hair of their heads shall be hurt; for I love those who are filled with integrity.
>
> And if your enemies should send unto you a warning, ordering you to move away from this place, you shall pay no attention to it, but tell them to "come on" as soon as they are ready. Those people who profess to be one with you will behold scenes that will cause their hearts to fail them. And as I have said unto you before, so I say unto you again, I will stand side by side with you in this place, and I will speak with you mouth to mouth, and you shall see the hosts of heaven go out to war.[12]

This revelation served as the basis for much of the Morrisite activity that followed and makes clear why they chose to continue a course almost certainly destined to produce open conflict. Morris's acts were consistent with this interpretation of Mormon-Morrisite relations until the very end. In sum, although he cast the Mormon church in the role of aggressor, he sought to provoke that aggression and felt secure that the Hosts of Heaven would protect him when the showdown came.

In the summer of 1861, when the army withdrew from Utah, Joseph Morris also understood the implications of their exit. He realized that the Morrisites were now placed in an extremely vulnerable position, but he saw this as a further unfolding of Christ's plan for deliverance. On August 3 he received a revelation which spoke directly to that point.

> I brought that army up to this place to rule over this people. That army has, therefore, done the work which I set it to do.
>
> And now, behold, I say unto you, my servant Joseph, that I have dispensed with that army which I brought up to this place, having done with them; and I will now take the old church into my mine own hands, and I will see if I cannot govern it.
>
> I have now removed everything out of their way, and they can come up against you whenever they are ready. I am ready now.
>
> And behold, . . . hold yourself in readiness for your enemies, for they will soon come up against you. And I, also, will come up to you, and you shall see me to your satisfaction. I will remove all fear both from you and

12 Morris, *The Spirit Prevails*, pp. 67–68.

> from all those people who trust in me. . . . I will make a slaughter among your enemies. They will not stand in your pathway two minutes after they are ready to strike the first blow. I shall try them to see what they will do; and when they make the attempt to kill, I will destroy them according to celestial law.[13]

Despite these many words of assurance, Morris and his followers were not free from fear and apprehension. Apparently they worried considerably about their personal safety, for numerous revelations during the summer and fall of 1861 mentioned the fears of Morris and his people and reminded them time and again that such fears were groundless, for divine power would protect and sustain them against all odds.

Perhaps part of the strain during this time was also due to the apostasy of some of Morris's followers who had become disenchanted with the way things were going at Kington Fort. Several revelations were directed toward "traitors" and "apostates" and gave instructions for dealing with them. The first apostates were severely criticized and condemned, but they were allowed to go their way in peace, taking at least some consecrated property with them. However, as time went by and relations between the Morrisites and their neighbors further deteriorated, Morris became less and less tolerant of apostates and less and less willing to allow them to take any property with them. By early 1862 a revelation went so far as to say that the wicked course of apostates should be stopped even if they had to be put to death to do so.[14] There is no evidence that such a penalty was ever invoked, but the threat must have been frightening for those who were weak or vacillating.

All was not smooth sailing within the ranks of the Morrisite leadership during this period either. Morris's counselors became more and more insistent upon advancing their own views concerning policy and administrative responsibility. Furthermore, it appears that Richard Cook and John Banks had never been especially fond of each other. Cook must have considered Banks something of an interloper, for, after all, he had appeared on the scene several months after Cook. The fact that Banks had been appointed "spokesman" for the church even though Cook was the senior counselor must also have been hard for Cook to accept. From time to time Morris produced revelations instructing his lieutenants to follow his counsel or suffer dire consequences, which seem to have worked, at least temporarily. By January 1862 this problem had come to a head, for Morris received a revelation directed specifically toward Cook and Banks.

> There are hard feelings existing between them. They do not see alike, neither do they work in union; they are not one in me . . . .

13 Morris, *The Spirit Prevails*, pp. 123–24.
14 Morris, *The Spirit Prevails*, p. 379.

> My servants should know better than to give way to such a spirit as that; for, by doing so they become my greatest enemies, and I shall be compelled to cast them off. If my servants will not put that spirit away from them, I will visit them, and I will remove it, and I will remove them with it.[15]

The revelation went on to specify the more important weaknesses of these two men. Cook was reprimanded for being too concerned about his own property, for failing to preach the law of consecration properly, and for tempering Morris's pronouncements to avoid hurting people's feelings. Banks was rebuked for his lack of humility and for thinking he was equal in knowledge to the prophet. He was told that although he did not like to acknowledge any man as his superior he must accept the authority of the prophet or be destroyed. The tone and specificity of this revelation produced the desired effect, for thereafter Cook and Banks appear to have gotten along better, and they continued to support the prophet until the day he died.

During this period Morris was not without personal problems, and one in particular was an embarrassment to the church. On August 23, 1861, Morris was commanded by revelation to look for a faithful companion. Apparently he had much less difficulty finding a willing bride among his followers than on earlier occasions, for he was shortly thereafter married to Mary Olsen, a Danish convert. Unfortunately, like several previous times, the marriage showed signs of disharmony almost before it was consummated. Less than a month after the wedding, Morris received a revelation that discussed Morris's problems.

> You wish to know my will concerning your companion. You are in trouble concerning her. What can I do with her, if she will not stand by you and take your counsel? If she fights against you, she fights against me. If she refuses to harken to you and obey you, she has no part with me, for I shall cast her off. . . .
>
> Let her harken unto my words, and I will be with her unto the end, and crown her with exaltation in the presence of her Father forever and forever, for I am the Lord, and I have spoken these things. Even so. Amen and Amen.[16]

Apparently this revelation had the desired effect, for Mary remained with him. Whether or not their marriage ever became one of bliss and harmony is unrecorded.

Sensing that a confrontation would ultimately grow out of legal disputes, Joseph Morris received a revelation in November 1861 outlining the

15 Morris, *The Spirit Prevails*, p. 364.

16 Morris, *The Spirit Prevails*, pp. 149–51.

procedure to be followed should their enemies come to arrest the prophet and his associates.

> You shall not be insulted and imposed upon by your enemies much longer. You need not fear the threats which they make against you, and think that, when they come up against you, I shall not be ready to meet them, for I shall. . . . They will pretend that what they do against my people will be done according to their law . . . . They will come up to this place and strive to lay hold of you and a few more chief men who are closely connected with you; and they will offer to spare the lives of all the rest of my people if they will deliver up to them those men who are the chief authorities of my Church . . . .
>
> And if they seek to arrest you, you shall call my people together, and they shall show themselves willing to stand by you, and prevent your arrest, if it becomes necessary. Should but few men come to arrest you, my people shall surround you, and when they see they cannot take you, they will go back without you; but when they come the second time, they will come with great force, feeling determined to take you. I wish to take a course to bring as many of them up to this place as I possibly can, in order to slay them.[17]

Regardless of how one might view the general prophetic abilities of Joseph Morris, the substance of this revelation is remarkable. It provides almost a flawless scenario of the actual confrontation between the Morrisites and the law that occurred six months later.

As the days grew shorter and shorter and the chill of winter began to envelop the camp, the Morrisites began looking anxiously toward the day of their deliverance. Their prophet continued to receive reassuring revelations concerning the welfare of his people, and numerous revelations made the time and circumstances of the Second Advent more explicit. Perhaps in response to inquiries from his people concerning the manner in which revelations were given, Morris produced a curious revelation on November 15 outlining the entire revelatory process.

The revelation explained that God had a high council in heaven where Christ and the other chief authorities met regularly. There they often considered the affairs of this earth and made decisions about its needs. All decisions were based upon eternal laws contained in great law books shelved in the council room and available for consultation from time to time. Morris was informed that no revelations were ever given until they had been passed through the council, recorded by an angel, tried by the law, and finally signed by the Father and Jesus Christ. Only after the lengthy process was completed were they then transmitted to Morris. The process of transmission was described thusly: "You should know that when you sit down to write

17 Morris, *The Spirit Prevails*, pp. 214–15.

a revelation, either myself [Christ] or one of my angels who belongs to the high council of heaven, is by your side dictating you. We put words into your mind, and we do all with the exception of writing them."[18]

Unfortunately, the revelation made no mention of any test to determine whether the source of the revelation was supernatural or not. At any rate, this revelation provides a fascinating view of the extremely anthropomorphic heaven Morris envisioned. For him heaven was as real and tangible as the old adobe fort where his council meetings were held.

As November wore on, expectations of the Second Advent continued to grow. Toward the end of the month Morris received a revelation that declared: "I am now at your side dictating you; therefore, hearken diligently to that which I am about to make known unto you; for you will soon witness great scenes. . . . I am now compelled to draw near unto you; therefore, prepare yourself to come into my presence, for in a few days I shall unveil my face unto you, and you shall see my glory."[19]

On the 24th he received similar assurance. "And now behold, I say unto you, my son, prepare yourself to meet me, for I am coming up to you quickly; for not many days will pass away before I shall visit you, and place the rod in your hand."[20]

On December 7, 1861, Morris was promised by revelation that he would see Christ "in a few hours." On December 12 and again on the 13th Christ said: "I shall come up to you in the course of a day or two." Several more days passed without the expected coming, but just before Christmas the Morrisites received news from two independent sources that seemed to confirm the imminent appearance of Christ. It was reported to them that on December 19 two hundred men had been called from Ogden and corresponding numbers from other nearby places to "clean out" the Morrisites. Forscutt said that because the Mormons could not obtain the requisite number "the Utah Church dignitaries wisely refused to assume the consequences and gave the necessary orders, so the Morrisites then were spared."[21]

Whether or not this report was true, it helped keep the Morrisites in a constant state of anxiety and anticipation. Concurrent with the report of the abortive invasion, another incident occurred that further excited the people of Weber Camp. A large band of Indians came into and passed through the fort. They moved so slowly that the Morrisites thought they were taking a mental inventory of everything within the camp. When their explorations were completed, they moved down the river and camped within sight of the fort. The Morrisites were convinced these were the same Indians that

18 Morris, *The Spirit Prevails*, p. 229.
19 Morris, *The Spirit Prevails*, p. 236.
20 Morris, *The Spirit Prevails*, p. 245.
21 Forscutt Manuscript, p. 40.

had participated in the massacre at Mountain Meadows and that they had again allied themselves with the Mormons to repeat the bloody deed. The Morrisites posted a double guard and spent several days in fear of invasion, but the Indians moved on without incident.

Forscutt made an interesting observation concerning the threatened Mormon invasion:

> It is a remarkable coincidence that though the Morrisites knew nothing of these things till afterwards, the prophet received a revelation commanding them all to be washed and dressed in their best apparel, for "their enemies would come against them that day, and the Lord would deliver them." When afterwards it was learned that preparations (for an invasion) had been recently made, it served not a little to strengthen faith in the word of the Prophet.[22]

On December 22 a revelation again affirmed that Christ would appear in a few days but that the people needed to be united in their faith before Christ could come. Morris was also told to call his people together and instruct them in their faith and call for a public vote of confidence.

> You shall stand upon your feet and ask my people how many of them are willing to believe and live by every word that proceeds from my mouth; and you shall ascertain by a vote how many of my people there are who believe that I mean what I say when I speak to them, when I say days. I want to know how many of my people have a correct faith. To have a correct faith they must believe that I mean days when I say days. To have a correct faith they must be looking out for me to come day by day. To have a correct faith they must believe that I shall not be more than two or three days at the farthest . . . . To have a correct faith they must begin to look out for me after Monday, and they must continue to look out for me until I come.[23]

The Lord spoke a second time to Morris on December 22. This time He sought to bolster the prophet's sagging spirits and to assure him that He would come after all. "O, my son, I will satisfy you in the course of two or three days at the farthest. . . . I will come unto you and deliver my people according to my promise."[24]

On December 24 even more urgency was stressed.

> I shall take my people away from this place very soon after I have moved the obstacles out of their way. I told my people some days ago to get their wagons ready for a quick move. . . . I shall soon gather them together, for I have nothing to wait for now.

---

22 Forscutt Manuscript, p. 41.
23 Morris, *The Spirit Prevails*, p. 315.
24 Morris, *The Spirit Prevails*, p. 312

> My people are moving about after wood and other things. I wish that they were through with that work, so that all things in this place might be perfectly calm and quiet; for I do not like to come unto my people while they are all in a bustle and confusion. As soon as they can bring themselves into perfect order and quietude, I will come unto them.[25]

In this same revelation the Saints were also instructed to clothe themselves in white linen to await Christ's appearance.

On Christmas Day the weather turned very cold and stormy, and the people began to complain, for it was the worst weather they had experienced since coming into camp. They felt that the Lord was being unfair to send such bad weather right at the time when they expected to be delivered. The Lord replied that He certainly had the power to moderate the weather in their behalf, but that He had sent the inclement weather instead for a wise purpose known only to Himself. The Saints were then advised to get in a wood supply sufficient for several days in order that He might come to them without delay.

On December 28, after justifying the further delay in making His appearance, the Lord declared:

> . . . you may begin to look out for me the day after the vote is taken. I will not disappoint you as I have done before when I was disappointing my people on purpose to bring them to a knowledge of the truth . . . .
>
> You may possibly see me on Monday. I may deliver my people on Monday; but if I should not come on Monday, I shall surely come on Tuesday; that you may depend upon. As I live, I will come and deliver my people either on Monday or on Tuesday.[26]

The next revelation, on December 30, begins with something of an excuse or apology.

> I wish to speak to you, my servant Joseph, for your own satisfaction. You know that I told you that I intended to deliver my people on Monday or Tuesday. But you see for yourself that I have not had the opportunity to deliver my people today. I swore an oath to you that I would deliver my people either on Monday or on Tuesday if my people were ready to meet me. I did not mean that I would come and deliver my people if they were not ready for me. I shall fulfill the promise that I made unto you, when my people are ready for me. . . . but if they cannot make themselves ready to meet me . . . I shall come upon them when they are unprepared; for I shall not wait more than two or three days under any circumstances whatever.[27]

---

25 Morris, *The Spirit Prevails*, pp. 319–20.
26 Morris, *The Spirit Prevails*, p. 337.
27 Morris, *The Spirit Prevails*, pp. 337–38.

On the last day of 1861 Morris received a revelation that held great promise for the New Year. It said: "Let all my people settle up their accounts today, and prepare themselves for a visit from me tomorrow morning.[28]

The dawning of the New Year came, but it was not the dawning of the Millennial Day. The Morrisites waited, shivering in the cold, but their Savior did not appear.

This bitter and crushing disappointment was almost more than the people could bear. The fervor, the fear, the heightened expectations, and the many disappointments of the previous weeks combined with their want and misery to produce a situation that strained the very limits of human endurance. The gravity of this situation was acknowledged in a revelation given on January 1, 1862.

> My people are unsettled in their minds, and there are a number of them who wish to leave this place, for their faith is failing them. They begin to think I never intend to come. Others of my people wish to leave this place for a few days; and my people in general wish to scatter. What shall I do with them? Shall I let them scatter? I know that they want both food to eat, and wood to burn; and I know also that they cannot hold together more than a few days longer . . . . As I have gathered them together, so I will take care of them, but they must not go away from this place.[29]

Surprisingly, only a few of the most discouraged left Weber Camp at that time. By some strange alchemy of the human spirit, the great majority of the Saints maintained their trust in the prophet, Joseph Morris. Somehow they found the strength to get through each day and to help one another in their time of trial. And the camp did hold together, not only for a few days or weeks but right on through the winter of 1862.

It appears that the Morrisites were left pretty much to themselves during the winter months. And, except for some local millers refusing to grind their wheat, they were harassed only by snow and cold and privation. Forscutt noted: "It was a sorry winter for the Morrisites, but they bore up as only men and women of undying faith can bear. Many of them lived in tents and through the bleak winter months. Stakes were driven down around the tents, and between these stakes and the tents, earth was packed down to keep out the cold. In times of cold there was much suffering, some complaining and considerable sickness. Others lived in plastered wickiups, an occupant of one of these describes it":

> My only tools for building were an ax, a spade, and a common table knife. I first planted posts, the thickest willows I could get, firmly in the ground. These I put about ten inches apart. I then wove willows in,

28 Morris, *The Spirit Prevails*, p. 341.
29 Morris, *The Spirit Prevails*, pp. 343–44.

> as they are wove in a willow basket, inside one post, outside the other, cutting the ends of square against the upright post. These I knocked down firmly with an axe. When completed to my cross beam, I built up my roof, then laid the straightest willows I could get on that, running down back and front as roofs usually do. These roof willows I covered with straw, and the straw with earth. With the spade I mixed earth and water into mortar and threw in double handfulls in every crevice, one coat inside and one coat out. I smoothed this surface with my case knife. When sufficiently dry, I put on a second coat, inside and outside smoothing it carefully this time. When dry, I whitened it inside and out, and for fine weather, I had a cozy little home. But the earth was so sandy and porous [that] when it rained . . . the water came through. But we got along nicely, wife, baby and I because we were happy. At night—[for once it rained three days and nights] I would hold an umbrella over wife and baby in bed while they slept. Then wife would hold it over baby and I while we slept. We were so much better off than those in tents, and those others in wickiups, for we had an umbrella to shelter us; they had none. And hard as it now seems, the thought then that this was so much better with our conscience approving us as suffering privation for the truth's sake, that we would not have exchanged homes if faith must go with it, for the best Brighamite home in Utah. We felt that [even] should we fail, we were laying the foundation for future triumphs in Utah over the terrible bondage of sin the people were under; and we were comparatively happy.

Forscutt then resumed his own narrative: "The sufferings of the winter tried the faith of some beyond endurance, and in the spring, a few unable to endure any further test, left the camp, and reunited with the Brighamites. The distinction between the two churches was so marked, and the bitterness of feelings against the Morrisites so intense, that the backsliders could only find sympathy among their enemies by warmly espousing their cause and being foremost in denouncing those whom they had forsaken."[30]

After the disappointment of New Year's Day, the revelations of Morris focused for a time more upon the material needs of the people, problems with apostates, and solving internal difficulties than upon the imminence of the Second Advent. The millennial theme was not forgotten, but it was temporarily minimized as more pressing matters were confronted. On January 11, 1862, a revelation said: "The hour of my coming is nearer than many of my people suppose that it is. I shall not tell my people to prepare for me any more .. I shall come as a thief in the night upon some of them, and I shall catch them going to sleep; for when some of my people little expect me, lo, I come."[31]

30 Forscutt Manuscript, pp. 42–44.
31 Morris, *The Spirit Prevails*, p. 360.

The substance of that revelation was that Christ would not make any additional promises concerning the specific time of His coming. Yet less than two weeks later the people were told He would come to deliver them as soon as they had all sworn to a special oath of allegiance. The oath required that they promise to faithfully abide all the counsels of the Lord (past, present, and future) and walk blamelessly before Him until the day of their deaths. This oath was never to be broken upon penalty of death, and it was to be administered by Morris or one of his counselors in the presence of all the Morrisite leaders and faithful church members. After taking the oath, the recipient was required to seal it by touching his or her lips to the Book of Revelation.

During the succeeding fortnight, numerous related revelations were received, and preparations were made for administering the oath. By the middle of February all preparations were completed, and the oath was administered to the people over a period of two or three days. (No more than twelve individuals were permitted to receive the oath at any one time.)

On February 15 a revelation declared:

> I see, my son, that you are about through with administering the oath unto my people. I have been present all the time, and I have seen all that my people have done; and, as far as they have gone, I am well pleased with them . . . .
>
> And inasmuch as my people are through with the taking of the oath, you wish to know what I am about to do now. What can I say unto you upon this matter? I know that you want me to come. You do not want to hear of anything else. Nothing else will satisfy you but my coming. You say in your feelings that my people have endured as long as they can endure; that those who own mills will not suffer their miller to grind for my people; and you want to know what they must do. They must put down the name of every miller who refuses to grind for them . . . . If all those millers refuse to grind for my people, I will come and cut them off, and also the owners of the mills, and I will deliver the mills into the hands of my people. But if there should be one miller found . . . who will grind for my people with a willing and generous mind, I will save the life of that miller. Let my people do as I command them in this respect, and I will come and deliver them before they suffer for want of food.[32]

On February 18 a revelation again referred to the consequences of taking the oath. "My people need not to hang their heads, and conclude that I am not coming yet; for, as I have said, I am coming as soon as the oath is well through with. Let my people set all things in order in the Camp, and have their bodies and clothing as clean as possible . . . let them rest in me, and I will not betray their confidence; for lo, I come quickly."[33]

32 Morris, *The Spirit Prevails*, p. 418.
33 Morris, *The Spirit Prevails*, pp. 421–22.

But despite this promise the winter wore on toward spring, and still the Savior failed to make His appearance. Food was scarce, and the closing of the mills to the Morrisites was indeed a critical matter. What wheat they had they could not get ground into flour. They finally found a miller willing to grind for them, but the mill was in Kaysville, several miles from the fort. Soon they ran out of wheat altogether and had to barter livestock to replenish their supply. Eardley reported that they also found this to be difficult, "owing to the counsels of the Church to have no dealings with the Morrisites."[34]

Given the Morrisites' critical need for flour, it is not surprising that it was an incident over a load of wheat that set the stage for their final confrontation.

34 Eardley, *Gems of Inspiration*, p. 22.

7 The Storm Descends

The several accounts describing events leading up to armed confrontation are extremely partisan and sometimes contradictory. Those who gave accounts represented various perspectives and seem to have been more interested in fixing blame than in providing accurate information. In any case, discerning the facts about the affair is a complex matter requiring careful comparison and assessment. For this reason all or part of several versions are presented here.

As the weather began to warm in the spring of 1862, the Morrisites once more began to experience problems with the law as well as with some of their own dissatisfied fellows. Richard W. Young wrote: "Lot Smith, sheriff of Davis County, while attempting to levy an execution, was met by armed men and ordered away from the place."[1]

The Morrisite account of this same incident provides us with considerable more detail and reveals the justification for resisting the officer. Whether the resistance was, in fact, as justified as the Morrisites believed is difficult to determine, but the important point is that they felt justified and were determined to continue such resistance. Eardley wrote:

> For some weeks there was no resistance to this systematic robbery [attachment of property] of the people, until Smith on one of his visits espied a very valuable horse belonging to one David Parks and his brothers. Smith notified Parks that on his next visit he wanted that horse. He had taken a liking for the horse and must have him. Parks informed Smith that he could never have the horse, and, moreover that he had taken the last hoof out of camp that he would be permitted to take; that this systematic plunder of the people would eventually bring them to starvation, and they had determined to stand it no longer.
>
> In the course of another week, Smith again made his appearance with several companions, all armed with revolvers, and riding fine horses, and carrying more executions, and according to promise, he had brought one for David Parks . . . . Parks, knowing [the reputation of] the man he had to deal with, took the precaution of having a dozen of his brethren

1 Richard Young, "The Morrisite War," p. 348.

> armed and ready to protect him, . . . and these were waiting in a tent near by where they could watch the proceedings. Smith and his companions alighted and hitched their horses, and the former stepped to Parks' horse, and began to untie him, to lead him away. Parks also stepped up, and taking the halter out of Smith's hands . . . [refused to allow it]. Smith seemed nonplused and astonished that anyone should have the boldness to interfere with him in the discharge of his mission, and again attempted to untie the horse, and again was prevented by Parks. At this second rebuff, Smith turned toward his companions, who were apparently awaiting his orders, and caught sight of the armed men in the tent. He exclaimed, "Oh, I see you really mean what you say. You are all prepared to resist the execution of the writ." Parks replied that he was correct. Then, turning to his companions [Smith] said they had better go, and they went, foiled and humiliated, to enter a complaint against Parks for resisting an officer.[2]

This resistance undoubtedly gave the Morrisites a sense of triumph over those they regarded as enemies, but it added fuel to the fire of hatred and distrust already blazing between themselves and the Mormons. Whether justified or not, the Morrisites were clearly in violation of the law and were fast gaining the reputation of "Davis County Bandits." Their decision to resist all legal attachments and writs placed them in a most delicate position, for it could only be a matter of time before they would be brought to account. Whether impartial or not, the law would have its day.

The suffering, privation, and disappointment of the winter had taken its toll among Morris's followers, and as the weather became more favorable, a few of them determined to leave the settlement. Among these was William Jones, a highly pragmatic man who had become thoroughly disenchanted with Morris. Ironically, Jones was the same man who had been the first to acknowledge Morris as a prophet of God and had been one of the original converts to the Morrisite church.[3]

Jones was also one of the more wealthy Morrisite converts, having consecrated considerable property, including household effects and some sixteen head of cattle when he moved into Kington Fort.[4] He also had a small

---

2 Eardley, *Gems of Inspiration*, pp. 21–22.

3 Richard Young, "The Morrisite War," p. 349.

4 The Law of Consecration and Stewardship dated back to 9 February 1831, when Joseph Smith received a revelation instructing all church members or those who would subsequently join the Mormon church to give a deed or "consecrate" all their property to the bishop as representative of the church. The bishop would then return an inheritance or stewardship to every family according to its needs. Any surplus would be held in reserve and apportioned to those without property.

This law was followed by some Mormons in Ohio, Missouri, Illinois, and later in Utah, but it was never universally applied. Eventually it was replaced

farm nearby from which he harvested about two hundred bushels of wheat in the fall of 1861. Although Richard Young questioned Jones's faith for having sowed and reaped crops contrary to the teachings of the prophet since Jones was not an apostle, such action was actually in accord with Morris's instructions. Whatever the case, William Jones had cheerfully shared his wheat and other property with needy members of the camp, and he was generally well regarded by his fellows.

When he decided to leave the community, he announced that he planned to take with him what was left of his consecrated property. This, however, was forbidden by the Morrisite leaders. Young wrote that Jones then resorted to stratagem to recover as much of his property as possible. He volunteered to lend to a faithful member a yoke of oxen and wagon to take into the canyon to haul wood, as he knew he would not be allowed to take the wagon outside the fort by himself. After the wagon was outside the enclosure, Jones slipped out another way and soon intercepted it. When he was some distance from the fort, he told his companion that he had left the fort for good and that he was now going to take the team and wagon for himself. The faithful Morrisite got off the wagon and returned on foot to the fort, where he related the story to his brethren. Soon about fifteen Morrisites armed themselves and rode out in pursuit. In anticipation of this, Jones had left the road and hid the wagon in the brush hoping to return later and recover it. However, his pursuers were not deceived and were soon on his trail. Finally, they surrounded Jones in a ravine, eventually forcing him to turn the oxen loose. With no more property at stake, Jones was allowed to escape to Kaysville, where he found temporary shelter with two other Morrisite defectors—John Jensen and Lars Gurtsen. Young reported:

> Jones having safely escaped was now desirous of getting his family away. He made several requests of a number of Morrisite men, who were hauling flour from Kaysville to the Morrisite camp to bring his family down, but to no purpose. [His wife, mother, and three children were still at the fort.] Finally, exasperated, he told the teamsters that if they did not bring his family down on a certain day, he would prevent them from hauling any more flour. Still the family did not come, and true to his word, Jones, by threatening the use of a club, caused the Morrisites to abandon their wagon and return to their camp. Jones then unhitched the team, turned the animals loose on the range and left the wagon on the road.

---

by the Law of Tithing.

Joseph Morris made the Law of Consecration the cornerstone of his communal doctrine at Kington Fort.

For a thorough discussion of this principle see Arrington, Fox, and May, *Building the City of God.*

> . . . one night soon after Jones' interference with the teamsters, the camp [of Jones, Jensen, and Gurtsen] was surprised by an armed party of about thirty men, under Peter Klemgaard, and the malefactors were captured, tied, thrown into a wagon and conveyed over the Sand Ridge to Kington, where they were cast into a log house, used temporarily as a calaboose.[5]

The several Morrisite versions provided a considerably different slant to the story, but all agree with Young on the outcome. Dove mentioned the incident briefly, stressing the destitute condition of the Morrisites, but failed to mention Jones's previous association and trouble with them.

> In the latter part of April 1862, teams were sent to the grist mill with wheat to be ground for the use of the Camp. As the men were returning home, the teams were taken away from them. The children were without bread, and the Camp much in need. To go to the courts of Utah for redress was useless, so twenty-five men were sent to Kaysward to take the men prisoner who had taken the flour, and bring them back to camp; but there were no legal papers for doing these things.[6]

In regard to the same incident, Eardley also failed to mention the previous Morrisite associations of William Jones and his two conspirators. In fact, he called them "Mormons." Calling them Mormons may have been done to prejudice the reader. However, such reference was not inconsistent with Morrisite thinking at that time. Those who defected from their ranks were automatically considered to be Mormons regardless of how the defectors might be regarded by themselves or by non-Morrisites. Eardley said:

> Upon returning from the mill, the teamster was accosted by a party of Mormons who seized the team and flour. As numerous appeals for justice had been previously made to the courts [?] without avail, it was deemed useless to attempt it in this instance. They were thoroughly convinced that there was no law for apostates in Utah. A posse of the brethren was immediately dispatched to recover the team and wagon. They overtook the men at Kaysward, and not only brought back the team and flour, but also the three thieves who had been the cause of so much annoyance to the camp, with the intention of confining them, to keep them from perpetrating any further depredations.[7]

Forscutt, who perhaps provided the most objective account, reported that when William Jones left Weber Camp, his wife and family refused to accompany him. In consequence of this, the Morrisites decided that Jones's remaining property should remain in the camp to take care of his family.

5 Richard Young, "The Morrisite War," pp. 349–50.
6 Morris, *The Spirit Prevails*, p. 5.
7 Eardley, *Gems of Inspiration*, pp. 22–23.

Forscutt wrote:

> In the spring of 1862 Elijah Chappell, a Morrisite, went to the mill at Kaysward with a load of wheat. Returning without the flour, he reported that William Jones met him, [and] demanded whip, team and flour. Chappell refused to give them until a revolver was pointed at his head. He then submitted. Jones took possession and Chappell went to the camp and reported. A "posse" of fifteen men started in quick pursuit, overtook Jones and his comrades, and as this was the second time such a step had been made necessary, they marched him and his associates to camp with the rescued team and flour. That he was determined to continue his policy he avowed openly and fearlessly. There was sympathy for him in the breasts of many Morrisites, because they regarded him as a brave and openhearted man. But for the men returned with him, there was little or none. One of them had stolen the community's stock in sneak-thief style. It was decided that these men should be held prisoners, for if set free, they would associate [with] the villainous element around .. . there and carry out a policy avowed to either starve the Morrisites out, or make them live on boiled wheat. Already it was known that about twelve had confederated for this and other aggressive purposes. Pursuit of them had been made once and stolen stock recovered. A log house calaboose was improvised and the three prisoners were confined there.[8]

Surprisingly, the briefest account of the capture was that given by William Jones himself. He said simply: "I had a yoke of cattle and a wagon. These I took and left the fort. I was pursued. The Morrisites captured me together with Lewis C. Gurtsen and John Jensen. They brought us back to the fort and put us in jail, where I remained until the thirteenth of June."[9] Regardless of the rationale for illegally confining the apostates, that action set into motion the legal machinery of the territory, which was soon to be the undoing of the Morrisites at Kington Fort.

The prisoners remained under confinement for several days, and then Gurtsen and Jensen formulated a plan of escape. Undoubtedly, Jones would have liked to accompany them, but he was heavily chained and, therefore, unable to do so. The two unchained prisoners cut a hole through the log wall and crawled through after dark. Gurtsen made good his escape, but Jensen stumbled into a sentry whom he took to be his companion. His identity was immediately discovered and he was returned once more to jail.

In the meantime, friends and relatives of the prisoners had filed a complaint with John F. Kinney, chief justice of the Third District Court at Salt Lake City. Although not a Mormon, Kinney was friendly toward them and was said by some to be under the influence of Brigham Young. Collusion

---

8 Forscutt Manuscript, pp. 45–46.

9 Banks, "A Document History of the Morrisites in Utah," pp. 36, 39.

among Young, Kinney, and Robert T. Burton, another principal actor in the unfolding drama, was taken for granted by the Morrisites and was strongly suspected by several non-Mormon observers. Since the possibility of such collusion is of considerable importance in understanding the outcome of the Morrisite affair, it will be dealt with in some detail later.

Whatever the case, there is no need to charge Kinney with anything but proper motives in regard to his initial action against the Morrisites. They were, in fact, holding prisoners in violation of the law. Kinney would have been derelict in his duty if he had failed to take action.

On May 22, 1862, he issued a writ of habeas corpus to Joseph Morris, Richard Cook, John Banks, and Peter Klemgaard commanding them to set the prisoners free. Henry W. Lawrence, territorial marshal, was ordered by the court to serve the writ, either in person or by deputy. Lawrence appointed Judson L. Stoddard, his deputy, to serve the document. Stoddard, accompanied by two other deputies, Thomas Abbott and Wells Smith, proceeded to Kington Fort, a distance of some thirty-five miles, to deliver the writ.

The party of law officers was permitted to enter the fort, but the Morrisites refused to receive the writ, insisting that they were no longer subject to the law. Nevertheless, Stoddard read the document to an assembled group of Morrisites, which included all or most of those named in it. (Eardley said that Joseph Morris was not present.)[10] Stoddard later reported that he attempted to hand the writ to one of the Morrisites, but that it fell to the ground. One of the men reached to pick it up but was forbidden by Klemgaard. One of them brought a shovelful of live coals from the house and dropped it on the paper, burning it. Stoddard also reported that the Morrisites not only refused to receive the writ and destroyed it but spoke insultingly to the officers. According to him, John Banks as spokesman had said: "You leave and tell Judge Kinney to do his best to enforce it. We will not release the prisoners nor give them up. We neither fear nor regard any governor, judge, or law, except our own law and that we will maintain."[11]

Whether or not the refusal of the writ was as disrespectful as Stoddard maintained is of small consequence. The Morrisites did indeed refuse to receive it and thus were clearly in contempt. The officers then departed and made their report to Judge Kinney. In the meantime the prisoners remained in confinement contemplating their fate. And, in theory at least, the fate designed for them was not a pleasant one. On May 9 Morris had received a revelation instructing him how to deal with the prisoners. It said:

10 Eardley, *Gems of Inspiration*, p. 23.
11 Richard Young, "The Morrisite War," p. 350.

> They are condemned by my law to perish, and they shall perish at the right time. They are traitors to my government, and death is the traitor's doom. . . I do not wish you to punish those three men until I tell you, and then you must do as I command you. You must keep a good guard over them, and treat them properly, and I will keep your enemies off until I am fully ready to destroy them, and then I will let them all loose, and smite them all dead as soon as I have done so.[12]

If the prisoners were made aware of this revelation, it could hardly have given them comfort, for it suggested most strongly that they would be killed when the proper time came. Although Morris himself was a mild man and unaccustomed to violent acts, he did believe in a violent and vengeful God. The revelation suggested that the prisoners and other hypocrites would be smitten by God, not by the Morrisites. Yet as time went on, Morris was becoming more and more fanatical. The safety of the prisoners or other apostates might not have been assured if the word of the Lord should ever have demanded that the Morrisites participate in their destruction.

On the day the law officers had been thwarted in their attempt to serve the writ of habeas corpus, Morris received another revelation referring to them and to the prisoners.

> And behold, I give unto you a commandment, my son. You shall pay no attention to sheriffs, lawyers, petty governors, and devil's slaves; for I will pay them all off at once. They will never trouble you at all. You should hold those prisoners until I tell you what to do with them; and what I command you to do you must do. Should any officers of the law command you to let these prisoners go, and threaten you with the consequences if you continue to hold them, you must tell these officers that you fear no consequences, and that you pay no more regard to them than what you do to the dirt under your feet; and should they threaten to send up a mob against these people, to sweep them off, tell them to send it as soon as they can. You need not be afraid, my son . . . for should they attempt to come up against you to-morrow, . . . I would cut them all off.[13]

Clearly, the Morrisite refusal to receive the writ was not based simply upon previous unfortunate encounters with the law, but was also based upon specific instructions given by revelation. Furthermore, the Morrisites were convinced that the Second Coming would very quickly supersede all civil authority.

By May 1862 most of the Morrisites had recovered from the disappointments of the previous winter and were once more eagerly awaiting the day of deliverance. Morris had received numerous revelations earlier in the

12 Morris, *The Spirit Prevails*, pp. 549–50.
13 Morris, *The Spirit Prevails*, p. 574.

spring that again specified the time of the advent. The people were told that it would occur just a few days after a spectacular pageant called the "Foreshadowing of the Kingdom of God Day," scheduled for May 30, 1862.

John Eardley painted a vivid picture of the preparations for and enactment of the "foreshadowing."

> Many revelations had been received giving every minute detail for this important event. It was declared to be a principle of heaven that "coming events cast their shadows before them," and therefore the coming of our Lord Jesus Christ and the establishment of His Kingdom must be foreshadowed.
>
> When the time appointed arrived, all was in perfect readiness, and the ceremony, occupying nearly the whole day, passed off with the regularity of a clock. Joseph Morris represented the Lord Jesus Christ, and was hailed as Lord over the whole earth, amid the shouts of the people and the blowing of the trumpets.
>
> The high priesthood in its perfect organization was represented [by] twelve generals [apostles] riding on horseback around the square and the high priests following, four abreast . . . . They marched around the square seven times, glorifying God and praising the Lamb. Numerous proclamations were read, and after the marching was completed, the twelve alighted from their horses, and Joseph Morris, clad in his high priest's robes, withdrew a short distance from his fellows and stood still while the twelve approached him, and hailed him again the Lord of the earth, as a representative of Jesus Christ, and the twelve, leading him back again, introduced him to the people as such . . . .
>
> There were many interested spectators assembled from the surrounding towns and settlements to watch the ceremonies, and many ridiculous stories became circulated as to the intentions of the Morrisites afterwards, all of which were intended to injure them and widen the breach between them and the Mormons.[14]

These stories may indeed have been ridiculous, but to the outside observer the great foreshadowing pageant may well have appeared ominous. The participation of the Morrisite "army," which had been organized a few weeks earlier, had added to the precision and grandeur of the ceremony. The Morrisites had been commanded by revelation to organize seven companies of soldiers as a commencement of the "Army of the Kingdom." Richard Young put special stress on the mobilization of this 142-man army, which appeared ready to do battle with the Mormons.[15] Undoubtedly, many of those present at the foreshadowing also reached the same conclusion.

---

14 Eardley, Gems of Inspiration, pp. 23–24.

15 Richard Young, "The Morrisite War," pp. 283–84.

Morris did not intend a violent confrontation at this time. He reported that he received a revelation on May 2, 1862, in which the Lord had said: "Mine army consists of holy angels, who are celestial beings; but your army will consist of mortal men. It is my duty to bring mine army to assist you, because your people are in the hands of the devil; they are now his slaves; consequently, they are of no use to you. You cannot use your own people until I have delivered them into your hands by destroying the power of the devil."[16]

Morris did not expect his army to serve as either an offensive or defensive force—at least not until after the deliverance. It was organized for ceremonial purposes such as the foreshadowing day and for the specific purpose of eliminating hypocrites (apostates). A revelation explained: "The duty of this army will be to cleanse my kingdom by cutting off all hypocrites who may embrace the fullness of my gospel, and afterwards will not abide my law; all such characters shall be cut off by this army."[17]

But even this duty, a bloody one to be sure, was ultimately qualified by revelation. The Lord made a provision for getting the job done Himself if the army could not bring itself to act against the hypocrites.

> And when the division shall be called out to cut off the hypocrites, . . . if after the seventh captain shall have given his command to the six companies the hypocrites should not be cut off, he shall give his command to his own company, and should they fail to do their duty, *you must give your command to me* [emphasis added] . . . .
>
> If the army which you have will not cut off the hypocrites after you have gone the regular round with them, then I will cut them off instantly.[18]

Morris expected great numbers of people to be destroyed at the time of the Second Coming, but nowhere did he indicate that a mortal army would bring this about. Clearly he had no taste for being personally involved in bloodshed. Nevertheless, his words were inflammatory and could hardly be dismissed by outsiders as entirely symbolic—especially in the presence of the very real and threatening "Army of the Kingdom."

Although these were exciting days at Kington Fort, they were sometimes touched with tragedy. It was almost as though an even greater tragedy was also being foreshadowed. Not only had Joseph Morris suffered many marital problems, he had never been able to live more than briefly with his children. His only living child, a daughter, lived with his former wife and stepfather, but he had not seen her for several years. When he found that his wife, Mary, was with child, he was overjoyed; but this joy was to be short-lived. His

16 Morris, *The Spirit Prevails*, p. 536.
17 Morris, *The Spirit Prevails*, p. 535.
18 Morris, *The Spirit Prevails*, pp. 556–57.

infant son died soon after birth in May 1862. On May 19 Morris received a lengthy revelation concerning the recent death of his son. It is both tender and touching, showing how deeply he felt about the loss and how difficult it was for him to reconcile God's will with his own. He sought a satisfying explanation from the Lord and received this reply:

> I can assure you that I have not taken your children from you to afflict you; but I have done it because you were not placed in a position to take care of them. . . . I took your children off the earth in order that they may not be ill-treated by those people into whose hands they might have fallen; for I can assure you that if I had suffered them to have lived, they would have suffered great affliction and abuse; but knowing that you could not have taken care of them yourself, it was my duty to take them to myself and take care of them for you.[19]

The revelation then goes on to explain that his son had been sent to him once before for a short time and then had been taken back to heaven to fulfill a mission there. He had been sent back to earth once more for only a brief time, and he was presently in heaven counseling with God the Father. Morris was then promised that his son would be sent to earth again just as soon as possible and that he would become a great and powerful servant of God who would have the power to turn water into blood, to bless or curse others at will, and to destroy thousands of evil people. All this he was destined to do in the name and power of his father Joseph. Apparently, this explanation satisfied the prophet, for he complained no more to God about his loss.

Meanwhile, things were beginning to move in the Third District Court of Judge Kinney. On May 24 Judson L. Stoddard returned the writ to the court. Although Stoddard made his report to the court immediately after serving the writ, it was not until June 10, 1862, almost three weeks after the trip that he made an official complaint about the conduct of the Morrisites at the time of his visit. On that date he swore out the following affidavit:

> Territory of Utah, Great Salt Lake Co. On the 10th day of June A.D. 1862 personally appeared before me Judson L. Stoddard who, on oath states that as Deputy Territorial Marshall, on the 24th day of May last [probably the 22nd] he was directed to serve a writ of habeas corpus, issued by Judge Kinney, directed to Joseph Morris, John Banks, Richard Cook, and Peter Klemgaard, who as was alleged, had imprisoned William Jones, John Jensen and Lewis C. Gurtsen, and had them confined without any lawful authority. That in pursuance of his authority, he proceeded on the 24th day of May to a place known as the Morrisite Camp, in Davis County, in said Territory, to serve said writ in company with two assistants.

19 Morris, *The Spirit Prevails*, p. 562.

> Affiant further states that when he arrived within 200 yards of said camp, he was met in the lane, leading to the camp by twelve men who passed by him, halted and formed, some of them having arms. As affiant proceeded to carry, he encountered about sixty men, most of them armed with guns, pistols, and swords, who retreated as afliant advanced and formed in a line around the house occupied by said defendants in said writ of habeas corpus. Affiant approached within hearing distance of said Joseph Morris and the other defendants, and said to them that he had a writ of habeas corpus issued by Judge Kinney, for the release of the persons they had in prison, and proceeded to read the writ to them which was listened to by said defendants.
>
> After said writ was read and a copy tendered them, John Banks appeared as a speaker for himself and the defendants, and used the following language: He said they would not obey the writ nor the law, that they neither feared nor regarded the writ of Judge Kinney, nor the law. You leave and tell Judge Kinney to do his best to enforce it. We will not release the prisoners, nor give them up. We neither fear nor regard any Governor, Judge or Law except our own law, and that we will maintain.
>
> Affiant further states that the defendant would not receive a copy of the writ, or the original, but treated it and the authority that issued it with the grossest contempt, and some of them said that no more writ should be served in the camp.
>
> Affiant further says that from reliable information there are in said Morrisite Camp, about one hundred armed men; that said Morris and his deluded followers have placed themselves in utter defiance of the law and legal authority, and with a view of defending themselves against any legal processes, they are well armed and are drilled every day in the use of arms and in military science.
>
> Affiant further states that he resides in near proximity to said camp, and he is well satisfied from the defiant position of said Morris and others that it would not be safe for any other to attempt to serve any writ without a strong posse of men, well armed, to assist in executing the process. Judson L. Stoddard
>
> Sworn to and subscribed before me this 10th day of June A.D. 1862. J. F. Kinney, Judge.[20]

Wells Smith and Thomas Abbott, who accompanied Stoddard, provided much briefer, more informal accounts. Neither mentioned meeting armed men outside the fort, and only Smith referred to the armed men within. Instead of sixty, Smith wrote: "We went in and were directed to where Banks lived. At the front of the house were two guards with double barreled shotguns, and a man with a drawn sword."[21]

---

20 Banks, "A Document History of the Morrisites in Utah," pp. 41–43.

21 Banks, "A Document History of the Morrisites in Utah," p. 44.

Both Smith and Abbott reported that the Morrisites refused to receive a copy of the writ, so Stoddard threw it on the ground and a man burned it. No explanation was given for Stoddard's first report that the writ had been delivered, being modified to a complaint detailing the many defiant acts of the Morrisites.

On June 10 H. O. Hansen and Philo Allen, both residents of Davis County, also filed separate affidavits before Judge Kinney, describing the circumstances of the capture and detention of Jones and Jensen. They alleged that the two men were confined in a log house, heavily chained, and under constant guard. They also swore that no one but the guards were allowed to converse with them, that they were threatened with instant death if they tried to escape, and that they were in danger of being murdered unless their release could soon be effected.

Richard Young commented that Judge Kinney "was highly enraged at the defiant attitude of the Morrisites" and issued a writ on the same day the affidavits were filed. The writ was addressed to Henry W. Lawrence, territorial marshal, or Robert T. Burton. It read:

> Whereas, Philo T. Allen, of Davis County and Territory of Utah, hath this day filed a complaint, on oath, before me, that on or about the 1st day of May, A.D., 1862, in County of Davis, and Territory of Utah, one Joseph Morris, John Banks, Richard Cook, John Parsons and Peter Klemgaard, did then and there willfully and without lawful authority, forcibly and against the will of William Jones and John Jensen [imprison said William Jones and John Jensen] and have kept them in close confinement ever since, therefore, you are hereby commanded to arrest said Joseph Morris, John Banks, Richard Cook, John Parson and Peter Klemgaard, if they be found in their bailiwick, and have them before me forthwith, at the Court House in Great Salt Lake City, then and there to be dealt with according to law, and have you then and there this writ with your return thereon enclosed. Hereof fail not under the penalty of law.
>
> Given under my hand and the seal of the Third Judicial Court, at Great Salt Lake City, this 10th day of June, A.D., 1862. [Seal] John F. Kinney, Judge, Third Judicial Court, Utah. Attest: Patrick Lynch, Clerk.[22]

Despite the urgency with which this writ was issued, there is no evidence that any effort was made to enforce it. Indeed, Marshal Lawrence believed that too much haste and use of force would provoke armed resistance and that the innocent would suffer. He was absent from Utah when the second writ was issued. Kinney was, of course, aware of Lawrence's absence when he issued the second writ, otherwise Burton's name would not have appeared on it. Forscutt stated:

22 Richard Young, "The Morrisite War," p. 369.

> At the time of the issue and return of Judge Kinney's first writ, armed subjection was averted by his [Lawrence's] wisdom and justice. . . . his liberal and enlarged view enabled him to grasp the situation, and avert bloodshed. He was a block in the wheel, but he was a merchant, and as such, business would call him shortly to the Eastern States. Postponement of issue of the second writ was therefore deferred till his absence should make his chief deputy, Col. Robert T. Burton, acting Territorial Marshal1.[23]

Since Richard Young concurred with Forscutt's assessment that Lawrence was opposed to the use of excessive force in enforcing the writs, no doubt Lawrence was truly a "break in the wheel," and his absence from the territory was a necessary requisite to an armed confrontation with the Morrisites.[24] It is also of some interest that Lawrence was a Mormon at the time of the Morrisite affair, but that he subsequently apostatized from the faith. Whether or not this disaffection was influenced by the Morrisite encounter is unknown.

On June 11, the day after issuing the second writ, Judge Kinney issued a writ of attachment, which recited the issuance of the writ, the contemptuous treatment of the authority issuing the writ, the failure to obey the mandate of the court, and other pertinent matters. Joseph Morris, John Banks, Richard Cook, John Parson, and Peter Klemgaard were then cited for contempt of court. Richard Young wrote:

> Judge Kinney was burning with indignation at the highly contemptuous course of the Morrisites, and insisted that the governor should call out a part of the militia as a *posse comitatus* in the enforcement of the latter process of the court.
>
> Secretary Frank Fuller, who in the absence of Governor Dawson, was acting Governor, issued the necessary order calling out a force of militia to act in conjunction with the marshall in the enforcement of the writ.[25]

It is difficult to tell whether Judge Kinney was as incensed with the Morrisites as Young contends or if he was personally desirous of precipitating an armed confrontation with them. Certainly there is some evidence that he delayed the confrontation as long as possible and then took action only under pressure from the Mormon leadership. At any rate, the following statement attributed to Judge Kinney by the Mormon apostle Wilford Woodruff would seem to bear this out. "I have not taken any steps without counseling President Young and when the men came to swear out their affidavit, I told them they must ask President Young. When they came back,

23 Forscutt Manuscript, p. 48.
24 Richard Young, "The Morrisite War," p. 370.
25 Richard Young, "The Morrisite War," p. 369.

they said they had done so and President Young told them to go to Judge Kinney and get out their affidavits."[26]

Apparently, the issuance of the June 10 writ was little more than a legal formality to justify the writ of attachment of June 11, for as Forscutt had pointed out, there was hardly sufficient time to serve it on the 10th and get a reply back to the judge by the 11th. The deputy marshal would have had to ride over thirty-five miles, attempt to serve it, and then return, covering a total of at least seventy miles in a matter of hours. Although not an impossible ride, it would certainly have been a most difficult one. Furthermore, there appears to be no documentary evidence that anyone tried to deliver the writ to the Morrisites.

Forscutt also called into question the logistics of mobilizing the militia to serve as a *posse comitatus* on such short notice. He was of the opinion that the posse was already mobilized before the writ of attachment was issued. He says it would have required:

> . . . the call on the Governor in due form for troops; next the call by the Governor on the Militia Officers; then the gathering together [of] the troops, the arming and equipping and provisioning of them; and lastly the taking of them with the ordinance over a rough road, receiving and mustering in companies from settlements enroute, and landing them there just out of sight of the [Weber] camp . . . and all this from the afternoon of the 11th to the evening of the 12th.[27]

Again, while this much accelerated action might have been possible, it certainly would have required remarkable cooperation among the principals and remarkably favorable conditions to bring everything together on such short notice. Forscutt's assessment is not without merit, but it must be realized that concerted action could have been carried out rapidly if the Mormon church organization had been involved.

Eardley reported that a posse of 200 picked men was chosen, "and this task was given to ten bishops of ten different wards to choose 20 men each who could be depended upon to carry out instructions."[28] In a broad sense, Eardley may have been right, for the men selected for the posse were Mormons and may well have come from ten different wards. To what extent the church organization was used to recruit the posse is unknown, but in all likelihood, it played a significant role. This seems likely for several reasons. First, the territorial militia was an official military unit of the United States, but it had only recently achieved that status. Previously it had been called

26 Journal of Wilford Woodruff, 26 June 1862, Archives, Historical Department, Church of Jesus Christ of Latter-day Saints, Salt Lake City, Utah.

27 Forscutt Manuscript, p. 48.

28 Eardley, *Gems of Inspiration*, p. 25.

the Nauvoo Legion and had been a Mormon military organization dating back to the 1840s when the Mormons were in Illinois. On April 28, 1862, the Nauvoo Legion had been officially called by the U.S. Adjutant General to protect the telegraph and mail route east through Wyoming. The call had irritated the non-Mormons in Utah, for it was issued to Brigham Young, president of the church, not to Frank Fuller, acting governor. This was taken as clear evidence that the militia was a church army, not a territorial one. No doubt the church organization that had controlled the Nauvoo Legion was still viable in June 1862.[29]

Second, although the militia was officially constituted, it had few, if any, standing members assigned to the Salt Lake area. Therefore, it was necessary to recruit members to form the posse from the Mormon settlements, and they had to provide their own arms and provisions. The quickest way to reach potential recruits would have been through the local church organizations.

Third, actual accounts from personal diaries seem to imply that calls to serve came through the church wards. For example, the journal of John L. Blyth, a Mormon residing in Salt Lake City, noted: "June 12th [1862] Thursday, was called upon to furnish a man and team to go up to the Weber with a posse of men sent to take Joseph Morris, the professing prophet of that district. I furnished a good team and man armed and equipped with 5 days rations for the trip."[30]

Jacob Miller, a Mormon from Davis County, provided this account: "[June 11, 1862] This evening call for volunteers to take Morris, Banks and others as the Morrisites are defying the law and refusing arrests . . . 12th, about 200 armed men with 2 cannons from S. L. City also 200 from this [Davis] County and 100 from Weber Co."[31]

On June 11 Hans Magleby of Salt Lake City, wrote: "I was called to go with a troop to the Morris Camp in Weber Valley. Left early in the morning [June 12] with about two hundred soldiers. Toward evening we left the city and camped about two miles from the city."[32]

Richard Young reported that the posse consisted of "one skeleton company of riflemen, one full company and a detachment of artillery; in all about two hundred and fifty men. The artillerymen had a six-pound gun and brass howitzer."[33]

---

29 Nels Anderson, *Desert Saints*, p. 216.

30 Journal of John L. Blyth, 1858–1863, p. 84, Special Collections, University of Utah Library, Salt Lake City, Utah.

31 Pioneer Journal of Jacob Miller, p. 88, Special Collections, University of Utah Library, Salt Lake City, Utah.

32 Diary of Hans Olsen Magleby, p. 72, Special Collections, University of Utah Library, Salt Lake City, Utah.

33 Richard Young, "The Morrisite War," p. 370.

Although reports disagree concerning numbers, it is clear that the official posse was a large and well-armed force and that it was considerably augmented with unofficial volunteers by the time it reached South Weber. Eardley maintained that "their numbers were greatly increased as they passed through the various settlements by armed volunteers, until they arrived near the Morrisite settlement with a force of fully 1,000 well-armed men and five pieces of cannon." On the other hand, he reported that "the able-bodied men of the Morrisites numbered about 90, . . . [they had] a poor collection of arms among them, such as shotguns, revolvers, pepperbox pistols, a very small assortment of rifles."[34]

Eardley was at the fort at the time the posse appeared, but he was hardly in a position to obtain an accurate count of the participants. If, as indicated, recruits volunteered along the way, it is doubtful if anyone, even the posse leader, Deputy Marshal Robert T. Burton, possessed an accurate tally of the size of the force. Morris himself received a revelation stating there were fewer than 700 in all, but unless one believes in his prophetic powers, that estimate would have to be placed beside Eardley's in terms of accuracy. Nevertheless, in all likelihood, there *were* fewer than 700 in the posse. Perhaps 500 is as reasonable an estimate as any.

Eardley's figure of ninety able-bodied Morrisite males seems to be accurate. Richard Young reported that there were 140 males at the fort, but only 94 were enrolled in the Morrisite army.[35] In any case, there can be no doubt that the posse greatly exceeded the Morrisites both in numbers and fire power. As far as is known, the posse's officers and men were all Mormons.

Robert T. Burton, chief deputy to Marshal Lawrence and a colonel in the territorial militia with many years of service in the Nauvoo Legion, led the posse. His chief aide on the expedition was Theodore McKean, also a deputy to Lawrence. Richard Young reported that Burton had been reluctant to serve the attachment, but that when he finally agreed to do so it was upon the condition that a massive force be used.[36]

The overwhelming size of the posse was calculated by Burton to frighten the Morrisites into submission without the use of force. Against a different foe such a tactic might have been successful, but Joseph Morris had already received several revelations anticipating the appearance of a large force. These revelations promised that his enemies would be destroyed by the armies of God coming to rescue the Morrisites. Morris saw the appearance of the "Mormon army" as a certain sign that the time of the Second

34 Eardley, *Gems of Inspiration*, p. 26.

35 Richard Young, "The Morrisite War," p. 430.

36 Richard Young, "The Morrisite War," p. 370.

Coming had arrived. In that sense, he actually welcomed its appearance. It is clear that he had no fear of the overwhelming numbers.[37]

The posse took a position on the bluffs south of Kington Fort early on the morning of June 13, 1862. Then, instead of delivering an ultimatum directly to the Morrisites named in the writs, Burton's men apprehended a Morrisite herdboy and instructed him to deliver a message to Morris. The message demanded that Morris and his lieutenants surrender themselves and their prisoners immediately. It continued:

> An answer is required in 30 minutes after the receipt of this document, if not forcible measures will be taken for your arrest. Should you disregard this proposition and place yourselves in jeopardy, you are hereby required to remove your women and children; and all persons peaceably disposed are hereby notified to forthwith leave your encampment, and are informed that they can find protection with the posse.[38]

The herdboy, Jacob Johnson, provided this personal account: "I was herding stock when a number of men, [Judson] Stoddard among them, rode up and said they wanted me to take a paper into camp. I said I could not leave my stock, but they said I must either take it into camp or be killed. So I took it and gave it to John Banks. The latter was being read when the first cannon was fired."[39]

The posse leaders have been severely criticized for the impropriety of sending the herdboy to the Morrisite camp instead of properly qualified officers, but at least the message reached the Morrisite leaders. However, the amount of time allowed to elapse between the sending of the message and the commencement of firing is even more controversial and important.

Forscutt gave the following account from his perspective within the fort:

> On the 13th of June, as the Apostles of the Weber church were returning from their morning prayer meeting—for they had day-dawn services—the first intimation of an approaching army was seen on the southern "bluff" or mountain. Soon many [Morrisites] were out wondering what hundreds of men were doing up there, wondering more when [upon] looking through a fieldglass the discovery was made that they were all armed and had cannon with them. The remembrance of revelations and of threats pointing to such a gathering was vivid. The Prophet was sought and the answer was given that he was receiving *a revelation* [emphasis added]. . . . [before] long . . . the Prophet appeared and handed to Mr. Forscutt, the Clerk of the Council, the revelation received. He read it to the Council. It affirmed the gathering to be that threatened so long. These men on the "bench" would demand the giving up of God's servants.

---

37 Morris, *The Spirit Prevails*, pp. 238–40, 257–58, 629.

38 Richard Young, "The Morrisite War," p. 370.

39 Banks, "The Document History of the Morrisites in Utah," p. 67.

> They were to be denied. The enemy would then attempt the destruction of the saints; but God would deliver them out of their hands. None of the faithful should be destroyed.[40]

At about this time the herdboy brought the message to the Morrisites. Forscutt wrote:

> In answer to inquiry, the boy, evidently terrified, told the Council the strength of the command was very great. That he objected to come down to camp if they were intending to destroy it. That he was in charge of the herd, and could not leave it. They evidently thought his life less precious than theirs; as to the herd, they would take care of that.
>
> The people had mostly gathered in the bowery by this time, all on the quiver for news. The Council repaired there. A brief prayer for Divine guidance was offered. It had been decided to lay both the marshall's document and the revelation before the people; the last named first. Mr. Parsons, who was blessed with a remarkably clear voice, read the revelation . . . but before he had time to present [the marshal's document] and obtain the decision of the people, the boom of a cannon was heard, and almost simultaneously, terrific and heart-rending screams from a young girl who sat on the third seat from the speaker's stand. For the moment it was thought to be from fear, but looking on her, the fearful sight of two dead women by her side and of her lower jaw hanging only by a narrow strip of skin, proclaimed the fact and the barbarity of the horde whose first salutation was a well aimed cannon ball into an assembly of worshippers.[41]

Exactly how much time elapsed between the sending of the message and the firing of the first shot is strongly disputed. Banks reported that several of Burton's soldiers testified that the cannon was fired thirty minutes after Stoddard left the herdboy.[42] Richard Young contended, however, that the demand for surrender must have been in the hands of Banks not later than 8:00 A.M. and that it was two hours later before the first shot was fired. Young wrote that Burton "sent men down the lane to the vicinity of the fort at least twice, but they returned without the expected reply. The General then directed Major Lodd, who was in command of the artillery, to fire two shots over the fort. This was at 10 A.M."[43]

Burton claimed he waited ninety minutes before he ordered the firing to commence, and Richard Young reasoned that at least two hours must have elapsed between delivery of the message and commencement of firing because there had been time within the fort "for consultation, for 'solemn prayer,' to write a revelation, to read it and submit it to the Council,

40 Forscutt Manuscript, pp. 51–52.

41 Forscutt Manuscript, p. 54.

42 Banks, "A Document History of the Morrisites in Utah," p. 68.

43 Richard Young, "The Morrisite War."

to call the people together, to open the meeting with ceremonies, to again read the revelation, and for Mr. Cook to submit the question of submission to the people."[44] However, if Forscutt's account is accurate, most of these activities had actually occurred prior to the arrival of the herdboy. Certainly, the presence of so many armed men on a hill less than a mile away could hardly have gone unnoticed by the Morrisites, and Morris's revelation had too much precedent in earlier ones to require additional information from the herdboy before it could be produced.

One Morrisite, Niels Anderson, who was at the fort, claimed later that not only was there not ample time given to surrender, but, in fact, the Morrisites in general "had no notice whatever; the only notice was a cannon ball." He wrote that he first learned of the notice to surrender at his trial.[45]

Anderson's statement may be basically correct; for if John Parson, the Morrisite apostle, was just beginning to read Burton's communication to the congregation when the first cannonball struck, a majority of those assembled probably never did hear the terms and conditions specified. In any case, there was certainly no time for the women and children to be safely removed from the battle area before the first shots were fired. Regardless of how much time elapsed between sending the surrender demand and the commencement of firing, it was not enough. The fact remains that the cannonball struck in the middle of unarmed Morrisites who had shown no overt resistance.

Perhaps the most charitable conclusion would be that Colonel Burton grew weary of the delay in responding to his demands and ordered that two warning shots be fired to speed up the Morrisite decision. Richard Young reported that "the first shot went over the fort into the bluff beyond; the gun must have been re-aimed before the second shot, for the projectile struck the plowed ground in front of the settlement and riccochetted striking an old house or corral, where it disappeared from the sight of the posse."[46]

It might, of course, be easy to suppose that the militia gunners were not well trained and that their lack of skill resulted in a warning shot accidentally becoming an instrument of destruction. (Their second shot did not strike precisely where aimed.) However, regardless of Burton's testimony, the gunners *intended* to hit the fort with their second shot. William H. Hunt, who assisted in firing the first two shots, made the following statement:

> I was captain of ten men in the artillery company. We had three pieces of artillery, one long black gun, a short gun, the old saw and a brass howitzer.

44 Richard Young, "The Morrisite War," p. 371.

45 Niels Anderson to Joseph F. Smith, 3 March 1903, Archives, Historical Department, Church of Jesus Christ of Latter-day Saints, Salt Lake City, Utah.

46 Richard Young, "The Morrisite War," pp. 371–72.

> The long black gun was a twelve pounder and it was there the first day. I served under Major Lodd, General Burton being commander. The first shot from the cannon went entirely over the camp. The second time *the cannon was aimed* at [emphasis added] a log house in the fort.[47]

Although their aim was imperfect, the gunners achieved their goal. The cannonball struck the plowed field and bounded into the fort, killing and maiming as it went.

Richard Young described the scene in the words of an unnamed Morrisite observer. He stated that immediately the scene became one of utter confusion. Richard Cook shouted for everyone to go home at once and for each man to take care of his own family as best he could.

> Men and women, panic-stricken, rushed hither and thither, some seeking safety in cellars, some in potato pits—in short, anywhere or in any place in which security could be . . . hoped for.
>
> There was not a Morrisite in the fort that was armed, or that thought of arming. They met to consider the question [of surrender] and to pray over it: . . . the first salutation they had was a cannon ball in the assembly.
>
> *About an hour and a half* [emphasis added] after the firing commenced, the Morrisites got their arms, each man determining to defend his own family, if the posse came sufficiently near to attack them. From this was effected an organization and a regular defense was made. But at the time of the attack there was not a man armed.[48]

The long-predicted storm had at last broken upon the heads of the people. But its fury was not to be spent upon the Mormons, but upon the Morrisites themselves.

47 Banks, "A Document History of the Morrisites in Utah," p. 68.
48 Richard Young, "The Morrisite War," p. 372.

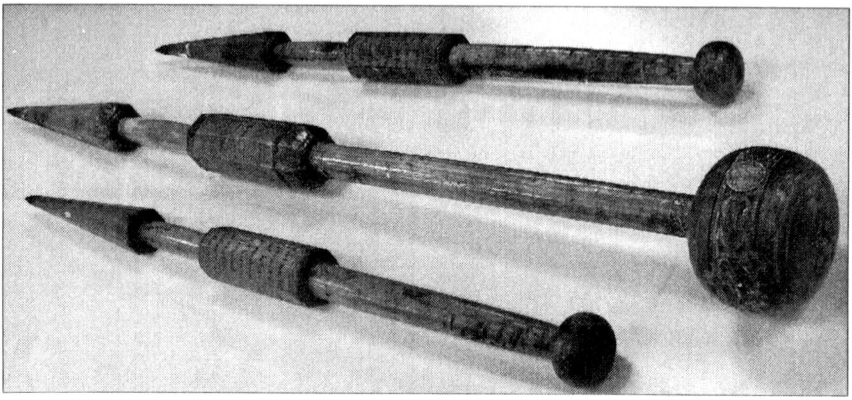

These scepters were designated by revelation to be five feet long and to bear specific explanatory inscriptions. They were used in the militant, Morrisite Foreshadowing Ceremony held May 30, 1862. One part of the ceremony required that Joseph Morris and eleven mounted Morrisite officials ride around Kington Fort seven times, each carrying a scepter and shouting, "Hosanna." The entire Foreshadowing Ceremony was intended to foreshadow the imminent second advent of Christ and the imminent presentation by a heavenly being to Joseph Morris of a divine scepter signifying his authority as God's supreme representative on earth. Immediately after the Morrisite War, these scepters were confiscated by the Mormon posse and displayed along with the bodies of Joseph Morris and John Banks in the Salt Lake City Council Hall. Other ceremonial articles such as Morris's official robe and crown were also displayed. Originally there were twelve scepters, representing the twelve tribes of Israel. Apparently, only three have survived. Courtesy of the Church History Museum, The Church of Jesus Christ of Latter-day Saints.

The text written on the scepters, as transcribed by Eric Paul Rogers, states the following:

TO ALL NATIONS AND PEOPLE
OF ALL LANGUAGES THAT NOW DWELL UPON THE EARTH
Be it known unto you that I am sent by the GREAT
KING OF KINGS, and LORD of LORDS to RULE
over all ADAM'S posterity. And being his REPRESENTATIVE
I hold in my hand this emblem of power, unto which all of the NATIONS and KINGDOMS
of
the EARTH
must BOW; for I am the legitimate RULER over all the EARTH, And my authority is
sanctioned
by
the FIRST GOD; therefore, I hold in my hand / an emblem of POWER to represent his
CEPTRE which will shortly, be given

unto me. I am Joseph Morris [name is signed] PRESIDENT of the Melchisidec Priesthood.

Behold! I am Hugh Park [name overlays original inscription] even
number five. And I present myself,
with this rod in my hand, before
this people, and, also before all man-
-kind, in the stead of the fifth
born son of Adam, to represe[n inserted]t or fore-
-shadow his name, number, and in-
-scription, he being the fifth ruler over all
Abraham's seed _ even over the
elect of God.

Behold! I am Daniel Smith even number seven. And I present myself with this rod in my hand, before this people, and, also, before all mankind in the stead of the seventh firstborn son of Adam, to represent or foreshadow his name, number, and inscription, he being the seventh ruler over all Abraham's seed _ even over the elect of God.

The only known photograph of Joseph Morris, left, taken in England, circa 1841, before he migrated to the United States. To the right is his older brother William, who did not migrate to the United States until after Joseph's death.

The first cannon fired in the Morrisite War left seventeen-year-old Mary Christofferson's chin dangling by a flap of skin. She was fortunate: the young mother sitting next to her was killed.

An English emigrant disillustioned with Mormonism, George Thompson was one of the first to join the Morrisite Army and later succeeded the Prophet Cainan as leader of the Morrisites.

John R. Eardley, George Williams (the Prophet Cainan), and George Thompson, in England, circa 1873, where a missionary effort had been initiated during the leadership of Williams.

Christ was expected to make His Second Advent at Dempsey Creek in this humble meeting house built in 1877 and photographed here in 2009.

The door of the Morrisite meeting house at Dempsey Creek, Montana, 2009.

George Johnson, the last official leader of the Morrisites, was a Danish emigrant who was never a Mormon. As a result, his teachings reflected his more liberal background. (left)

Andrew Henrikson was a Danish emigrant who never knew Morris and was never affiliated with the Mormon church. He served as president of the Montana Morrisites from 1866 until his death in 1921. (right)

III *The Morrisite War*

8 The Last Revelation

When the cannonball landed in the Morrisite congregation, it not only threw the assembled worshippers into confusion, it instantly convinced them that the attacking force was bent upon their destruction and that they must now fight for their lives. Peter Anderson, son of the girl whose chin was struck by the cannonball, later wrote that "rumors of the Mountain Meadows Massacre were fresh in the minds of all the Morrisites. None of them were convinced that if they did surrender they might not be letting themselves and their families in for a similar fate."[1] They were dazed by the sudden turn of events. Not only had the posse fired upon them, it had done so with deadly effect despite the prophet's assurance that none of the righteous would be harmed. For some of them the cannonball swept away much more than the life of two friends and the beauty of a young girl. The direct attack also took its toll in the Morrisites' faith in their prophet and their fierce dedication to a way of life that had been filled with unbounded hope and built upon unspeakable sacrifice. The realization of this truth left some in total shock.

For others, the destruction about them suggested that they must place even more faith in their prophet and in their God. For it was clear that nothing short of Divine Providence could save them from destruction at the hands of so formidable a foe. They had trusted in the Lord with all their hearts and now they must trust Him with their very lives. It was in this same spirit that the prophet Joseph Morris entreated with God immediately after the first casualties occurred, and he received only words of comfort and reassurance.

> Behold, I am Jesus Christ, and I come near unto you. I know your condition. I wish to try this people before I deliver them. I will put a stop to the present course in a short time. The enemies shall go so far, and then I will stop them—they have almost gone far enough—I will stop them at the right time. I know you feel discouraged, and feel as though I had forsaken you and this people; but I have not, and that you shall soon see. Be still,

---

1 Peter Anderson, "The Wound that Never Healed," *Frontier Times* (July 1965):44.

> and faint not. They have commenced the work, but I will finish it. As soon as this scrimmage is over, I will give unto you my Father's message, and then I will sweep them off. You need not fear; I will stop them at the right time. The hypocrites that are in the midst of this people will go over to the other side. As soon as they have drawn from among this people all the hypocrites, then I will put a stop to the present course. I have suffered them to come and do what they have done, in order that they may draw out all the hypocrites. None will leave me and go over to the other side but those people who are false before me—who have not my spirit to strengthen them. The true and faithful will stand firm; but the false-hearted will go. Those that stand faithful . . . through this, I will deliver. You do not think that I should suffer this to take place; but I have suffered it for a wise purpose. This is a trying day to some. The clouds all around appear dark to my people; but a bright cloud will soon make its appearance.
>
> Both you and the faithful must depend on me, and you will be right. You must not give up to them, but stand them out, and I will sustain you.[2]

And how the Morrisites needed that sustenance. Their arms were poor and mostly short range, and their ammunition was in short supply. They were already short of food when the attack commenced. Soon they would be out of food altogether. But most of all, the flimsy fort could provide them with scant protection from the rifles and cannon of the militia. Not only was the fort poorly built but it sat in a virtually indefensible location. The sandy bluffs to the south and west encircled the fort on two sides. They were only about half a mile distant and rose some two hundred feet in height, providing a direct view of the fort and its interior. The Weber River, swollen with spring rains and melting snow, swept ominously within a few yards of the fort's northern perimeter, discouraging any thought of escape in that direction. Furthermore, more than a hundred volunteers from the Ogden area had positioned themselves on the bluff near the north bank of the river. They, too, were greatly elevated above the fort and had a clear view of it, inside and out. They had brought a cannon with them, which they occasionally fired but apparently with little effect. For all practical purposes the fort sat in the bottom of a bowl, open and vulnerable from three sides. Small wonder that the Morrisites prayed fervently for intervention from the Hosts of Heaven.

The time at which the Morrisites began to return fire is a matter of dispute. Robert Burton, in testimony given seventeen years after the Morrisite affair, said:

> The first firing from the small arms came from the fort, perhaps twenty minutes after the first cannon was fired. I interpreted this as an indication that they did not intend to surrender. I then directed Major Howard

2 Morris, *The Spirit Prevails*, pp. 627–28.

> Egan, with considerable force, to form a line around the east side of the fort, and Major Cunningham was sent to the west side and both received heavy fire before they got into position. I supposed that the river would prevent escape on the north side, for the stream was high. When we got into position firing was done on both sides, and my orders were to the officers, if not to the men where I remained the night before, to avoid the shedding of blood as far as possible, but see that the prisoners in no way escaped. I thought that the leaders would probably surrender, but we discovered that they were not inclined to yield.
>
> The forces on the west were under Col. Ross who was directed to get a position near an old wall and in doing so he received a pretty heavy fire, in which Jerrod Smith was killed, at the mouth of the west lane in the afternoon of the first day.[3]

Burton's testimony, however, was contradicted by John C. Chambers, a Mormon participant in the hostilities. He reported:

> After the first cannon was fired, the Colonel called for a company with long range rifles to take possession of a ravine in close proximity to the main body of infantry, which, being done they received the word to fire, and immediately there was considerable agility observed in the occupants of the fort, who hurried from the bowery where they had been assembled to their houses and prepared themselves for resistance to the law of the land which was about to be enforced.
>
> Col. Ross in company with Major Stoddard took command of the long-range rifles and cautiously advanced upon the fort, hoping to make their fire more effective and finally gained a position on the north side of the fort near the river which was held until the surrender. As they were approaching two men with their wives and children were seen waving a handkerchief as they left the fort, who came forward and gave themselves up. The name of one of them was Eardley; the other name I did not ascertain. The Colonel took them into custody and placed a guard over them until the surrender of the fort.
>
> The whole body of infantry were then marched down to the brush skirting the Weber River where they lay in ambush most of the day, being on hand in case of emergency, the 1st rifle company being engaged on the north side shooting down any of the rebellious horde they might observe, whilst Capt. Jack's Enfield Rifle Company on the south kept them on a continual flutter and curtailed their intercourse very materially. The artillery had by this time caused some deaths in the fort. The prisoners were then set free who came forth waving a white flag. This was done apparently to see if this would not cause a cessation of hostilities, but the posse were there for the apprehension of Morris and his counselors, and nothing less than their surrender would satisfy Sheriff Burton.[4]

3 Banks, "A Document History of the Morrisites in Utah," pp. 71–72.

4 Journal History of the Church of Jesus Christ of Latter-day Saints, 1830–

This account corresponded much more closely with that of John Eardley in the Morrisite camp than with Colonel Burton's. Eardley recalled:

> Scarcely had they assembled than a cannon ball came bounding into the congregation, killing two women, one an elderly lady, the other with a nursing babe in her arms. A young lady, sixteen years of age, was struck by the same shot, carrying away her chin. The shot was accompanied by the yells of the posse, in imitation of the Indians. The meeting was brought to a sudden close, and all were counseled to go to their respective homes.

The booming of cannon and the firing of rifles continued for nearly two hours before any attempt was made by the Morrisites to defend themselves. In the meantime the mob approached the camp and took shelter behind the mud walls of the old Fort, where they could better locate the position of the men, women, and children. Then they would fire a cannon ball through the building, and the rifles would stand ready to shoot the inmates as they would flee to some other place of safety. The question then arose, "What shall we do, they are close upon us?" The counsel was then given: "Protect your families in the best way you can, but avoid shedding blood, if possible." This counsel was strictly obeyed; for when they took up what arms they had, they would invariably fire over the heads of the posse, and this was found a sufficient deterrent for the first day.[5]

George Dove, also a Morrisite eyewitness, agreed with Eardley and Chambers. He remembered:

> . . . a cannon ball came in our midst, and it killed two women, one a nursing mother, with a babe in her arms, and the other an old lady. A girl sixteen years of age, had her chin shattered by the same shot. The yells of the attacking party were heard all around us. For an hour and a half after they commenced firing, not a man in the Camp of Weber took up arms, while the Mormon Militia poured in cannon and rifle shot on every side; then the men said: "What shall we do"; and the word was given: "Protect your families the best way you can, but avoid shedding blood if possible." This was carried out to the letter; for had the Morrisites been so disposed, they could have done much execution.[6]

Since all Morrisite accounts (including one cited by Richard Young) and the account of John C. Chambers, a Mormon, agree substantially concerning the time when the Morrisites commenced armed resistance, the accuracy of Robert Burton's account is doubtful. If those accounts are basically

1872, compiled by the Church Historian's Office, 13 June 1862 to 15 June 1862, Archives, Historical Department, Church of Jesus Christ of Latter-day Saints, Salt Lake City, Utah.

5 Eardley, *Gems of Inspiration*, pp. 26–27.

6 Morris, *The Spirit Prevails*, pp. 6–7.

correct, it also casts serious doubts on Burton's contention that the cannon was originally fired with the sole intention of frightening the Morrisites into surrender. If the posse commenced small-arms fire immediately after the cannon discharge and before the Morrisite assembly had dispersed from the bowery, there must have been malicious intent from the beginning. Certainly Chambers's statement that riflemen on the north side were "shooting down any of the rebellious horde they might observe" seems to contradict Burton's assertion that he had counseled them to "avoid the shedding of blood as far as possible." Chambers also casts some interesting light on the circumstances under which the cannon was originally fired.

> Immediately on arranging his plan of attack, Col. Burton deputed Major Howard Egan and another to proceed towards the fort with a white flag, anticipating to be met half way by a like deputation from the fort; but as no notice was taken of the circumstances, the party returned and waved the flag that had been insulted and threw it down upon the ground before the cannon. The attack was commenced by the artillery, the ball striking the bowery in which some of the fanatical people had assembled . . . . Whilst the cannonading was proceeding Col. Ross formed his infantry upon the hills further to the southwest of the fort.[7]

It is instructive that Chambers used the term *attack* and that he then asserted, as previously noted, that the colonel called for a company of long-range rifles and they began firing at the fort as soon as they were in position—long before the Morrisites responded in like manner. Perhaps the militia gunners were more skillful than they were previously given credit for, and perhaps Robert Burton's memory had partially failed him when he related the story seventeen years later. It must also be recognized that Burton's testimony was presented at a time when he was on trial charged with the murder of a Morrisite woman who died on June 15, 1862. Under such circumstances he was under considerable pressure to make the entire Morrisite episode appear as properly handled and lawful as possible.[8]

Although Chambers believed that the Morrisites' release of the two prisoners was for the purpose of inducing the posse to cease their attack on the fort, such was not the case, at least not as far as Joseph Morris was concerned.

---

7 Journal History, 13 June 1862 to 15 June 1862.

8 It should be noted that in an account given just a few days after the affair, Burton said: "I sent a communication to them and waited 90 minutes and received no answer. Then I fired a cannon ball and they returned the fire with small arms and the fire kept up through the day." See Journal of Wilford Woodruff, 18 June 1862. This account implies that the Morrisites were the first to use small-arms fire, but it does not say so specifically. In fact, the wording does not obviate the possibility that the Morrisites responded to small-arms fire as well as to the cannon fire.

Sometime in the morning of June 13 he had received a revelation instructing him to release the prisoners, for they had already served their purpose. "The object I [Jesus Christ] had in view in retaining those prisoners, was to bring up mine enemies to this place, in order to fulfill my words; therefore, I have accomplished what I wished to do through those prisoners. I can dispense with them now. . . . You may let out those prisoners, for I do not want them any longer. I will cut them off myself when I come.[9]

The death of Jared Smith on the afternoon of the first day of battle was the first posse fatality. Evidently the Morrisites also were not unanimous in adhering to the injunction to avoid the shedding of blood. Richard Young reported that Smith died instantly, but the Journal History presented the following account:

> The soldiers had strict orders not to expose themselves unnecessarily, but Jared Smith, son of Arthur Smith, after having fired, rose up to see the effect of his shot and was immediately struck in the breast with a bullet. Private Whitehead saw that he was mortally wounded and so asked him if he had any word to send to his father; he replied, "Tell them it is all right, Mormonism is just as good today as it ever was." These were the last words he spoke and he died five minutes afterwards.[10]

Although a variety of interpretations of Jared Smith's last words might be made, one in particular seems very much worth considering. Given the circumstance of his death, it certainly might be inferred that he believed he had given his life in support of his religion, and therefore his death was not a tragedy but a heroic and worthy act. How widely such a view might have been shared by other posse members can never be known, but given the strong religious overtones of the encounter, it is inconceivable that the issue of law and order was the only one motivating the recruits. At issue, of course, is the attitude of the posse, for the Morrisites were convinced it was a religious war from beginning to end. They were sure that the posse was simply an arm of the Mormon church that, incidentally, had the force of law behind it. Aside from the words of Jared Smith, other evidence tends to support the assumption that at least some of the posse members believed that religious as well as legal principles were at stake in the encounter. For example, John C. Chambers usually referred to the posse members as troops, but on one occasion, when he was commending them for their endurance in very inclement weather, he wrote: "The brethren were very devoted to the cause.[11] Unfortunately, Chambers did not specify the "cause," but the use of the term *brethren* certainly helped establish the posse's religious identity.

---

9 Morris, *The Spirit Prevails*, p. 626.

10 Journal History, 13 June 1862 to 15 June 1862.

11 Journal History, 13 June 1862 to 15 June 1862.

Robert Burton used the same term in referring to some men who came to join the posse after the encounter had begun. He said: "Some brethren came to inquire so I organized them into my posse."[12]

John Eardley reported that on the third day, when the Morrisites were in the process of surrendering, Robert Burton "told them he wanted no more of their 'damned apostacy.'"[13] If this report is accurate, it clearly shows that the leader of the posse was, in fact, deeply concerned with the religious as well as legal issues involved. Eardley was not present when the alleged words were spoken; however, they were reported in exactly the same terms by George Dove, who was an eyewitness.[14] It is also of interest to note that another Morrisite eyewitness, Alexander Dow, reported in a sworn statement on April 18, 1863, that when Burton came into the camp he "rode his horse upon Morris, and commanded him to give himself up, in the name of the Lord."[15]

The firing of cannon and the exchange of small-arms fire continued throughout the day. At dusk most of the posse members withdrew from their positions, leaving only a strong guard to prevent escape from the fort and to show the Morrisites that they could expect more action on the morrow. The Morrisites took advantage of the cover of darkness to improve their defenses. They enlarged the shallow trenches that were already dug and scooped out more dirt from the floors of their houses and banked it against the walls to provide more protection.

That evening Robert Burton sent a letter to Acting Governor Fuller reporting on the day's proceedings and asking for further instructions. He was concerned about the strong resistance encountered, the death of a posse member, and the possibility of several more days of hostilities. On the following day he received the governor's answer: "Sir—the shedding of blood in resistance to civil authority renders execution of the law imperative. The service of the writs submitted to you is expected at your hands and you have been empowered to call to your aid a sufficient force for the purpose. Let your acts be tempered with mercy; but see that the laws are vindicated."[16]

Colonel Burton took the message to heart. However, he was hindered in carrying it out by a heavy rain that started about 10:00 P.M. Friday and fell throughout the day of Saturday, June 14. Burton reported that the Morrisites began firing at four o'clock in the morning, as soon as the posse members showed themselves, but neither side could do much damage because of the

12 Journal of Wilford Woodruff, 18 June 1862.

13 Eardley, *Gems of Inspiration*, p. 28.

14 Morris, *The Spirit Prevails*, p. 27.

15 Richard Young, "The Morrisite War," pp. 470–71.

16 Richard Young, "The Morrisite War," pp. 438–39.

heavy downpour. Burton's forces were also reinforced by an additional cannon on Saturday.[17]

Apparently, many of the posse members saw the siege as something of a lark or holiday, for John Chambers gave the following account:

> The artillery were inactive the whole day [June 14]. Just as we had gathered to camp and were endeavoring to start fires to dry our wet clothes and cook a little supper, the Ogden cannon roared forth, awakening the stillness and varying the otherwise monotonous nature of the day and exciting the military aspirations of the city [Salt Lake City] artillery. A loud "huzza" arose from the camp in honor of the "north." The "south" being determined not to be a whit behind, made a rush for the "old sow" [the nickname of the large cannon, which had been expressly sent up from the city to aid in the siege] and replied by a louder roar that made the mountains tremble and intimated to the yet deluded people that there was a little more thunder in store for them on the morrow.

Chambers also reported that the siege of the Morrisites had attracted a large group of spectators, who came in holiday fashion to witness the event. The bluffs on the north side of the river were covered with spectators and troops from Ogden, while "the surrounding heights on the south side of the river were dotted over with small parties witnessing the siege of the fort."[18]

For the Morrisites, however, the day was anything but a holiday. They continued to improve their fortification, but the rain, which provided a welcome respite, also caused great suffering. The previous day's cannonade had torn great holes in many of the rooftops within the fort, allowing rain to pour through into the rooms below. The recently dug pits soon became muddy quagmires filled with several inches of water. In these the wounded and dying, the men, women, and children lay or crouched for protection. Under these circumstances it was impossible to build fires, so there was no warm food to eat and no way to dry out soaked clothing and bedding. Small wonder they were worn out and discouraged and that a number of them surrendered before the day was over.[19]

During the night the rain ceased falling, and the Sabbath dawn broke clear and beautiful. Colonel Burton was determined his orders would be carried out and the siege brought to an end, so he called his officers and troops together in preparation for storming the fort.

Chambers wrote:

> The troops were accordingly called together, and after prayer by Bishop Cunningham were briefly assured by the Colonel who said, in substance

17 Banks, "A Document History of the Morrisites in Utah," p. 73.

18 Journal History, 13 June 1862 to 15 June 1862.

19 Banks, "A Document History of the Morrisites in Utah," p. 69.

> that: if the business they were called upon to do was right, it would be right to do it on Sunday, and if it were not right, it would be wrong to do it on any day. So he wished them to be prepared for a good day's work; he instructed the officers to be careful with their men and urged the men to be obedient to their officers, and he felt positive no lives would be lost.
>
> The officers having then received orders, the troops were then marched to their different positions.[20]

Burton wrote that "on Sunday at four o'clock they opened fire on us again, and it was kept up all day, they doing their best to hold the fort, while I did my best to close in on them with as little loss as possible."[21]

Again Chambers flatly contradicted Burton's statement. "About seven o'clock A.M. the *stillness* [emphasis added] of the Sabbath morn was broken by the firing of cannon and the cracking of the rifle, which had the effect of rousing the devoted disciples of Morris to a sense of the danger that awaited them, which was evident from the rapid running from one place to another, and they were in turn fired upon by Capt. Jack's sharpshooters."[22]

This statement provides very compelling evidence that once again the firing was commenced by the posse, not by the Morrisites. Chambers continued:

> As the fort could not be reduced by cannonading it was found necessary to storm the fort and in order to accomplish this without loss of life on our part, a rolling battery was constructed consisting of willows placed lengthwise through three hind wheels of a wagon making a battery of about six feet thick. As soon as the battery was made ready Col. Burton gave orders for the whole command to advance in order to storm the fort. The advance was immediately made and soon the entire fort was surrounded by skirmishing parties under the command of Col. Ross on the north, on the south and east sides under the command of Major Howard Egan and Col. Merrill [of Ogden] together with Capt. Jack's Enfield Rifles.[23]

Although the posse was determined to take the fort and was making steady headway, this was not taken as cause for despair by the faithful Morrisites. On the contrary, they saw it as a certain sign that the time of their deliverance had at last arrived. Dove reported that the people had been almost without food, that they were weary, and that their ammunition was about exhausted. But again this was seen as a positive sign by the believers.[24] The advancing posse, the shortage of food, the fatigue, and the dwindling supply of ammunition seemed to conform perfectly to a revelation Joseph Morris had received that very morning. The revelation was profoundly optimistic,

20 Journal History, 13 June 1862 to 15 June 1862.
21 Banks, "A Document History of the Morrisites in Utah," p. 74.
22 Journal History, 13 June 1862 to 15 June 1862.
23 Journal History, 13 June 1862 to 15 June 1862.
24 Morris, *The Spirit Prevails*, p. 7.

assuring the faithful Morrisites that all would be well and that Christ would deliver them that very day—for after all, it was Sunday, and Christ was the Lord of the Sabbath.

> I wish to speak unto you this morning to encourage you . . . I heard the prayer that you offered up this morning, and I will answer every word of it ..
>
> This is the third day of the war; it is my day [Sunday] . . . . Everything is about ready, and the time is come when I shall have to come and show myself plainly unto you.
>
> My faithful people have nearly spent their physical strength and used up their ammunition, and when they have done so, and are not able to defend themselves against their enemies any longer, they will have done their own part, and will be pronounced faithful before me, having done their duty. Until my people have come to this point, I cannot lawfully come to their release. A people must spend their own strength and means before they have a lawful claim on me for assistance, and when they have done so, I am compelled by law to come and assist them.
>
> When you see the ammunition of my people used up, and they have no means left to defend themselves, and mine enemies begin to make headway and force themselves into this camp, you may know that the time of my coming has arrived . . . .
>
> Look out for me; for lo, I come unto you quickly. I am Jesus Christ. Even so. Amen and Amen.[25]

This revelation gave the faithful Morrisites the fanatic will to continue resistance to the very end. Joseph Morris was assured that his hour of triumph had arrived. He was convinced that on that very day he would be crowned by Christ as Lord of all the Earth. He was so certain that his cause was just and so confident of ultimate victory that he could hardly have suspected that on that beautiful Sabbath morning he had just produced his last revelation.

In the afternoon considerable resistance was encountered by the posse from the west side of the fort where the Morrisites had made portholes for firing through the walls of several cabins. Accordingly, Colonel Burton ordered a charge upon these buildings. Seventeen men, under the command of Lieutenant James Lewis, advanced quickly and safely to the nearest cabin, but found it locked and empty. They came under heavy fire while attempting to force an entry, and just as they broke open the door, John Peter Wahlin, a member of the attacking force, was struck in the head by a bullet and died instantly.

The occupation of the cabin gave the posse direct access to the fort and made it possible to greatly hinder the defenses of the Morrisites. To stop the fire from the other cabins, the rolling shield or battery was then pushed

25 Morris, *The Spirit Prevails*, pp. 629–32.

as close as possible to the fort wall. Upon seeing the battery descend upon them, the Morrisites in the adjacent cabins ran hastily from their positions and retreated in near panic to the farther reaches of the fort. Apparently they thought the battery was not only a shield but was filled with explosives and combustibles designed to burn the Morrisites out.

The effect of the ominous-appearing battery and the occupation of the westside cabins was immediate. The Morrisites realized that further resistance on their part was hopeless—they had done all they could and must now wait upon divine intervention. George Dove recounted the following:

> Late in the afternoon the bugle sounded in the Fort [playing "A Cottage by the Wood," the signal calling the Morrisites to assembly] and a white flag was raised and carried by Alonzo Brown to the western part of the Fort. The order to do this was given by brother John Parson and others, who stated to Joseph that they thought the men had done all they could, and that they were willing to surrender and give their lives for the sake of the people if necessary. Orders were given to cease firing. Robert Farley continued to blow the bugle while bullets were flying around him, but he remained unhurt. While the white flag was being carried to the western part of the Fort, Burton and his men continued to advance toward us firing all the time. John Parson called out: "For God's sake and the sake of humanity stop your firing!" Then Burton and many of his men rushed into the Fort and ordered the Morrisites to stack arms, which was done by them without hesitation. After they had done this, Burton called out for Joseph Morris, John Banks, Richard Cook, John Parson and Peter Klemgard. When they presented themselves before him he said, "I want no more of your apostacy."[26]

Burton's account of the entry into the fort corresponded closely with that given by Dove:

> Brown, who bore the flag, asked me what was wanted. I told him it was an unconditional surrender, that they were requested to stack their arms in a conspicuous place from where I was . . . . In a few minutes I discovered that some of the Morrisites were stacking their arms in the fort near the white flag. This was a little after seven o'clock P.M. All the arrangements for securing the arms had to be made before dark. I, therefore, started into the fort with Golding, Croxall, and Stoddard by my side on horseback, saying to the men behind the breastworks that they must follow me into the fort.[27]

Burton reported (seventeen years later) that about twelve men besides the officers entered the fort with him and that he immediately sent back for ten more but deliberately kept the number small so that an excessive

26 Morris, *The Spirit Prevails*, p. 7.
27 Banks, "A Document History of the Morrisites in Utah," p. 76.

number would not retard the work and create trouble. However, James Ashman, a member of the posse who entered the fort with Burton, reported that a hundred men entered with Burton. Most Morrisite accounts say that Burton entered with a large force. Richard Young, a Mormon, said that more than a score entered with Burton, but that only a few were placed in a position to guard the stacked arms and that they were faced by more than a hundred Morrisite men, while others were approaching from various parts of the fort still carrying their arms. Eardley, on the other hand, stated that "a detail of the posse was placed in file between the people and their arms, so as to preclude them any attempts at regaining them. After taking every precaution, Burton called for Joseph Morris . . . [and the others]."[28]

From this point on the accounts of what happened vary greatly depending upon whether they are given by Morrisites or Mormons. On June 18, 1862, Burton gave his version of what happened at a hearing before Judge Kinney.

> I placed some men to take charge of the arms or guard them. Then Mr. Morris made some remarks and asked me what I wanted. I said I wanted all the men who had taken up arms against me. Then Morris said to the crowd, "all who will stand by me to the death lift up their hands" and all as far as I could see lifted up their hands and made a push as though they were going to the school house or some place to defend themselves. I ordered Morris to stop . . . and followed him up. I had no arms but my revolver and as he would not stop I stopped him with my revolver. He was shot dead. Banks was also shot through the neck from which wound he died.
>
> Two women were shot at the same time which I very much regret but it could not be helped.[29]

The Morrisite version, also based on eyewitness reports, differed from the above. For example, John L. Bear, who lost his wife and child in the battle at Kington Fort, recorded the following account of Morris's death:

> Four men on horseback initially entered, followed by the mob. Then Burton hollered out, "Where is Joe?" Someone answered, turning his face southward, "There, he is coming."
>
> He and Banks came arm in arm; then Burton gave his horse the spurs, like he was was going to ride over him, but Morris did not flinch or move, but took hold of the bit of the bridle and forced the horse back, saying "I want to know what you are going to do with this people. They have done no wrong. They are innocent."
>
> Burton answered, "It's none of your G - - d - - - business." Morris replied, "I want to speak to them."

28 Eardley, *Gems of Inspiration*, p. 28.
29 Journal of Wilford Woodruff, 18 June 1862.

> "Be d - - - quick about it," was the response.
>
> So Morris said, "Brethren, I have taught you the true principles." Then the people said, "Hail to the prophet. Hallelujah!"
>
> Morris said: "Now, who will die with me, come and die with me." A number came and shook hands as a parting farewell. I wanted to also but could not on account of the crowd.
>
> Then Burton, leveling his revolver shouted, "Will you give up, Sir?"
>
> "I will never give up my principles; they are eternal truth!"
>
> With the words, "God damn you," Burton shot him.[30]

The widely publicized affidavit of Alexander Dow, also a Morrisite eyewitness, did not differ in substance with Bear's account. Dow, however, stated that upon Burton's shooting of Morris and Banks, Mrs. Bowman called Burton a "blood-thirsty wretch," which prompted him to shoot her too.[31]

Though the Mormon and Morrisite descriptions of what happened differ, there are several points of agreement. Morris did make a speech to his followers, after which there was movement among the Morrisites. Whether this movement was toward arms stacked nearby, or to some of the buildings within the fort, or just to Morris's side in a symbolic gesture of solidarity, it is not known. It is a fact that the speech made by Morris and the subsequent movement of the Morrisites precipitated the action taken by Burton. It is another fact that Burton did kill Morris and that others were shot in the same incident.

Although we cannot know for certain what prompted movement among the Morrisites, it should not be surprising if Burton did in fact interpret it as a dangerous and hostile act rather than merely an excuse for silencing the prophet, as most Morrisites believed. Tactically, his entry into the fort may well have been hasty and ill advised. Apparently he entered the fort with a relatively undisciplined force, and adequate precautions for guarding the arms and prisoners were not initially taken. Any movement by the Morrisites might indeed have appeared to be a threat to the safety of himself and his men.

Certainly Morris had been undaunted by the appearance of the posse within his gates, and he was still defiant. Judging from the account of Dove, the surrender had been made over his objections, and certainly he had received enough reassuring revelations to convince him that his hour of triumph had arrived now that the posse was upon him. To the very end, the Prophet Joseph Morris expected to be delivered by divine intervention, which would result in the destruction of his enemies. His last mortal thought must have been that finally his victory had been won.

---

30 John L. Bear, "The Autobiography of John L. Bear," *Journal of History* (Lamoni, Iowa: 1911–12), pp. 207–8.

31 Richard Young, "The Morrisite War," pp. 470–71.

Clearly many of the Morrisites also shared Morris's interpretation of the events that were taking place. Mary Christofferson Anderson, the girl whose chin had been shattered by the cannonball, reported: "I had been in a cellar, and came out, having heard that deliverance was at hand. I saw Burton fire three shots at Morris." Mrs. Emma Thompson Just, another Morrisite witness to the shooting, said:

> We Morrisites thought that none of our number who were faithful could be killed. Even when Morris was shot and fell lifeless to the ground we did not think him dead. I saw the wadding fly back from his clothes and thought it was the bullets rebounding from him. We considered him invulnerable, or that if he should be killed he would be immediately restored to life. When Morris was killed my father sat upon his body saying, "Now kill me, for I have nothing more to live for."[32]

Writing twenty-four years later, George Dove related simply: "Such was the earthly end of Joseph Morris, but he still lives in the hearts of those who received his teachings.[33]

Most accounts, including that of Richard Young, indicate that with the death of the prophet all resistance ceased and the Morrisites became fully tractable. However, apparently such was not the case. Burton reported that he had "ordered Col. Ross to detail four unarmed men to separate the women from the men, as the women were terribly excited; and the men were drawn up in a line to be marched off as prisoners."[34]

John Chambers gave a much more colorful account of the proceedings:

> Col. Burton then called for fifty more men and afterwards the whole of the command who were drawn up in line across the fort, facing the Morrisites.
>
> A scene then follows which can better be imagined than described. Those who still resisted were placed under a heavy guard, and a guard had also been put over the arms. It was extremely difficult to separate the men from the women and to get them to come out of the school house. In order to do this Col. Ross called for a party of men and these went at it with a will; for those who were stubborn were dragged by the hair of their heads which according to their custom was exceedingly long and afforded a good hold. Women screamed, children cried and the officers of the law labored with some difficulty to quell the riot and confusion until dusk which was now nearly approaching and rendered the scene still more confused.
>
> The brass howitzer being called for, the artillerymen were on hand in a few minutes with a load of grape to belch forth more thunder, if needed.

32 Banks, "A Document History of the Morrisites in Utah," pp. 80–81.

33 Morris, *The Spirit Prevails*, p. 8.

34 Banks, "A Document History of the Morrisites in Utah," p. 81.

> Col. Burton then contended with the deluded people and told them that they would be immediately destroyed, if they did not surrender. This had the effect of staying the further shedding of blood and the whole of the Morrisites [with the exception of the women and children] were placed under a strong guard.[35]

With the Morrisites finally under control, the "Morrisite War" ended. All those who had borne arms or whose name appeared on the rolls of the Morrisite army were taken to Salt Lake to stand trial for murder or resisting due process. The posse arrived in Salt Lake City on the evening of June 17, 1862. The next morning the prisoners (about ninety in number) were taken before Judge Kinney's court and imprisoned or placed under bond to appear at the next session of court, March 1863. Richard Young reported:

> Early in the morning of the sixteenth, the general dispatched Albert Dewey to Salt Lake City with the bodies of Morris and Banks . . . .
>
> About two o'clock of that day, the posse started towards the Territorial Capital, with those of the Morrisite male prisoners, who had been enrolled in the army, exclusive of the wounded and of those who had surrendered in obedience to the proclamation previous to final capitulation. The start was not made, however, until ample provision for the temporary needs of the women and children left had been made.
>
> The bodies of the Prophet and his first Counselor were taken to the city hall, where they were viewed by thousands of people.[36]

Hubert Howe Bancroft, in his *History of Utah*, has given a more graphic account. "The camp was then plundered, and the dead conveyed to Salt Lake City, where the bodies of Morris and his lieutenant were exposed at the city hall, the robe, crown, and rod of the former being laid in mockery by his side, and his fate regarded by the saints as the just punishment of one who 'had set himself up to teach heresy in Zion, and oppose the Lord's annointed.'"[37]

Whether or not Bancroft's appraisal of the feelings of the Mormon people concerning Morris is accurate is a matter for conjecture, but it is of some interest that his body and the accoutrements of his holy office were displayed publically and viewed by thousands. There can be no doubt that to the Mormons Joseph Morris was an object of great curiosity, if not of scorn.

---

35 Journal History, 13 June 1862 to 15 June 1862.

36 Richard Young, "The Morrisite War," p. 466.

37 Hubert Howe Bancroft, *History of Utah, 1540–1886*, vol. 26 (San Francisco: History Company, Publishers, 1890), p. 618.

9 Aftermath

The unexpected death of Joseph Morris, the destruction of Kington Fort, and the hasty separation of the men from their wives and children left the Morrisites in an untenable position. Although they were outcasts, they had no one aside from the Mormons to turn to. They were desperately in need of help, for nearly all of them were without adequate shelter, food, and clothing. More than half of them were absolutely destitute. Many Mormons came to their aid during this time, and Brigham Young himself sent a physician to the jail to dress the wounds of the Morrisite prisoners, yet the Morrisites were still considered deluded untouchables by many of their Mormon neighbors.

A number of the Morrisites who had stood faithful during the long winter of privation at Weber Camp found the death and destruction of the war more than they could bear. They surrendered their faith and rejoined the Mormons, or sought to hide their identity, or left the territory. Among the more prominent of these was Apostle Mark A. Forscutt, who eventually became closely identified with the Reorganized Church of Jesus Christ of Latter Day Saints.

A surprisingly large number of Morrisites, although shocked by the sudden turn of events, remained loyal to the teachings and memory of their fallen prophet, Joseph Morris. For them, the death of their leader was interpreted as the result of God's will. Joseph Morris was soon acclaimed as a martyr who had given his life in the service of God, just as Joseph Smith had done two decades earlier. It was believed that he had fulfilled his earthly mission when the great foreshadowing ceremony had been performed at the end of May 1862. Thus, Joseph Morris's mission was seen as being entirely symbolic. He had been chosen of God to foreshadow the glorious day of deliverance, but it had never been intended by God that Morris should actually reign supreme as Lord of all the Earth. It was believed that the Second Coming was still to occur—that it would speedily take place now that the foreshadowing had been accomplished and the testimony of Joseph Morris had been sanctified by the shedding of his own blood. By interpreting the events in this way, many of the Morrisites were able to retain their faith and to maintain a sense of group identity and loyalty even though they were deprived of a leader and were beginning to disperse.

When the Morrisite men who had borne arms against the posse appeared before Judge Kinney on June 18, they were bound over to the Third Judicial Court preparatory to standing trial at the next court session scheduled for March 1863. Except for Richard Cook, Peter Klemgaard, and Christian Neilsen, considered leaders in the uprising, the men were freed on bond of $1,500 each. James Dove (an apostle) and his son George, two of those released on bond, wrote that "the majority appeared for trial, but some few went East and others went West to Carson Valley and California."[1]

A few years later James Dove admitted to being among "the few" when he wrote:

> The people of Weber began to wander into the wilderness in July 1862, and in November, James and George Dove started for Nevada, and having passed through a part of the winter in the woods, near Virginia, came down to Carson Valley, there finding John Livingstone talking to the people, who were anxious for us to preach and John E. Jones, James Dove and John Livingstone met in prayer in Father Jones' house.[2]

Ultimately, seven of the Morrisites were convicted of murder in the second degree and received sentences ranging from ten to fifteen years. Sixty-six of the remainder were convicted of resistance and fined $100, and two were acquitted.

The imposition of these sentences was not unduly harsh considering the crimes for which the men had been convicted, but by March 1863 the Morrisite affair was no longer entirely in the hands of Mormons or Mormon sympathizers. The political climate and power structure had changed dramatically in Utah Territory since the previous June. Stephen S. Harding had arrived as newly appointed governor on July 7, 1862, and he was immediately struck by what he believed were the antigovernment sentiments of the Mormon church and people. He was shocked to find that the Mormons had been involved in what had every appearance of a religious war but seemed indifferent at best to the Civil War raging in the East. He wrote to the secretary of state on August 3:

> . . . [the Mormons take it for granted that] the United States as a nation is to be destroyed, that the Gentiles will continue to fight each other until they are exhausted, and then the Saints are to step in and quietly enjoy

1 George S. Dove and James Dove, *A Voice from the West* (San Francisco: Church of the Firstborn, 1879), p. 12.

2 James Dove, *A Few Items in the History of the Morrisites* (San Francisco: Church of the Firstborn, 1892), p. 1.

> the possession of the land, and also what is left of the ruined cities and desolate fields; . . . .
>
> Brigham Young and the other teachers are constantly inculcating in the minds of the crowded audiences who sit beneath their teachings every Sabbath, that the government of the United States is of no consequence, that it lies in ruins.[3]

Governor Harding took a keen interest in the Morrisite affair but from a very different perspective than that of Frank Fuller, who had dispatched the posse to Kington Fort. He came to the conclusion that the Mormons were religious fanatics as well as disloyal and therefore worthy of reproach in all their actions. When Colonel Patrick E. Connor arrived in Utah in November 1862 with a troop of California volunteers, the governor concurred with his decision to locate the garrison on the bench above Salt Lake City rather than in the isolated Cedar Valley where Johnston's Army had been stationed. Colonel Connor's command replaced the Nauvoo Legion as the official armed force in Utah, and with this replacement both civil and military control once more returned to Gentile hands.

The church leaders opposed the location of a military post literally within gunshot of the city, but Harding and Connor were convinced the Mormons needed police supervision, and a new fort was begun immediately. It was named Camp Douglas in honor of Senator Stephen A. Douglas. Soon after his arrival, the new military commander served notice on the Mormons that he would tolerate no disloyal behavior and that he would arrest anyone "guilty of uttering treasonable talk." Shortly thereafter, Governor Harding addressed the territorial legislature (comprised mostly of polygamous church leaders) and gave them a stern lecture on patriotism and polygamy. He said: "I am sorry to say that since my sojourn among you, I have heard no sentiments, either publically or privately expressed, that would lead me to believe that much sympathy is felt by any number of your people in favor of the Government of the United States, now struggling for its very existence." He then denounced polygamy as a wicked institution and said that the marriage of one man to a mother and daughter was "no less a marvel in morals than in matters of taste."[4]

Perhaps the governor knew that the Morrisites had also opposed the institution of polygamy, but he probably failed to understand that the Morrisites were also quite indifferent to the Civil War and that they, too, had expected to inherit the land left desolate by it, once the Mormons were swept out of their way.

Whatever the case, Governor Harding was ready and willing to blame and condemn the Mormons for the heavy-handed treatment of the Morrisites,

---

3 Nels Anderson, *Desert Saints*, pp. 216–26.

4 Nels Anderson, *Desert Saints*, p. 225.

and he was sympathetic when the Gentiles at Camp Douglas and other friends of the Morrisites circulated a petition asking for the pardoning of those convicted. Within three days of the sentencing, the governor issued a proclamation listing the names of all the recently convicted Morrisites. It said simply:

> . . . to each of them full and perfect pardon for the offense of which they stand convicted, and they are, and each one of them is hereby forever exonerated, discharged and absolved from the fine, costs, and charges imposed upon them or either of them in pursuance of said conviction.
>
> In testimony whereof I have hereunto set my hand, and caused the Great Seal of the Territory of Utah to be affixed at Great Salt Lake City this 31st day of March A.D. 1863. Stephen S. Harding, Governor Utah Territory.

Ironically, the pardon was witnessed and also signed by Frank Fuller, secretary, the man who had been in the governor's chair when the Morrisite War took place. This action fanned into flame the smoldering anti-Morrisite sentiment in Utah and virtually forced many of the dissidents to seek governmental protection or flee the territory. John R. Eardley, Morrisite apostle and apologist for the movement, wrote concerning the outcome of the pardoning:

> The feelings of bitterness and hatred had now received a new impetus, and began to make themselves felt more directly than ever. Persecution ran high in many instances, compelling many to apply to General Connor for protection and means of living. He told all such to move their families up to the Fort, which was then under construction, and he would give them employment. Many availed themselves of this opportunity, and moved their families and effects up to Fort Douglas, where they were free from their persecutors. A few, however, remained in Salt Lake City until the Spring of 1863, when they were informed that General Connor was about to send a large government train to Carson City, Nevada.[5]

The Morrisite pardoning not only disturbed the Mormon populace in general but dismayed Judge Kinney and the grand jury then in session. Immediately the grand jury, consisting of many prominent Mormons, censured the governor.

> . . . the Governor, clothed with the pardoning power, interposed to prevent the punishment due to rebels against the law. He sanctions and sustains their rebellion and by pardoning them, proclaims to the world that they have acted rightly, wisely and lawfully. No time is allowed for investigation, none for repentence or reformation; but in less than three days from the time of the sentence of the court, are all of them pardoned

5 Eardley, *Gems of Inspiration*, p. 32.

> by the Executive, to renew their armed resistance against the power of Government, a pardon, which not only seeks to release them from fine and punishment, but the costs due to the officers and witnesses.
>
> *Therefore, we the United States Grand Jury for the Third Judicial District for the Territory of Utah, present his "Excellency" Stephen S. Harding, Governor of Utah,* as we would an unsafe bridge over a dangerous stream, jeopardizing the lives of all who pass over it, or as we would a pestiferous cesspool in our district, breading disease and death.
>
> Believing him to be an officer dangerous to the peace and prosperity of this Territory; refusing, as he has, his assent to wholesome and needed legislation, treating nearly all the legislative acts with contumely; and last of all, as the crowning triumph of his inglorious career, turning loose upon the community a large number of convicted criminals; we cannot do less than present his Excellency as not only a dangerous man, but also as one unworthy the confidence and respect of a free and enlightened people.[6]

Before long the Mormons circulated a petition calling for Governor Harding's removal from office, and this was forwarded to President Lincoln. The non-Mormons in the territory countered by demanding that Judge Kinney be removed from office because, in their opinion, he was under the influence and direction of Brigham Young. Perhaps as a sign of equity, President Lincoln complied with both requests, for both men were removed from office. He transferred Harding to Colorado, where he was appointed chief justice.[7] Kinney was not given another federal appointment by Lincoln, but the Mormon people still had the last word. They selected Kinney to be Utah's delegate to Congress for the next term.

Eight years later, in 1871, Steven S. Harding was residing in Milan, Indiana, where H. H. Beadle contacted him regarding Bill Hickman's truthfulness and basic character. Beadle was in the process of authenticating a manuscript that he claimed had been written by Hickman, which disclosed, among other things, Hickman's services as a hit man, or assassin, for Brigham Young. The manuscript was published under the title *Brigham's Destroying Angel: Life, Confessions and Startling Disclosures of the Notorious Bill Hickman.* My reprint of the 1904 edition contains, in appendix K, a reprint of a letter from Harding to Beadle written on December 23, 1871. Among others things, the letter outlines the basic events leading up to the Morrisite War, those of the war itself, and Harding's role in pardoning the militant Morrisites. Although some Mormons have dismissed the entire Hickman work as a fraud and some have insisted that Beadle wrote

6 Richard Young, "The Morrisite War," p. 468.

7 Bancroft stated that Harding left Utah 11 June 1863, upon being appointed consul at Valparaiso. Bancroft, *History of Utah,* 26:621.

it himself, the material in it referring to the Morrisites generally conforms to known facts.[8]

Harding gives a dramatic account of Hickman coming to Harding's house in the middle of the night to sign in large letters the petition to pardon the convicted Morrisites. Harding asserts that Hickman signed in defiance of Brigham Young and was the only Mormon to do so. On the other hand, Hickman's account of his signing is much more bland. He says: "Their friends got up a petition for their relief and most of the gentiles signed it, but very *few* [emphasis added] Mormons attached their names. The governor asked me if I was going to sign it. I told him I was. He then asked me if I was not afraid of Brigham Young, knowing it was in opposition to his counsel to have any Mormons sign it. I told him no; that 'Brigham Young was as afraid of me as I was of him,' meaning that we were not afraid of each other."[9]

Regardless of the veracity of his memoir, Bill Hickman clearly had sympathy for the Morrisites and had been for many years closely associated with Brigham Young. The signing of the petition seems to have nearly completed his estrangement from the L.D.S. leader. Soon afterward, Hickman gained employment as a guide for Colonel Connor.

Clearly Judge Kinney was very popular with the Mormons, but if he conspired with Brigham Young in the Morrisite affair, no documentary evidence of it has been found. Perhaps the closest thing to documentary evidence is the absolute lack of it. Brigham Young's correspondence contains three letters from J. F. Kinney in the last half of 1861, but not a single line from him during 1862, the year of the Morrisite War. The same is true for the first several months of 1863. This, of course, would not be worthy of note if it were not for the fact that beginning on September 14, 1863, a flood of correspondence from Kinney was received by Brigham Young. Between September 1863 and February 1864, Kinney sent Young no less than twenty-three very warm and cordial letters. Sometimes he wrote more than one letter a day. His letters continued almost daily throughout the winter and early spring of 1864 and then tapered off, continuing intermittently throughout the remainder of the year. This lack of correspondence during the crucial Morrisite period is circumstantial evidence at best, but it does seem curious that the chief judicial officer in the Morrisite case, who frequently wrote to Brigham Young at other times, would-have had nothing to say to the Mormon leader concerning a matter of considerable importance to them both. Certainly it raises the real possibility that such correspondence did once exist and that sometime in the ensuing century it was discreetly removed from the record.

8 Hickman, *Brigham's Destroying Angel*, pp. 161–63 and appendix K.

9 Hickman, Brigham's Destroying Angel, p. 163.

Of course, the pardoning of the convicted Morrisites immeasurably improved their legal status and gave them confidence that they were not without friends in Utah. However, for those who had failed to appear for trial, the matter was somewhat different. Since the governor's proclamation made no provision for the bonds that the Morrisites had forfeited, those who escaped trial actually ended up in worse condition than those who had been convicted. Bancroft cited the case of Abraham Taylor, who had posted a bail bond but failed to appear for trial. His homestead was sold to Joseph A. Johnson, clerk of Judge Kinney's court for $200, and his family was turned out in the street. Taylor appealed the sale to Judge Kinney on the grounds that no judgment had been recorded and asked for an injunction. However, Kinney replied that "if there was no judgment, he could render one, as the court had not permanently adjourned, but [had] only to meet on its motion." Presumably Kinney was not as concerned with the letter of the law in this circumstance as he had been in the case of the resistant Morrisites. At any rate, in 1868 the sale was declared illegal, and Taylor recovered his property and back rent for five years.[10]

Encouraged by the new political climate, Alexander Dow, a devout follower of Joseph Morris and one of those pardoned by Governor Harding, swore out an affidavit on April 11, 1863, in which he alleged that Robert T. Burton had wantonly assassinated the Morrisite prophet and three of his followers. He swore that this had occurred after the Morrisites had surrendered—when they were helpless before the guns of the posse. His affidavit affirmed:

> Morris said he wanted to speak to the people. Burton said, "Be d - - - - d quick about it." Morris said, "Brethren, I've taught you true principles." He had scarcely got the words out of his mouth before Burton fired his revolver. The ball passed in his neck and shoulder. Burton exclaimed: "There's your prophet." He fired again, saying: "What do you think of your prophet now?"
>
> Burton then turned suddenly and shot Banks, who was standing five or six paces distant. Banks fell. Mrs. Bowman, wife of James Bowman, came running up crying, "Oh! You blood-thirsty wretch." Burton said, "No one shall tell me that and live," and shot her dead. A Danish woman then came running up to Morris, crying, and Burton shot her dead also. Burton could easily have taken Morris and Banks prisoners, if he had tried. I was standing but a few feet from Burton all this time.[11]

This affidavit became the main basis for a grand jury indictment for murder against Robert Burton in 1870. Richard Young stated:

10 Bancroft, *History of Utah*, 26: 620.
11 Richard Young, "The Morrisite War," pp. 470–71.

> Inflamed by an anti-Mormon sentiment, of which the pardon of the Morrisites had been the chief cause, a grand jury was led in the fall of 1870 to bring in an indictment for murder against General Burton, and for a year and a half, the latter thought himself compelled by circumstances to evade arrest. The grand jury that found the indictment was a packed jury selected on open venire contrary to statutory provisions. The petit jury, before which the defendant would have been brought, would, in all likelihood, have been selected in the same manner, with a view to convict. The judge was the most relentless and unjust magistrate that had been upon the Territorial bench. Public sentiment was inflamed. Under such circumstances, General Burton wisely kept beyond the reach of the officers.[12]

Whether the judge and jury were actually as prejudiced as Young suggested is difficult to determine, but it is true that the United States Supreme Court in 1872 faulted the procedure used in selecting the grand jury and thus rendered their indictment null and void. Burton then returned home from exile.[13]

Young did not explain why it took the "inflamed—anti-Mormon sentiment," inspired by the trial of the Morrisites, seven years before a grand jury was impaneled to investigate the allegations against Burton, or why nearly another decade was to pass before another grand jury was to find another indictment for murder against him.

On February 18, 1879, nearly seventeen years after the alleged occurrence, Robert T. Burton was brought to trial for the murder of Mrs. Isabella Bowman, one of the two Morrisite women killed during the surrender proceedings at Kington Fort. The prosecution attempted to prove its case primarily along the lines presented by the Dow affidavit. The U.S. district attorney felt confident he could secure a conviction, based largely on the testimony of a key witness, S. D. Sirrene, who had testified before the grand jury. However, he failed to appear at the trial itself. There was also contradiction of testimony on the part of certain Morrisite witnesses, including Emma Thompson Just, who was confused about the identity of Burton and Judson Stoddard, one of the deputies who accompanied him. The trial lasted several weeks, but in the end the jury, comprised equally of Mormons and non-Mormons, brought in a verdict of not guilty.[14]

Even though the jury returned a legal verdict of "not guilty," the question still remains, was Burton guilty of murder in the surrender proceedings at

12 Richard Young, "The Morrisite War," p. 470.

13 Richard Young, "The Morrisite War," p. 470.

14 See Sumner Howard, U.S. District Attorney, to Charles Devens, Attorney-General, 28 July 1877, Chronological Files, Utah, Box 683, General Records of the Department of Justice, Record Group 60, National Archives, Washington, D.C.

Kington Fort? Many people, of course, believed that he was. Burton, however, even avowed on his deathbed that he had not shot either woman. Although the matter can never be absolutely settled, the preponderance of evidence seems to support the verdict of the jury.

First of all, Burton was a devout Mormon, but even Morrisites seemed mostly to agree with Stenhouse, that "General Burton is not a bloodthirsty man, he is not a low blackguard, and is much respected as an honorable, good citizen."[15] Of course, even an honorable gentleman might be moved to extreme measures if adequately provoked, but the behavior of the women (even if accurately described by Dow) would hardly seem sufficient to warrant firing at them by a man such as Burton.

Second, although Forscutt and others have alleged that Burton was a gentleman in private life, but absolutely sold in the services of Brigham Young, the killing of the women would still make no sense. Even if Young had instructed him (for which there is no evidence) to get rid of a troublesome rival—Joseph Morris—such instructions would not have included the slaying of the women.

Third, the sudden and confused circumstances surrounding the deaths of Morris, Banks, and the two women suggest that the women were probably killed accidentally, and quite possibly by someone other than Burton. It must be remembered that Burton was on horseback and as such had to manage his horse as well as shoot at moving targets. The likelihood that in the rush and confusion he could have managed to selectively kill four people with a six-shooter (even at close range) is doubtful. Actually, most accounts agree that there was renewed firing by several posse members when Burton fired at Morris, and at least eight or ten shots were fired by the posse. There is no doubt that Morris fell under Burton's bullets, but in all likelihood the others were shot by other posse members. For example, Eardley said that "John Banks was calmly standing a short distance away, and some one of the posse stepped behind him, and shot him in the back of the neck."[16]

The wound was not immediately fatal, but Banks died during the night. There is much disagreement about the specific action of the Morrisites that provoked the first shots from Burton, but once the firing from the posse commenced there is no telling who was shot by whom. Even if Burton's bullets actually did strike one or both of the women, it was probably an unfortunate accident resulting from the attempt to stop Morris.

Burton was probably guilty of haste and overzealousness in his initial decision to fire the cannon at the fort without allowing more time for negotiations, and he probably sanctioned the use of small arms against the

---

15 T. B. H. Stenhouse, *Rocky Mountain Saints* (London: n.p., 1872), p. 599.

16 Eardley, *Gems of Inspiration*, p. 29.

Morrisites before they returned the posse fire, both of which set the stage for active Morrisite resistance. Furthermore, he probably took inadequate precautions during the surrender proceedings to assure that they could be successfully terminated without incident. Nevertheless, the evidence strongly suggests that he should be exonerated of the purposeful slaying of the two Morrisite women who fell by the side of their prophet on that fateful day in June 1862.

Joseph Morris's brother, George, attended the trial and remarked about it in his "Life History." He referred to his brother's death as "murder." He wrote that after listening to the testimony of the witnesses and carefully reading the accounts of Burton's trial in the newspapers, his feelings had not changed from his first impression (some seventeen years earlier), namely that no effort had been made to take the Morrisite leaders alive. George felt Joseph's crime was not worthy of death.

George said that he did not approve of what Joseph did, but neither could he approve of what Burton did. He felt Joseph's crimes were religious enthusiasm, bigotry, and fanaticism and that those on the other side may have been guilty of the same things. He asserted that those were very dangerous attributes and that they sometimes made people do inappropriate things in the name of God. George also intimated that he intended to keep his concerns about the Morrisite War to himself.[17]

In the winter of 1876, George Morris reported that he had been thinking a good deal about his late brother Joseph and wondered if he could help him by doing his temple work. (The Mormons believe that the dead may be baptized and have other sacred ordinances performed in their behalf by proxy in a sacred temple or the endowment house, thereby making their salvation possible.) Consequently, George wrote to Brigham Young on March 15. He stated that his brother Joseph had not received his endowments and that surely the shedding of his blood had atoned for all of the sins he had committed. George requested that he be allowed to officiate in temple ordinances on behalf of his brother.

Given Brigham Young's earlier pronouncement of anathemas against all Morrisites and especially Joseph Morris, his reply to George Morris might seem incongruous. But apparently the removal of the Morrisite threat and the passing of more than a decade had softened Young's feelings for he readily gave his permission. Young noted that performing the ordinances for Joseph could do George no harm and might benefit Joseph.

On September 6, 1876, George Morris and his oldest daughter, Lavina, went to the Salt Lake Endowment House and performed the sacred ordinances for Joseph Morris; his wife, Mary; and some forty other deceased

17 "History of George Morris," pp. 198 – 200.

family members. In the eyes of George Morris, he had now done all he could to bring about a reconciliation between Joseph and the Mormon Church.[18]

18 "History of George Morris," pp. 178, 179, 186–91.

IV The Dispersion

10 Exodus

By the time the imprisonment, trial, sentencing, pardoning, and other immediate consequences of the Morrisite War had culminated in the spring of 1863, the Morrisite movement was in disarray and near collapse. Faithful Morrisites still held many previous expectations about the imminent Second Advent, and they had successfully redefined the role of Joseph Morris as martyr and foreshadower instead of deliverer, but they lacked a cogent ideology and competent leadership to sustain them until the expected millennium should arrive.

Joseph Morris had been so sure of his divine right to leadership and so convinced of his own role in personally leading his people into and through the millennium that he had made no provisions whatsoever for a successor. Furthermore, his faithful disciples had given no thought to such a need either.

At this point the Morrisites were in much the same situation as the Mormons had been in Illinois in 1844 when Joseph Smith was assassinated. What they desperately needed was another Brigham Young or at least a Sidney Rigdon. Instead, the most logical successor to leadership, the eloquent John Banks, had died along with Morris at Kington Fort. Moreover, the twelve apostles, who might have assumed leadership, were rendered virtually inoperative for several months because of imprisonment, indictment, or having fled the territory. Furthermore, by definition, Morrisite leadership required a prophet and a special kind of prophet at that. Joseph Morris had insisted that a living prophet who could regularly produce revelations was mandatory. During Morris's reign there had been no need and no place for another prophet, but his unexpected death had created a vacuum that no one was immediately prepared to fill. Consequently, the Morrisites turned their immediate attention to basic survival needs.

Certainly from the Morrisite perspective, the political climate in Utah had immeasurably improved from the previous year, for they now had a supportive governor and a protective military force supporting them. Despite these political changes, the economic and religious institutions were as firmly in Mormon hands as ever. A majority of the Morrisites who had gathered at South Weber were either penniless or had consecrated what wealth they had to the church. Only a small minority had retained much personal property, and with few exceptions they owned no land, livestock, or tools for making a living. Of course a few of the earlier settlers around Slaterville, Ogden, and South Weber had joined the Morrisites, and some of them retained their lands even after the war.

For the majority of the Morrisites the most pressing problem was how and where to make a living, and that problem dominated their efforts to the exclusion of nearly all other immediate postwar considerations. Clearly Utah, with its scant water resources, limited arable land, undeveloped industry, and openly hostile populace, was not a promising environment for the Morrisites. Except for the temporary employment opportunity while Camp Douglas was under construction, the economic prospects for Utah Morrisites could hardly have been worse. Consequently, when Connor announced he was sending a large government wagon train to Carson City, Nevada, and that Morrisites could travel along under its protection, the response was immediate. John Eardley stated:

> They made application for transportation for themselves and families, which the General very generously granted, and told them not only to come themselves, but to tell all others who wanted to leave Utah that there was room enough for all in the train he was about to send out.
>
> The news spread rapidly, and the Morrisites and others availed themselves of this opportunity of leaving Utah. So many came that the General found it necessary to order a second train, and determined to send one to Soda Springs, Idaho with a view of establishing a colony. Rations were furnished to those who were destitute, and each person chose the route they wished to take.
>
> On the 5th day of May, 1863, both trains moved out of the Fort together, one going north, and the other going south, like the *"two wings of a great eagle,"* both accompanied by a company of troops as a guard. The northern bound train arriving at Soda Springs, its passengers were induced to remain there by the government officers, and were fed and supported, and furnished with teams and seed by the government until they became self-supporting. This settlement continues to exist and flourish and has become a permanent point on the Short Line Railroad.[1]

Eardley's publication in 1899 gave the impression that the Morrisites generally believed in 1863 that the gospel, as restored through Joseph Morris, would be nourished in the wilderness after they departed from Utah and that two centers of Morrisite strength (two wings of the Great Eagle) would ultimately encompass and enfold the world. However, there seems to be little if any direct evidence that such an ideology was the principal reason

1 Eardley, *Gems of Inspiration*, pp. 32–33.

for the Morrisites to separate into two divisions. More likely, the divisions resulted from the practical decision of Colonel Connor to keep the Nevada wagon train of manageable size and to encourage settlement of the middle Bear River Valley by non-Mormons. Certainly there was nothing in Morris's teachings to suggest a coming geographic separation of the Morrisites. In all likelihood, the division came about primarily for logistical, political, and economic reasons, and its religious significance was not a factor until the Morrisite condition was compared post factum to the allegorical reference in the Thirteenth Chapter of Revelation which says: "And to the woman [the church] were given two wings of a great eagle, that she might fly into the wilderness into her place where she is nourished for a time, and times and half a time, from the face of the serpent."

In any case, the notion that the Morrisites would form two divisions and enter the wilderness for a time as wings of the Great Eagle gained considerable symbolic significance for the movement soon after the exodus from Utah. Perhaps the Morrisites expected that the two wings of the Great Eagle would miraculously result in unity, but instead, the division paved the way for disunity, factionalism, and competing leadership.

Actually, the Morrisites were not limited to two divisions even in May 1863. Although most of them soon departed, a few chose to remain in Utah. In fact, the single most successful contender for leadership, George Williams, remained there for seven years before moving elsewhere. William Davies, who was also destined to head a sizable Morrisite faction, was already in Montana when the two wagon trains departed. Several apostles were in Nevada at that time, and they had already begun to effect an organization there. Before long, pretenders to leadership were in California, Washington, Idaho, and elsewhere.

The Morrisites seem to have made little effort to settle the issue of general leadership prior to the departure of the two wagon trains, and though they later tried to unite they were never very successful. Eventually, more than a dozen men contended for leadership, but none of them could garner more than a plurality of support at any one time.

The principal contenders for Morrisite leadership did not declare their candidacy simultaneously, but rather emerged over a period of some twenty years as dissatisfactions, disagreements, and disillusionments developed. Several of those claiming leadership did not actually define themselves as general leaders, at least not initially, for some of them were leaders of local congregations who for various reasons gained wider prominence and influence. Among these were John Livingstone, Goodmund Gudmundsen, John Parson, Joseph Warner, and George Dove. Except for Warner and Dove, all had been ordained apostles by Joseph Morris and therefore could buttress their claims to leadership through direct authority. Although this group of contenders claimed to have received spiritual guidance and to have experienced many things they believed to be of supernatural origin, none of them were able to successfully establish themselves as anything more than ordinary spiritual leaders. Most made no pretense to prophethood.

On the other hand, the two contenders previously mentioned—George Williams and William W. Davies—not only claimed moderate spiritual gifts, they insisted they were chosen prophets of God. In addition to the above contenders for leadership, the names of several other Morrisites appear prominently in the records. Among these are John Eardley, William James, George Thompson, Andrew Hendrikson, George Johnson, Alexander Dow, and Almerian Grow.

The members of the two wagon trains were primarily interested in finding a place where they could start once again and earn a reasonable livelihood. They had not forgotten Joseph Morris nor the millennial hopes he had generated, but in the absence of strong and effective spiritual leadership, they looked first to physical survival. Undoubtedly they hoped that the Morrisite church would prosper, but there were no well-formulated plans calculated to bring that about when the two wings of the Great Eagle departed into the wilderness.

Perhaps the physical privations at Kington Fort and the economic uncertainty in the months following the final encounter were partially responsible for this more materialistic and secular orientation. At any rate, it is impressive that although many of the Morrisites turned to agriculture many also sought the mining camps and gold fields of Nevada and Montana. And with but one exception, none of the groups that later formed tried to revive the Law of Consecration. Instead, most became devoted to free enterprise and absolute control over their own personal property.

The bitter experience of Kington Fort not only encouraged most Morrisites to emulate conventional nineteenth-century American economic practices, it also produced more reluctance to surrender personal autonomy to religious leaders. Thereafter, prophetic claims were greeted with caution, if not with open, and sometimes bitter, skepticism. The Morrisites desperately needed a talented leader, but they were not ready to uncritically accept just any prophet pretender.

11 The Soda Springs Settlement

Although the issue of general leadership had not been settled when the two wagon trains left Salt Lake City in May 1863, it was necessary for someone to serve as spokesman for the emigrants. The Morrisite leadership of the Left Wing has not been recorded, but the spokesman selected for the Soda Springs group was Alexander Dow. Dow had joined the Morrisites in 1861 and had participated in the Morrisite War. No detailed record of his administration has survived, but Dow's tenure appears to have been undistinguished. He had gained some fame by issuing his affidavit against Burton. Perhaps this affidavit was the determining factor in Dow's selection as leader.

In a letter written June 2, 1863, Colonel Connor describes the expedition into the Bear River country, reaching into northern Utah and southern Idaho.

> On the 5th of May ultimo Company H, Third Infantry, California volunteers, under command of Captain Black, left this post pursuant to my orders, enroute, via Box Elder, Bear River, Cache and Marsh valleys, for a point at or near the great bend of Bear River known as Soda Springs, Idaho Territory, for the purpose of establishing a new post in that region for the protection of the overland emigration to Oregon, California and the Bannock City mines.
>
> Accompanying the expedition and under its protection were a large number of persons heretofore residents of this territory, Utah seceders under the name of Morrisites, from the Mormon Church.
>
> Some of them were able to furnish their own teams and wagons. They numbered in all 160 souls comprised of 53 families, seven single men and four widows.
>
> On the 20th, Company H, Third Infantry, arrived after a long and tedious trip, accompanied by their charges, the settlers for the new town. A suitable and eligible location was selected on the north bank of Bear River . . . . The water is good and abundant, as well from the river as from the numerous mountain streams—easily diverted for purposes of irrigation. The soil, judging from the growth of the native grasses is susceptible of cultivation and the raising of valuable crops.[1]

---

1 Quoted in Lula Barnard, Faundy Bybee, and Lola Walker, *Tosoiba* (Soda

This section of the Oregon Trail had for many years been famous for its mineral springs, abundant forage, and marauding Indians. In 1862 Connor had recognized the desirable but dangerous atmosphere of the area and decided to pave the way for peaceful white settlement. In late January 1863 he led a force of about 200 soldiers into the Bear River country intent upon pacifying the Indians. Just north of the present town of Preston, Idaho, they found a large concentration of Snake and Bannock Indians in winter camp. Connor's men surrounded the camp and attacked on January 29. The wintering natives were caught completely by surprise and were nearly annihilated. "Some little children 'played dead' and were passed by when the soldiers went over the campground shooting the wounded. Fourteen soldiers were killed, and seventy-nine were wounded in the fray."[2]

For this act of "pacification" Connor was elevated to the rank of brigadier general and gained immediate fame as an Indian fighter. Two years later, while directing a campaign against the Indians in the Powder River country, Connor told his officers to accept no offers of peace. "Attack and kill every male Indian over twelve years of age."[3]

This side of Connor's character is of interest here primarily because it is characteristic of attitudes held by many Americans in the nineteenth century. Although there were some in sympathy, others believed it to be appropriate, even laudable, for a military commander to devastate an Indian encampment with no more regard for men, women, or children than for vicious animals that posed some real or imagined threat. At the same time these commanders were expected to exercise great care over their command and treat white male civilians with respect, white children with kindness, and white women with courtesy and gallantry.

Connor displayed deep sympathy and concern for the refugee Morrisites. In fact, his order to kill the Indians was to reduce the dangers on the Oregon Trail and make the area safe for white habitation. To him it was a simple matter of expediency that 287 Indians were sacrificed to accomplish these objectives. Furthermore, there is no evidence that the Morrisites felt any moral conflict over the bloody proceedings of the previous winter. Although they probably knew few details of the encounter, they saw the "pacification" of the Indians as an absolute requisite to settlement at Soda Springs. If anything, that action increased their confidence in Colonel Connor. They regarded him as a kind and benevolent friend.

Springs, Idaho: Daughters of Utah Pioneers, 1958), pp. 50–52. See also *Soda Springs Sun*, 11 June 1931.

2 Nels Anderson, *Desert Saints*, p. 237.

3 Dee Brown, *Bury My Heart at Wounded Knee* (New York: Bantam Books, 1972), p. 103.

The Morrisites, accompanied by their military escort, arrived near Soda Springs on May 20, 1863. The 150-mile journey from Salt Lake City had taken fifteen days. At ten miles per day it is not surprising that Connor referred to the trip as "long and tedious." Emma Thompson Just, a young girl in the emigrant train, described the trip to her cousin in England a year later.

> We came in the spring, and most of our journey was made up the valley of the Bear River. It was a trip I shall always remember, for the hillsides were so green and flower-covered and the river so deep and blue.
>
> The mountains are not so steep and rugged as they were at Ogden, but it is a beautiful spot. There are heavily timbered hills stretching away to the south and beyond them, mountains that are also timbered. From these forests have come homes for us all. The first summer was spent mostly in building a log house for each family, and quarters for the soldiers.
>
> In the lower stretches nearer the river, there are miles and miles of cedar [juniper] which is not only very ornamental but also supplies us with all the fuel we need. It truly is a favored spot. The Creator must have designed it just for this little band: logs to build our houses; firewood to keep us warm; health giving [mineral] waters to drink, streams full of fish and mountains full of game.[4]

Emma Thompson Just, a year after arrival on the Bear River, still reflected the optimism of her people and Colonel Connor concerning the favored location of the new settlement. And much indeed had been accomplished during that year. The soldiers, under Connor's direction, had laid out a military reservation and constructed a log fort some 100 feet square, complete with living quarters and storage rooms. Some 300 soldiers were quartered there for the ensuing two winters and three summers. The fort was called the Soda Springs Post, but soon became known as "Connor's Fort," even though Connor himself had stayed at the post for only a few days before returning to his command at Camp Douglas.

In the meantime, 200 acres of land a few hundred yards west of the military reservation had been surveyed for a townsite. Each family had received a small parcel of land upon which to live, and before the first winter arrived all had been adequately (though modestly) housed.

Yet, despite this auspicious beginning, the new colony soon began to encounter difficulties. The climate proved to be much more severe than anticipated. A clue to its severity might have been recognized the first morning after arrival when the new settlers awoke to find several inches of snow covering their belongings.[5] Before many years it became evident that Connor and the Morrisites had misjudged the productive capability of the

4 Barnard, Bybee, Walker, *Tosoiba*, pp. 57–58.

5 Barnard, Bybee, Walker, *Tosoiba*, p. 59.

area, at least in terms of nineteenth-century farming technology. And John Eardley's assertions about the permanent nature of the Morrisite settlement were based more upon wishful thinking than fact. Morristown, as it came to be called, had been established on the north bank of the Bear River about a mile below the present townsite of Soda Springs. Lula Barnard and associates, local historians of the Soda Springs area, tell us that:

> Attempts at farming were very discouraging. Freezing temperatures occurred often, even during summer nights. Men tried building fires and smudges in an effort to ward off effects of the frost, but with small success. During the second winter, more than half the livestock was lost by reason of extreme cold and lack of feed. Five successive grain crops were destroyed by freezing weather.
>
> After this, most of the settlers moved away and their small holdings reverted to the government except for a few which were bought by loggers and miners who came later.
>
> Connor's Fort [which had been constructed east of Morristown in 1863] was abandoned in May 1865, Indian *atrocities* [emphasis added] having been reduced to a minimum.[6]

Among the few Morrisites who remained in the area and perhaps the most prominent were the Niels Andersons. Niels Anderson and Mary Christofferson had been married at the fort July 30, 1863. Their marriage was thought to be the first performed in the newly created Idaho Territory. Mary Christofferson was fifteen. The previous year she had been the first casualty of the Mormon-Morrisite War when a cannonball carried away most of her lower jaw. This wound resulted in a tragic disfiguration that plagued her throughout her life. Whenever she met a stranger she felt compelled to cover her mouth with a handkerchief. She had eight children and died at the age of eighty-three in 1928. James Dove visited Soda Springs in 1889 and later wrote: "[I] was received very kindly by the people, and especially by Bro. Bowman and Bro. Anderson and his wife. When I first saw her my tears came, for I remembered what she had suffered."[7] Peter Anderson, their fifth child reported that his father, Niels, was a blacksmith and that later he became known as the father of the anti-Mormon party in Idaho.[8]

It is evident that the Niels Anderson family maintained great bitterness toward the Mormons even after the death of their parents. A large bronze plaque bearing the eight children's names was commissioned and attached to the parents' tombstone in the Soda Springs cemetery.

---

6 Barnard, Bybee, Walker, *Tosoiba*, p. 62.

7 James Dove, *A Few Items in the History of the Morrisites*, pp. 14–15.

8 Peter Anderson, "The Wound that Never Healed," p. 46.

The 650-word inscription gives a bitter account and interpretation of the "Morrisite Massacre" and "the deception in Bringhamisms [sic] [teachings of Brigham Young]."[9]

Eventually Soda Springs became a sizable town. The few Morrisites who remained in the area largely abandoned diversified agriculture and turned to ranching or commerce. It must have angered and dismayed them to see the area they had pioneered eventually invaded and taken over by Mormons, whom they had hoped to leave behind in Utah.

In June 1870 Brigham Young and a contingent of Mormon church leaders visited Soda Springs with an eye to colonization. A special house, constructed virtually overnight, was erected by twenty stalwart Mormons from Paris, Idaho. The building materials and other supplies had been freighted in from Paris in seven wagons.

> The completed log cabin measured twenty-two by eighteen feet and had a good floor, windows, and shingle roof—a real luxury in those days. It was considered truly a fine house, and was furnished, even to calico ruffles at the windows.
>
> The purpose in building it was to have a comfortable place near the famed Soda Springs where President Young and other church leaders could stop for a few days . . . .
>
> The "Brigham Young Home," as it was always known, stood apparently firm until 1944.[10]

Brigham Young was favorably impressed with the area, for at the October General Conference of the Mormon church, held in Salt Lake City in 1870, a call went out for Mormons to colonize in the Soda Springs area. In the spring of 1871 the first permanent Mormon settlers arrived, and eventually Soda Springs became an important outpost of Mormonism. It is of some interest to note that two years earlier Brigham Young had invested in 650 acres of land that included part of the Soda Springs townsite.[11]

Although Soda Springs flourished, nothing now remains of old Morristown, which once lay a short distance downriver. The buildings were torn down or inundated when the waters of Alexander Reservoir flooded the old townsite shortly after the turn of the century.

The disenchanted pioneers who left that area in the mid-1860s seem to have dispersed in many directions, but many of them retained their Morrisite identity and passed it on for two or more generations. A number

9 Courtesy of Margaret M. Link, Lakewood, Colorado, and Helen Eliason, Deer Lodge, Montana. For the complete inscription see *Montana, the Magazine of Western History* 25 (Winter 1975):71.

10 Barnard, Bybee, Walker, *Tosoiba*, pp. 89–91.

11 Barnard, Bybee, Walker, *Tosoiba*, pp. 89–91.

of them moved east and established organizations in Iowa and Nebraska. Others settled around Malad City, Idaho, while others helped pioneer the Upper Snake River Valley, particularly in the vicinity of Firth, Blackfoot, and Idaho Falls. A few of them returned to Utah, some went to Nevada, and a rather large number settled in Montana's Deer Lodge Valley. A few even returned to their countries of origin in Europe.

12 The Prophet Cainan

The vacuum of general leadership created by the death of the Prophet Joseph Morris soon began attracting candidates. The first to volunteer his services as prophet, seer, and revelator was one George Williams. Williams is something of an enigma, for his first association with the Morrisites is unknown. In fact, his name appears nowhere in the Morrisite record prior to the death of Joseph Morris. Almost certainly he was not associated with the Morrisites at South Weber and was not directly involved in the conflict there.

At the time of the Morrisite War, George Williams was forty-eight years old and was living near Salt Lake City, possibly at Mill Creek. The 1860 census shows that he had two children, and there were two adult women living in his household—Susannah Woolfelt, whom he had married in England, and Louisa. Although this raises the possibility that he had plural wives, it seems more likely that Louisa was his daughter.

George Williams was born February 14, 1814, at Thorp, Surrey County, England, to James and Sarah Williams. His father was a gardener. George was baptized into the Mormon church May 4, 1848, and became a member of the Rotherham, England, branch. He had married prior to that time. On October 9, 1850, he registered with the Liverpool L.D.S. Mission Office to emigrate to the United States with his wife and aged mother-in-law. However, he did not leave England as scheduled.

The 1851 census shows him living at Bridgegate in Rotherham. He worked as a butcher and lived with his wife and mother-in-law. Williams was ordained a priest in the Aaronic priesthood May 18, 1851, but a year later he was excommunicated for "improper conduct." Apparently his conduct improved, for he was rebaptized into the Mormon church on December 17, 1852, and became a member of the Sheffield, England, branch.

On April 11, 1855, George and his wife, Susannah, boarded the S. Curling at Liverpool to immigrate to the United States. They joined a handcart company under Captain Moses Thurston, arriving in Salt Lake City on September 28, 1855.

Little is known of Williams's activities between 1855 and 1862. However, he participated in the reformation of 1856–57, for he was rebaptized on March 15, 1857. At that time he was a member of the Mill Creek Ward.

Perhaps Williams had met Joseph Morris when he was still living in Salt Lake City. However, neither Morris nor Williams acknowledged any such meeting. If Williams had any direct link with the Morrisites prior to the fall of 1862, there is no record of it. Perhaps he was simply an aspiring prophet looking for some people to lead.

Whatever the case, in the autumn of 1862 George Williams commenced a campaign to gain leadership of the Morrisite church, which was languishing in disarray. His claim to leadership was set forth in a remarkable document, "A Description of Interviews with Celestial Beings," which was first circulated by handwritten letter but eventually published by John Eardley in 1899.

The document began:

> After leading a blameless life, and searching after the treasures of eternity, through the gospel of Christ, under the guidance of the Holy Spirit, I was, on the 15th day of April, A.D. 1862, riding on my spirited mare by the slope of the western range of mountains, near Hacker's canyon, in Salt Lake Valley, Utah, when snow began to fall in a marvelous manner. A cloud appeared in the north and became agitated, and speedily formed an enormous archway, spanning the entire valley.
>
> On each side of this arch were massive pillars of light, constructed with fine skill, and folding doors studded with golden bolts. Beholding this heavenly appearance, I alighted from my horse, and allowed it to escape.
>
> While meditating this scene, the eyes of my understanding were opened by the spirit of God, so as to understand the things of God as they were from eternity.
>
> The folding doors were thrown back, and the highway to the eternal worlds was opened before me, and a voice strengthened me, saying: "Fear not, thou greatly beloved of the Lord, these are they that form a portion of the armies of heaven." Beyond the folding doors I saw a countless host of horses, and they who sat upon them had on breast-plates of fire, and diamonds, and helmets of precious stones, and out of the nostrils of the horses came fire and smoke, and their riders had large swords, and their faces were lightened as the sun.
>
> As soon as the first of this host reached the archway, they halted and formed a double line, the horses facing each other, and up this line I saw into the first heaven, from earth, and bear record of the same, God, the Eternal Father, standing on a throne of sapphire stone, and Christ seated at His right hand.[1]

1 Eardley, *Gems of Inspiration*, pp. 54–59.

Williams reported many other marvelous experiences. He was informed that his preparation for prophethood would commence at that time and that the knowledge he received was for the benefit of the Church of the Firstborn (the Morrisites) . He reported that two celestial beings, who identified themselves as Elias and Enoch, laid their hands upon his head and ordained him. Then Jesus of Nazareth addressed him saying:

> "All hail thou son of the Highest" and embracing me [Williams], he said: "I am that was and is to come, and for Me and My Father must you act while you remain upon the earth. The restoring of all things connnected with Adam's race has now to take place. Prepare yourself; for you are he, called and chosen from before the foundation of this earth, to bring to pass the purposes of my Father in this the evening of time."[2]

Williams claimed to have received "many other counsels," which he was commanded not to disclose. A second instructional meeting was scheduled for August 25, 1862. At the appointed time he returned to the same place where he claimed to have met John the Revelator, who gave him further instructions. Seth and Enos were also present. He reported that they laid their hands upon his head and declared him to be "the first-born son of the third God in the last quorum of heaven, even Cainan, then Melchisedec, now George Williams, and then conferred upon . .. [him] . . . all the keys of the holy priesthood that were ever given to mortal man."[3]

The reference here to Cainan and Melchisedec is a continuation of the principle of reincarnation or transmigration of spirits introduced by Joseph Morris. George Williams reported that this was his third incarnation. In his first incarnation he had been Cainan, one of the seven angels, and in his second one he was none other than Melchisedec, the great king of Salem. These previous incarnations, plus the authority granted to him during the two celestial interviews, entitled him to rule upon the earth as God's supreme representative "to put in motion and carry on the great gospel plan of saving, redeeming and exalting Adam's race, together with the planet on which they dwell."[4] From this time forward George Williams was also known as the *Prophet Cainan.*

Armed with this superlative description of his appointment to leadership, Williams—the Prophet Cainan—began corresponding with the Morrisites at Soda Springs and Carson Valley, attempting to assume his "rightful" position. A fragment of a letter dated August 12, 1863, and bearing a Soda Springs, Idaho Territory, postmark is evidence that he personally visited that outpost shortly after it was founded. The letter was a "General

2 Eardley, *Gems of Inspiration*, p. 56.
3 Eardley, *Gems of Inspiration*, pp. 58–59.
4 Eardley, *Gems of Inspiration*, p. 59.

Invitation to the scattered sheep of Joseph to come and meet the Prophet of the Lord."[5]

The degree of success enjoyed by Cainan at Soda Springs is unknown, yet it may be inferred that he was accepted by some if not most of the Morrisites living there. Later on a number of the Soda Springs pioneers found their way to Council Bluffs and Omaha, and Cainan was welcomed by them there. Some of these eventually retraced their steps and moved to Montana's Deer Lodge Valley. Others moved directly from Soda Springs to the Deer Lodge Valley, and still others arrived there via the goldfields of Bannack and Grasshopper Gulch. There is little doubt that most of the Morrisites who moved to Council Bluffs and Omaha supported Cainan, and by the mid-1870s a majority of those in Montana did likewise. His early proselytizing in Soda Springs must have initiated that support, for among others, Alexander Dow, the Morrisite leader there, accepted him as a prophet. The Prophet Cainan returned to Utah from Soda Springs and resumed his writing campaign among the scattered Morrisites. He lived in the Salt Lake area until 1869.

His campaign for Morrisite leadership seems to have been conducted mostly through correspondence. Although he was visited by representatives from various Morrisite outposts who were apparently instructed to bring back reports of the legitimacy of his claims, there is no evidence that he visited any of the scattered Morrisites in the interim. Among these visitors were Almerian Grow from California in 1864, George Dove from Nevada in 1865, and George Thompson and John Bowman from Soda Springs that same year. Cainan must have believed he had convinced or reconvinced these visitors of the authenticity of his claims to leadership, for his letters to the Morrisites in 1864 and 1865 are authoritative in tone. He seemed to take his own right to general leadership for granted as he appointed local leaders and traveling missionaries and gave organizational and spiritual instructions to the Saints. Nevertheless, there remained some questioners, if not doubters. For example, in October 1864 the Prophet Cainan addressed a letter to one Henry H. Wadman, whose inquiry had been forwarded through Mark Forscutt. Wadman wanted to know if Cainan had been sent legally by God to carry on the fullness of the everlasting gospel or if the people should look for someone else. Cainan's affirmative reply was lengthy and reasoned, but it contained no new substantial evidence to support his claim.

---

5 On 31 May 1969, Henry Hendrikson of Missoula, Montana, gave the author permission to copy and publish certain Morrisite church records and ecclesiastical letters from George Williams (Cainan) that had been in the possession of his father, Andrew Hendrikson. Certain other original documents were obtained in 1968 from Robert Johnson of Missoula. Copies of these materials are retained by the author. Hereafter they shall be referred to as the Morrisite Papers. Letters from the Prophet Cainan constitute File #1.

During his lifetime Cainan wrote hundreds of pages of instructions and revelations to his followers in the form of epistles styled after the King James version of the New Testament writings of Saint Paul. These were intended to be published as scripture for the edification of his disciples. Indeed, they were copied in longhand and stored in ledgers. Some were even translated to Danish, but apparently few were ever published. In keeping with the New Testament style, the epistles were often addressed to the Saints in a certain location or to individuals using only their first names. Unfortunately, such usage was not always consistent or clear. For example, he wrote to both John Parson and John Eardley in Nevada referring to both as "My Beloved John." He referred to James Dove as "My beloved James" or "Brother James." He then complicated the matter by referring to William James as "Brother William," but also as "Brother James." From time to time he referred to George Dove, George Thompson, and George Johnson as "Brother George." Sometimes he even referred to "Brother Dove" when it was not clear whether he was talking about James or George. The Prophet Cainan undoubtedly knew of whom he spoke, but his obscure and inconsistent style has added considerably to the list of "eternal mysteries."

In November 1865 Cainan wrote a letter to James Dove and John Eardley seeking to enlist their support and attempting to bolster their courage. Contained within it is a poem. The poem is a fascinating and fantastic description of the early hours of the Mormon Morrisite War. Apparently it was intended to serve as a rallying song for the Morrisites and to show Cainan's deep revulsion for the Weber Camp disaster. It is unclear whether certain of its inaccuracies are the result of ignorance, purposeful distortion, or poetic license, but on several points it is at variance with known fact. Nevertheless, the poem depicts the conflict in colorful, dramatic language and provides a valuable perspective for analysis not only of the conflict but also of the author himself. Apparently Cainan constructed the poem from the accounts of others and from his own fertile imagination. It may not be an accurate depiction of the facts, but it clearly illustrates his attitude toward the Weber tragedy and his characteristic tendency to write in a grandiose and heroic or epic style.[6]

---

6 The most notable discrepancies between this poem and known facts are: (1) Two women were killed while holding an infant, but in neither case was the child wounded or killed. (2) The posse was too far away to clearly see the recipients of the initial attack, who were also obscured by the bowery roof and other buildings and fences. Thus, their leader could hardly be "tempted with passions of lust" by viewing the "beautiful form" of a casualty. (3) The rain started at 10:00 in the evening, not the morning of the first day. (4) The maid's chin was hit with the *first* cannonball that entered the fort. Two other women were instantly killed by the same missile.

The Mormons came down like a wolf on the fold,
  On a morning in June that was glittering like gold.

As the sun darted forth from his place in the east,
  The hosts of fanatics, o'ercome by the Beast

Were gathered in ranks with axes and knives,
  And "death to the faithful" their watchword that flies

Through squadrons of rags, raw leather and hair,
  As the promise rung out of the spoil and the fair.

While the mountains were echoing their loud cannons roar
  The Daughters of Israel lay stretched in their gore!

Unconscious the babe with a smile on its face
  Was torn from the breast by a bombshell's embrace,

The parts of its body were scattered afar
  And trampled in dust to be gathered no more!

And there lay its parent distorted and pale!
  The blood on her brow and the ring in her nail!

Her beautiful form, as it lay in the dust,
  Yet tempted their leader with passions of lust!

The elements shaken unbinding the rain
  That horde of maneaters stretched their limbs on the plain

From Gethsemane's garden and Weber's low vale,
  The same Host of Angels presented the wail!

The trial is equal, the petitions alike,
  Round the throne of Jehovah the Armies unite:

Twelve legions are ready "Send us out to the foe
  "Thy Son was forsaken like thy servant is now!

"The females immortal are weeping to see
  On Adam's lone planet, a fair Gallilee,

"Not the nail, but revolver is chosen again
  "To insult and impede and wrong to maintain

"Give the Word, Oh dear Father, our Parent, our God!
  "That Seth may be loosed to act free with his rod

"On the path of the lightening thy message will take "
  And the shepherds of Baal in their prison-house wake

Thus spake the celestials as thru them a thrill
  Of righteous excitement; but awaiting his will!

But the morning broke out and the cannon again
  Set showers of iron, like the pelting of rain

On the house of the Prophet, the splinters and spars
  Retreated in haste on their way toward the stars.

The shrieks of the children and cries of the maid
  Whose chin was torn off by the fierce cannonade!

The flesh and the bone on the willows were flung!
  O'er the blood of this beauty the savages sung!

Then a Son of the Fullness (whose numbers were few)
  With muscles convulsed as the rifle he drew

Right firm to his shoulder and getting the line,
  Sent a messenger forth, dividing his spine!

And tossing with anguish and writhing in pain
  Sung his anthem and danced back in Lucifer's train!

"One atonement is made" whispered sisters at prayers,
  "The infidel garments must have slept unawares;

"His agreement with Death this covenant with Hell
  "Are covering too short—let Isaiah foretell!

This young sister sighed, then resuming again
  "Our Father in Heaven see thy house is in pain!

"Deliver us now from this murderous crew!"

At this point Cainan cut the poem short. He explained: "Here I end; not that the exercise tires; but that you may share the honor of placing in verse the terrible scene of immortal Weber. Finish the tragedy yourselves, and if your production is more preferable than mine, it shall be appended. I will try to finish; but not now."[7]

There is no indication that the Prophet Cainan ever returned to this task. In 1879 George and James Dove printed a song by Joseph Taylor that portrayed the same event. The song was historically more accurate but much more bland and of no higher literary quality. Perhaps this was James Dove's belated response to Cainan's challenge.[8]

In March 1864 Cainan addressed an epistle to "A portion of the Twelve and scattered disciples . . . [in Carson Valley] . . . that have held fast to the holy principles." In it he called for the inauguration of proselyting and called John Parson to be the first missionary. However, his faltering and equivocating call demanded little self-sacrifice on the part of missionaries, thus opening the door for excuse making and rationalized exemption from service. Cainan wrote:

7 Cainan to James Dove and John Eardley, November 1865, Great Salt Lake, Morrisite Papers, File #1.

8 Dove and Dove, *A Voice from the West*, p. 42.

> . . . let His servant John Parson, prepare himself, setting his house in order, that his consort and little ones may not suffer in his absence; but, as a wise man, make arrangements for their safety in every way. Should this hinder his departure, it can be excused. Let him not start till this is accomplished; then his burden will be light and his spirit free; for it is not meet in this day of abundance that the family of a faithful minister of Christ should suffer and pine while he is laboring for the Lord. And if any faithful brother of the twelve can be spared from his family, let him journey along with him; and if not one of the twelve, let a high priest whose resolves are firm to serve the Lord, take his departure with him; . . .
>
> Be not tempted to stand forth in angry debate with any man. In so doing you soil your dignity, and place yourselves on a level with fallen beings . . . .
>
> Do not placard the cities with the tidings you have to bear; but rather seek out for opportunities of mildly getting the principles before the people.
>
> Your mission is to the cities of California, beyond the Sierra Nevada Mountains; and you are sent, as in the day of old, like sheep among wolves.[9]

John Parson, accompanied by John Livingstone, responded to the call. Given these extremely soft-sell instructions, it is hardly surprising that the missionary efforts of Cainan's appointees bore few fruits. Eventually, missionaries went to several places in the United States and Europe, and even the Middle East, but few converts were made.

Of course, it would be inappropriate to conclude that the Morrisite missionaries were not dedicated or willing to make sacrifices. No matter how extensive their preparations may have been or how mild their instructions, the lot of Morrisite missionaries in the latter nineteenth century was not an easy one. Just to serve on a mission was a sacrifice. They almost always traveled without purse or scrip, which meant they received no salary and were entirely dependent upon charity for food, clothing, and shelter. Often they were forced by circumstances to sign on as seamen or other workers to pay for passage or other expenses. More often than not they walked.

In July 1874 Cainan wrote to John Eardley expressing his thankfulness that he (Eardley) had been able to travel safely from nation to nation while in the service of the Lord. Then, in what must be one of the understatements of all times, he briefly and matter of factly referred to an incredible missionary journey taken by two of his followers, Almerian and Hannah Grow. The reference apparently was not made for the purpose of praising the journey but rather to praise the Lord for His care and protection of those traveling in His service.

9 Eardley, *Gems of Inspiration*, pp. 60–63.

> Which of the ministers of the fullness has taken harm from the nation of people he has visited? Even Almerian with Sister Hannah, debilitated and weak, crossed from the extreme west [western United States] over the deep, through England, France, Austria, Turkey, to Constantinople, and delivered to the Sultan a portion of the fullness revealed by Mahomet, or Ishmael, to Cainan . . . . [They] did this, and returned unscathed, through Jerusalem, Malta, England, Scotland, New York, Omaha, San Francisco; and somewhere here in the camp of deceivers [San Francisco], our sister expired.[10]

In June 1868 Cainan had written to the Saints in Montana mentioning, almost incidentally, the prospective opening of a mission to the Middle East. Apparently his reference to "the hunter" was Almerian Grow. He wrote:

> Of late I have been laborously employed in preparing another mission to a branch of the House even Ishmael, the Son of Hagar by Abraham. These have to be visited by the hunters and from their members will be gathered Saints of the Most High . . . .
>
> . . . these are now called Mohamitans, [the] hunter has received his credentials and under my hand will start from New York and all the [House] of Israel must hear the voice of the Lord hissing from the West.[11]

Perhaps one reason Cainan did not use Grow's name in 1868 was because he had been criticized previously by some of his followers for allowing Grow to remain in fellowship even though his support of Cainan had several times waxed and waned. Cainan provides no clue in the letter of the content of the message he had received by divine revelation from the Prophet Mohamet. However, many years later he sent a copy of one of his 1867 journal entries to the Saints in Montana. This entry contained a full account of Cainan's interview with Mohamet and the message given by him.

According to that entry, sometime in 1867 Cainan was visiting a friend at the mouth of Little Cottonwood Canyon when a voice came to him bidding him to dismiss his friend, for he was about to receive an important message. Cainan recognized that the voice was not mortal, so he stopped the conversation and requested that his friend leave him and return to his home. The friend was surprised at the request, but immediately departed, leaving the prophet alone in a grove of cottonwood trees. Cainan reported:

> The voice presently came again saying: "fear not servant of the most high, we are your friends." And immediately I was strengthened spiritually. The things of the Earth was fled from my understanding and a soft unspeakable enveloped me. Something at a vast distance very bright was

10 Eardley, *Gems of Inspiration*, p. 75.

11 Cainan to the Saints in Montana, 16 June 1868, Great Salt Lake, Morrisite Papers, File #1.

> swiftly approaching me. Out of this bright body stepped one of beautiful countenance and massive stature with green garments flowing around him. Upon his head [was] a folded banner of white and green, in the center of a circle of a half-moon. His legs were bare up to his knee with threads of yellow bound here and there around them. Bending very low he came near me with a: "Hail servant of the Most High. I am Mohamet, and before I was Mohamet I was Ishmael the son of Abraham and Hagar, and I am also a servant of the Most High . . . [and] I am permitted to leave my Mansion in Paradise to visit the servant of the Most High now in mortality. . . . The son of Mary has sent [me] to warn, therefore, I need not give a sign or hand a key of priesthood. My raiment must show I am [of] another branch of priesthood and occupy a separate mansion in paradise; for there are many mansions. Jesus, son of Mary, is not divided in feeling with me. Therefore, both serve the Most High and by his appointment and according to the line of teaching shown us for we are dependent servants there [just] as you are here . . . . As my stay with you must be short, I lay before you my errand of Mercy the Most High and merciful God grants me to deliver.

According to Cainan, Mohamet then told him that the government of Turkey was in a dangerous state, having gotten into debt with many nations contrary to the law and doctrine he had given to their forefathers. Also, the harsh treatment of Christian peoples under Turkish domination had aroused the indignation of powerful nations, and they were planning to overthrow and destroy the Turkish government unless it reformed. He said that ministers from these powerful nations were planning to meet with the sultan and his ministers to arrange a better state of things. Mohamet then instructed Cainan to send a courier to Turkey with a message for the sultan to pay heed to the proposals from the ministers of the powerful nations and treat them with courtesy and respect lest they make a war of vengeance against him and destroy his government and people. This message was to be sewed inside the coat collar of the messenger and not looked at nor read again until it was delivered to the American minister in Turkey, who was to deliver it to the sultan. Mohamet promised that Cainan would in many days have the right person to serve as messenger pointed out to him. He then said: "Let him read my words and understand your interview with me, even Mohamet. Let him be sent without a preparation of money, and [if] he will do it his journeyings shall be protected and his wants supplied."[12] At the close of the entry Cainan wrote: "Almerian Grow was the person sent and [he] returned in safety. I have lost sight of him a long time." After returning from his incredible missionary journey, Grow moved to St. Louis, where he

12 Journal entry from Cainan, 1867, contained in the ledger of George Jansin, Morrisite Papers, File #8.

worked in the ministry for a time, but there is no further record of him or his ecclesiastical activities.

Apparently, the message was delivered, as prescribed, to the American minister in Istanbul, but whether he forwarded it to Abdul Aziz, the reigning sultan, is unknown. The sultan's reactions, if he ever received it, are also unknown. However, Cainan's report was not far from the mark. Abdul Aziz was the first and last sultan to travel abroad, and his western visits resulted in the first loans for the first railroads in the empire. He also instituted a number of western reforms, including the establishment of several schools and universities. Whether these reforms delayed the ultimate breakup of the empire is difficult to tell, but even if they did it is doubtful if the message sent by Cainan had any impact upon the outcome.

It is evident that the Prophet Cainan's sojourn in Utah was difficult both temporally and psychologically. He labored as a farmer but tried to keep his identity secret. If, as we have assumed, he did not participate in the Morrisite War and had not been identified initially with the Morrisite movement, the Mormons may have ignored or at least tolerated him for a time. Nevertheless, he often changed his address and employed the practice of having his mail addressed to confederates instead of himself. In 1864 his letters were to be sent to Philip Bery Chandler. In February 1868 he instructed his correspondents to write to Wellington Barr, and in June of that year he listed James Speaking. In August 1865 Cainan reported that he was living seven miles from the post office and was concerned that his mail was being opened.

On several occasions he expressed concern over his personal safety. In June 1865 he requested that "Brother Taylor not write one word respecting his views of me or this work to Camp Douglas. There lives an enemy to the Lord's servant, whose will is to destroy him from the earth."[13] On September 15, 1867, he wrote:

> Since I saw you I have been assailed by threats of law and death and my name and even parentage have been cursed by those who have taken sides with Lucifer to destroy me. . . . I am clear of all their slanders and spite and I rejoice to know that I gave none cause for bitterness, but labored diligently with all Weber House to lead them on to eternal lives and they would not; but sought to hinder the purposes of God in getting me slain.[14]

On June 16, 1868, Cainan wrote to the Saints in Montana: "I work incessantly on my little farm to support those entrusted to my care but expect

13 Cainan to James Dove and John Eardley, 4 August 1865, Morrisite Papers, File #1

14 Cainan to Brother James (probably William James), 15 September 1867, Morrisite Papers, File #1.

soon to be released from the Land of the Enemy where I live and [am] in jeopardy every hour and this is increased by those who once professed great love for the Lord and his work in my charge."[15]

It is difficult to tell whether Cainan was actually as harassed and in as much danger as he believed, but clearly by 1868 he was frightened and disillusioned. Although he seldom mentioned specifically who his enemies were, it is evident that some were Mormons but others were Morrisites. Many supporters had fallen away from him by this time, but, in characteristic fashion, he preferred to deal with them through letters rather than through direct confrontations. Although there had been much dissension in Nevada, California, and Montana, Cainan refused to engage in an active personal campaign for leadership. Perhaps he really did fear for his life and thus avoided personal contact with the Saints.

15 Cainan to the Saints in Montana, 16 June 1868, Morrisite Papers, File #1.

13 The Left Wing of the Great Eagle: Nevada and California

By autumn 1862 several Morrisite refugees from the Weber conflict could be found scattered among the mining camps of Nevada. Most of these had been active participants in the battle and had elected to skip bail rather than stand trial with their brethren the following spring. Several, in fact, had held high positions in Joseph Morris's organization and were still deeply committed to his teachings. Nevertheless, the traumatic experiences of battle, lost leadership, and exile had for the time being rendered them virtually incapable of continuing the work Morris had begun. Therefore, early spring found them still disorganized but filled with growing determination to carry Morris's message to others. Unfortunately, there are few extant records of their activities and none that could be considered unbiased. The only contemporaneous records are the letters of the Prophet Cainan, written from Utah, to various Morrisites in Nevada. At best they are useful for making inferences, but they can hardly be considered direct reports of activities in that area. Beginning in 1879 and continuing sporadically through 1892, James, George, and Joseph Dove wrote several pamphlets, which, among other things, dealt with Morrisite activity in Nevada and California beginning in 1862. Apparently these were reconstructed from memory or in some cases from entries in personal diaries. Undoubtedly the pamphlets have many deficiencies, but they constitute the chief source of information about the Nevada-California Morrisites.

When James and George Dove came down into Carson Valley in the spring of 1863, after having spent the winter in the woods near Virginia, they encountered John Livingstone. They found him:

> . . . talking to the people, who were anxious for us to preach; and John E. Jones, James Dove, and John Livingstone [all Morrisite apostles] met in prayer in Father Jones house, in Jack Valley, to inquire of the Lord; and it was decided that there should be a meeting on Sunday in the Jack Valley school house, and there was a large congregation, James Dove preaching first, John Livingstone followed with a few remarks, the people listening

> with great attention. We advanced the principles taught us in Weber. In April, some were baptized, namely, Robert Roberts, Jane Roberts and her daughter Jane. Soon after this a few more were baptized. Robert Ford, John Harvey, Sister Bell and her husband, were favorably inclined. John Bowman and wife, Mrs. Baxter and Henry Wadman were under the presidency of James Dove. John Livingstone, John Parson and Richard Cook formed a presidency, and did some work in Nevada; and they baptized a few, ...
>
> There were many persons who were very much interested in and favorable to the principles advocated and taught during the first two years. Bro. John Eardley came from Austin, Nev., in the fall, and took hold of the work with James Dove, and kept it up in Carson City till the latter left in November, 1865.[1]

This brief sketch written by James Dove in 1892 reveals a good deal about the beginning of the Morrisites in the Far West. However, it is almost as revealing for its significant omissions. No mention is made of the terminus of the wagon train that left Salt Lake City in May 1863. Apparently no new settlement was contemplated or attempted as had been the case in Soda Springs. It may be assumed that wagons left the train and dispersed throughout several burgeoning communities in Nevada, for we find Morrisites near Virginia City, in Carson Valley, in Jack Valley, and elsewhere. These were the bawdy, reckless, fevered sites of the first Nevada mining strikes. Nevada had been virtually without a white population in 1859, when the fabulous Comstock Lode was discovered at Virginia. This strike stimulated a huge influx of prospectors, speculators, and camp followers. By 1860 the population was 6,857. In 1861 Nevada was officially separated from Utah Territory and by 1864 had attained statehood, claiming a population in excess of 25,000. Perhaps the first Morrisites in Nevada were as much attracted by the lure of the "mother lode" as by the lure of permanent settlement, for there was little besides mining to recommend Nevada in the early 1860s.

Whatever the case, the Morrisites were scattered throughout the mining camps of western Nevada, and they could hardly avoid being influenced by the bustle, confusion, and excitement of this raw frontier. It is hardly surprising that their congregations were small, their leadership sporadic, and their loyalties fluctuating. In short, their theological fortunes were up against formidable secular odds.

Not only did James Dove omit reference to the wagon train and the Nevada "gold" rush, more significantly he failed to mention one word in his pamphlet about the impact of the Prophet Cainan upon the Nevada Saints. Yet, as previously noted, the Prophet Cainan was at that very time

1 James Dove, *A Few Items in the History of the Morrisites*, pp. 1–2.

conducting a vigorous letter-writing campaign calculated to capture their support. Obviously, by 1892 when his pamphlet was published, Dove was attempting to garner support for his son George, who sought from 1874 on to assume Morrisite leadership. He discounted the claims of the late George Williams by simply ignoring him. Actually, in an earlier publication George and James Dove acknowledged the work of George Williams (Cainan) and cast him as kindly though misguided. They also cast some light upon his first appearance among the Morrisites.

> In the year 1862, George Williams presented himself in Salt Lake City before some of our brethren. He claimed that the apostleship of Weber was given him for help and for government; when at the same time, the Lord had not told him that the apostleship of Weber had been broken up, and that by revelation, which was the fact. He made the mistake of being led by impression, and not by revelation. There was no word about George Williams, from Joseph Morris in Weber. There was a great deal of sound philosophy and good reason in his letters; hence he said, that it was "The Science of the Gospel!" He was a good, fatherly man. But the philosopher could not discern much spiritually, and he made some grave mistakes.[2]

The Doves had certainly not ignored Cainan in 1864 and 1865. George Dove had been sent to interview him in 1865 and apparently returned with a favorable report, for the missionary activities of the Doves correspond closely with instructions given them by Cainan. On July 4, 1864, Cainan wrote to James Dove and John Eardley rejoicing that they (and other Nevada Morrisites) had expressed a "unanimous feeling to conduct and act according to the requirements of the Lord from his Holy Priesthood." They were then instructed to close their affairs in Nevada and go on missions. James Dove obeyed that call, for he reported that he "left in November, 1865, to go on a mission to the Eastern States, in company with George S. Dove and Hugh Davies."[3]

During that same period many of Cainan's letters were addressed to "My Beloved James and John" (James Dove and John Eardley) , which indicates that James was his supporter for a time at least. This fact is of some interest when juxtaposed with Dove's solitary reference to Cainan in his 1892 pamphlet. While describing a visit to Montana in company with his son George in 1885, Dove said: "We called at Race Track; we wanted to get their meeting house, but they would not let us have it; *we did not trust in their leader, George Williams* [emphasis added]."[4]

2 Dove and Dove, *A Voice from the West*, pp. 13–14.
3 James Dove, *A Few Items in the History of the Morrisites*, p. 2.
4 James Dove, *A Few Items in the History of the Morrisites*, p. 10.

The Prophet John Livingstone

One of the problems hampering Cainan's initial efforts to gain the undivided support of the Nevada-California Morrisites was simply that he commenced his campaign there a few months too late. At least half of the Morrisite apostles were in Nevada in the winter of 1864 and felt the need for a more formal, centralized organization than had existed there previously. Therefore, "six apostles and Richard Cook, Morris's counselor, met in Bro. Neils Morrison's house to ordain Bro. John Livingstone to receive communications for the guidance of the apostles, John Parson and Richard Cook. John E. Jones objected, but complied afterwards and Bro. Livingstone filled the office to the satisfaction of John Parson."[5]

We find here a classic example of a rational-legal attempt to establish a prophet (i.e., one who receives communications from God). Although John Parson was satisfied with the appointment of Livingstone, obviously John Jones was not. It would be interesting to know how many other Morrisites had reservations about Livingstone's prophetic call. Certainly this was an inauspicious beginning for a neophyte prophet, yet at least the Nevada Morrisites now had one. Parson and Livingstone soon departed to California on a preaching mission, but later disagreed and "did not work together any longer."[6]

Within this context, it may have seemed to some that Cainan's letter of March 1864 appointing John Parson to be the first official Morrisite missionary was a bit presumptuous. After all, they had just appointed Livingstone to be their prophet, yet here was another prophet giving instruction.

John Parson complied with Cainan's request and in August 1864 was rewarded by being appointed president of the church at Carson. No doubt this contributed strongly to the disaffection between Parson and Livingstone. Parson had been appointed by the local apostles to be Livingstone's subordinate, yet he was now given the authority by Cainan to preside. Small wonder if Parson and Livingstone "no longer saw eye-to-eye."

Following instructions from Cainan, James and George Dove embarked at San Francisco for New York in December 1865. After a rough voyage, they landed safely in New Jersey. James Dove reported that he delivered a few lectures but met with poor success.

Dove's proselyting failures in the East must have shaken his confidence in the prophetic powers of Cainan, for he "returned to San Francisco in January 1868 and finding a few that accepted W. W. Davies as a leader, joined them, and began to preach the fullness of the gospel, and met with

5 James Dove, *A Few Items in the History of the Morrisites*, p. 2.
6 James Dove, *A Few Items in the History of the Morrisites*, p. 2.

success in convincing a few persons."[7] From this time on the Doves withdrew their support from Cainan and continued searching for an acceptable leader. Many other Nevada-California Morrisites did likewise. By 1873 John Parson had visited Davies in Walla Walla and temporarily accepted him. John Livingstone had accepted him earlier. However, for most of them the enchantment with Davies was short-lived.

In 1879 James and George Dove published a brief chronology of the pretenders to general Morrisite leadership. In addition to George Williams (Cainan), they listed John Livingstone, William Davies, John Parson, Joseph Warner, and George S. Dove. Presumably Dove was seen by them as the last and only legitimate heir to Joseph Morris.

The Stewardship of James and George Dove

James Dove and his son George were English converts to Mormonism. James was born December 2, 1819; George was born May 18, 1842. James and his wife, Alice, with their two children, George and Sarah, sailed for America in early 1856. After arriving on the Atlantic seaboard, they made their way to the L.D.S. gathering place near Iowa City and joined the Martin Handcart Company in August 1856. After a most difficult journey, they arrived in Salt Lake City in early December.

Shortly after arriving in the valley, they began to encounter some Mormons who were becoming disillusioned and disaffected. Questions concerning the prophetic abilities of Brigham Young and his authoritarian style, disparities between rich and poor, and concerns about polygamy became serious issues. George became acquainted with Joseph Morris and, against his father's advice, followed Morris from American Fork to Salt Lake City in the fall of 1859. After Morris moved to South Weber, George again followed. After his father, James, visited, he too became converted. James Dove joined the Morrisite Church and in September 1861, was ordained an apostle—a position he held until after the death of Morris.[8]

According to James Dove, his son George began receiving spiritual communications and having dreams and visions in 1873. "Bro. George continued to receive the word of the Lord, giving instructions how to proceed with the work, and giving light on many things. . .He was operated upon at times by the Holy Spirit, and the word of the Lord came that we

7 James Dove, *A Few Items in the History of the Morrisites*, p. 3.

8 See Richard N. Holzapfel. "The Flight Of the Doves From Utah Mormonism To California Mormonism: The Saga Of James and George Dove," pp. 196–219 in Roger D. Launius and Linda Thatcher, eds. *Differing Visions Dissenters In Mormon History* (Urbana and Chicago: University of Illinois Press, 1994).

were to organize into a church called the *Church of the Firstborn.*"[9] Given this impressive array of spiritual gifts, it is surprising that George Dove did not define himself as a prophet. However, he wrote in 1879, "George S. Dove does not pretend to be a prophet, in the general acceptation of the term, or to give revelations in writing."[10] The selection of a name for his church is also of some interest. Dove gave the "Spirit of the Lord" credit for originating the name, but perhaps the credit should have been given to another source, or at least to another spokesman. On August 28, 1868, the Prophet Cainan referred to his own mission as prophet to the Morrisite church and then declared: "This Church will also be called *The Church of the Firstborn—The Holiest of All,*[11] because it receives and will receive the greatest and most holy principles to be revealed to mankind."[12] Either Dove got his sources mixed or else the Spirit spoke with consistency through both Cainan and himself.

Sometime between 1874 and 1877, George S. Dove founded his Church of the Firstborn and baptized five believers, among them his father. He and his father subsequently proselytized in Fairmount Valley, Sacramento, and Pleasant Grove, California. James Dove reported that "about this time things seemed to be at a standstill, on account of the Doves having failed in business and were poor."[13]

After the Doves' financial fortunes improved, they resumed their proselytizing. In August 1885 James Dove visited Salt Lake City, and in October and November he and his son visited Morrisites at Deer Lodge, Race Track, Willow Glen, and Anaconda, Montana. Their reception was mixed. Some of the Morrisites opened their doors and hearts to them. Others were offended by their attempts to win converts and to discredit the Prophet Cainan. On October 7 they were kindly received by their old friend and associate John R. Eardley, who was operating a store at Willow Glen. From there he accompanied them to Anaconda. However, upon returning to Willow Glen a few days later, they engaged in a verbal altercation with Eardley, and he ordered them out of his store. For several days they held meetings and visited Morrisites, and on Sunday, October 25, they held two meetings in the Willow Glen schoolhouse. By then Eardley's feelings must have softened, for he attended the meetings.

---

9 James Dove, *A Few Items in the History of the Morrisites,* p. 5.

10 Dove and Dove, *A Voice from the West,* p. 15.

11 There is no evidence that either of these organizations had any connection with the present Church of the Firstborn. Both of them rejected the then current practice of polygamy, while the modern Church of the Firstborn strongly advocates that practice.

12 Eardley, *Gems of Inspiration,* p. 91.

13 James Dove, *A Few Items in the History of the Morrisites,* p. 6.

It is unknown how many followers the Doves attracted in Montana, but it is doubtful if they had much success. Nevertheless, one event of considerable importance to Morrisite history occurred while in Montana.

> . . . a number of brethren began to advocate the publishing of the revelations of Joseph Morris. We told them at first that we did not think they could understand them all; we were satisfied that such would be the case; but they felt determined to have them just as they were written. Finally arrangements were made for the means to conduct that part of the work, and the brothers at Montana would have George S. Dove pledge himself that he would publish the revelations in their crude state. He returned to San Francisco and commenced the work, and it took about seven months to accomplish it, as the revelations were in a very disordered condition. Some people have not felt satisfied with the publication, and others have, while some parties have found fault with George S. Dove for publishing them, and gave him no credit for the efforts put forth by him for the benefit of truth and the revival of the Morrisite people.[14]

The above publication came out under the title The Spirit Prevails in 1886. Perhaps some of the Morrisites were not pleased with the Doves' publishing efforts, but virtually every primary publication concerning the Morrisites came from their press. George Dove seems never to have attracted a very large following, but without the Dove publications the history of the Morrisites would have gone largely unrecorded.

In 1887 the Doves published Articles of Faith, which outlined the basic principles and doctrines of the Church of the Firstborn. Although many principles and doctrines corresponded with Mormon theology, from which the Morrisite movement emerged, there were several fundamental differences. Among these were the rejection of the principle of a literal resurrection after one life on earth in favor of a belief in reincarnation. It was believed that persons could not become perfected in one lifetime upon the earth, but that several sojourns would be required in different bodies and places before the eternal spirit would be prepared to dwell with the angels of heaven. Variations of this belief were found among nearly all the Morrisite factions, although it was emphasized much more by some than others.

The Doves taught that reincarnation was not only available to the righteous but was open to all. The Church of the Firstborn believed in rewards and punishments, but not in an endless hell. Sinners were given a second chance. "After we have cast off this mortal, the deeds done in the body come to memory, and if our deeds have been evil, we at once feel convicted, and fully realizing our condition, we are anxious to come in mortality to try again."[15]

---

14 James Dove, *A Few Items in the History of the Morrisites,* pp. 10–11.

15 Articles of Faith (San Francisco: Committee of the Firstborn, 1887), p. 15.

Another unique belief concerned the Godhead. God and Jesus Christ constituted the Godhead. "The Holy Ghosts, spoken of in the scriptures, are the angels of God who are sent to . . . be ministering spirits of the heirs of salvation upon this earth."

The Doves returned to Utah in late November 1885. James remained there until about 1891, and George apparently divided his time between there and San Francisco. James Dove believed that South Weber should again be a gathering place for the Morrisites, for he wrote concerning their activities.

> We traveled on till we came to Weber, and James Dove stayed a few days and then, went down to Salt Lake City and stopped there a few weeks; then went up to Weber for good, and in a few weeks Ellen Romstrom came up and brought some means to build a house, believing it was to make a home for the Morrisite people; but no one came to help, and we had to bear it alone. James Dove worked there for two years, and made a nice place, suffering considerable hardship in the winter, believing that he was doing the will of the Lord; but the old lady died, and the place went back into the hands of the man who owned the land, and Carlton took all the rest, cow, chickens and household furniture; but we firmly believe that it was a shadow of things to come, although it was not the spot of ground that the Lord called his; still it was in that valley where the Lord said that it was, and that he would march the people from there. James Dove came home to his family [in San Francisco] and has been preaching and writing for the promulgation of the truths of the fullness of the gospel ever since, and will continue to do so while life remains.[16]

There is little reason to doubt that James Dove, along with his son George, did continue to preach to the people, but the efficacy of their preaching seems doubtful. By the 1890s the Morrisites had been divided and subdivided for so many years there was little hope of reuniting them. Non-Morrisites simply were not interested. The Doves employed the power of the press and traveled widely making personal appeals, but to little avail. In 1892 James Dove wrote: "After years of separation in an unorganized condition, having been led hither and thither, without any central point in which to concentrate their energies, would it not be well for the Morrisite brethren to look unto the truths that are contained in the pamphlets that have lately been published by James Dove?"

It is clear that the author had become tired and discouraged, although he still held fast to the faith himself. He concluded his pamphlet with a veiled admission that the work of the Doves had been largely unproductive. "We know that men all over judge us by the success of our efforts; don't forget that God looks at the efforts themselves."[17]

---

16 Articles of Faith, p. 7.
17 Articles of Faith, p. 19.

Yet of all the followers of Joseph Morris, perhaps the Doves remained more faithful to his unadulterated teachings than any others. They insisted that the Second Coming could occur nowhere other than at South Weber, because that location had been so designated by his revelation. Consequently, they tried for years to encourage the Morrisites to return there to prepare for that great event. They expected that the Savior would return to earth at South Weber likely accompanied by Joseph Morris. From there the faithful would be escorted to the Salt Lake City Square, where the full contingent of Saints would gather. From there they would all depart for Jackson County, Missouri, where the New Jerusalem would be built and Christ would reign personally for a thousand years.

The pathos of their single-minded dedication, self-sacrifice, and diligent yet largely fruitless labors for more than three decades is almost overwhelming. They were truly voices crying out in the wilderness.

James Dove was more prophetic than he knew when he declared that what had been started at South Weber was "a shadow of things to come." He and his son, George, labored mightily to "make a home for the Morrisite people; but no one came to help."

If it had not been for their numerous publications, the stewardship of the Doves would have gone almost entirely unnoticed. Their publications not only recorded their involvement in the Morrisite movement, but constitute the most inclusive nineteenth-century references to Joseph Morris and his successors.

Holzapfel notes that James Dove died sometime before 1899 and that by then, George no longer claimed leadership of the Morrisite church or published on its behalf. The Church of the Firstborn lasted until 1910. Holzapfel suggests a useful theoretical framework for explaining the lack of success in promoting the Church of the Firstborn in Utah. Holzapfel notes that sociologists discuss the rise and fall of social movements in terms of "resource mobilization": material resources, number of potential converts, support or opposition of local government, and leadership pools. He asserts that the Doves' church was deficient in all of these dimensions. The Doves were very weak financially. Potential converts in Utah were greatly reduced because a new L.D.S. president was once more producing revelations by the late 1870s. The Doves antagonized most Mormons by siding with the U.S. Government's prosecution of polygamists. Second-level leaders were in short supply.[18]

The Doves' emphasis upon obedience to the federal law prohibiting polygamy antagonized Utah Mormons in the late 1870s and throughout the late 1880s. Yet by the 1890s and thereafter, the L.D.S. Church had reversed

18 Holzapfel. "The Flight Of the Doves," pp. 209–13.

its position on polygamy and begun emphasizing the need to obey all civil and criminal laws. Whether or not this was through revelation is not empirically verifiable, but clearly it was expedient if Utah were to become a state and the L.D.S. Church were once more to operate fully as a legal institution.

The Left Wing of the Great Eagle never materialized into a unified movement. From beginning to end it was factional and groping. Several men tried to assume leadership, but in competing with each other they attracted only a few followers, who often shifted loyalties. Their messages seem to have had virtually no appeal to non-Morrisites. Hence, the movement languished for lack of effective recruitment. In effect the would-be leaders were engaged in a zero-sum process in which nearly every convert was made at the expense of some other faction. Through the attrition associated with death, disinterest, migration, and disillusionment, the end result was as James Dove lamented: "No one came to help."

14 The Walla Walla Jesus

In a letter written from Great Salt Lake City dated August 9, 1865, addressed to James Dove and John Eardley (then in Nevada), the Prophet Cainan wrote: "As Deer Lodge Valley, Montana, is the nucleus, let all others begin to turn their attention that way as they tire in the wings. Brother Wm. Davis [Davies] presides there over temporalities and if a High Priest could journey there whose desire was to tarry on the land and to serve the Lord by blessing the brothers and sisters, there with the good things of the Priesthood." This is Cainan's first mention of William W. Davies, a man who he thought was a loyal supporter, but who was soon to become a competitor for the Morrisite leadership.

On August 21, 1865, Cainan wrote to Davies at Dance Stewart and Company, Deer Lodge City, Deer Lodge Valley, Montana Territory.

> Dear William, be prepared to receive Bros. S. Guhl and Sorenson whom I expect to winter with you on their way to Scandinavia, likewise Bro. Thompson on his way to England. These Brethren have been with me and bear from under my hands their appointments, and are the hunters of the Lord holding the keys of that office . . . . Listen to their teachings . . . , doing unto them as unto me . . . . Let your Priesthood have their regular meetings and be an example of goodness to all, that their faith may be great in your government *over temporalities.* Let Bro. Thomas preside in his priesthood. . . . Send on to Bro. Sven O. Hagg my invitation to prepare to journey in the spring with Bros. Guhl and Sorenson, and he shall be highly gifted with the everlasting gospel's power, if faithful. . . . You may expect an immigration next summer from Nev. and Cal. Are you ready to receive them? I will expect to hear from Deer Lodge at an early day. There the nucleus must be established.

Cainan wrote to Davies with authority, obviously expecting him to accept the instructions and appointees. Davies, however, had other plans, and he soon set the record straight. On April 30, 1866, Cainan reported to John (probably Eardley): "From W. Davis [Davies] comes a disgraceful and offensive missel, too much so to go on file, claiming another exaltation for himself, [with] Sven Hagg, counsellor." From that point on

Davies and Cainan were irreconcilable, and the die was cast for factionalism in Montana.

William W. Davies was born in Denbigh, North Wales, August 9, 1833. His parents were Wesleyan Methodists. He learned the trade of stonemason from his father. At the age of fourteen, young William was introduced to the Mormon faith by missionaries, and he was baptized two years later. In 1845 he married Sarah E. Jones, and ten years later they migrated to America, settling at Willard, some fifty miles north of Salt Lake City. His dedication to religion was evident, but he became more and more disillusioned with the leaders of Mormonism. When Joseph Morris began preaching in Slaterville and South Weber in the fall of 1860, Davies was attracted to him and joined the Morrisites in 1861. He moved to Kington Fort, consecrated his property to the Lord, and joined the Morrisite "army." There he participated in the Morrisite War and witnessed the death of the prophet.

William Davies and family were numbered among the Morrisite pioneers in Soda Springs in early 1863. In 1864, in company with several other Morrisite families, Davies moved to Virginia City, Montana, and from there took up residence in the Deer Lodge Valley in 1865.

After arriving in Deer Lodge, Davies became greatly depressed. He still believed in Mormonism and in the teachings of Joseph Morris, but he felt alone and leaderless. He determined to seek an answer to his problems by turning directly to God. Therefore, on January 24, 1866, he prayed long and earnestly and was rewarded by a vision convincing him that his prayers had been answered and that he would be the instrument through which God would impart his will to the children of men. Davies believed he was to usher in a new era, to establish for a thousand years the Kingdom of Heaven upon the earth. Davies claimed that from that time forward he communed directly with the Godhead, receiving from time to time instructions concerning his appointment.[1] (Undoubtedly it was a report of this vision and prophetic calling that so disturbed the Prophet Cainan in April 1866.)

One of Davies's revelations directed him to establish the Kingdom of Heaven in the region of Walla Walla. In obedience to that dictum, and in company with some forty followers, some of whom had been sent to Montana by Cainan, Davies took to the Mullan Road and arrived in Walla Walla, Washington Territory, in 1867. At that time Walla Walla was the largest city in the territory, having enjoyed a huge boom as chief supply point for the newly discovered gold and silver mines in Idaho.

When Davies was shown eighty acres upon which to develop his colony, he looked it over carefully and proclaimed: "This is the Place." Even here the

---

1 Russell Blankenship, *And There Were Men* (New York: Alfred A. Knopf, (1942), pp. 79–94.

Morrisites could not escape all of Brigham Young's influence, for these are the precise words attributed to Brigham Young when he first surveyed the Salt Lake Valley exactly twenty years earlier. Although conventional wisdom and a large monument in Salt Lake City's Emigration Canyon now attest to Brigham Young's "This is the Place" pronouncement, it appears that those words were first attributed to Young by Wilford Woodruff several years after Young's death. Could Woodruff have borrowed the phrase from Davies?

As soon as the land was purchased, his followers moved onto it. All things were consecrated to the Lord and held in common. This seems to have been the only Morrisite faction that tried to revive the law of consecration as practiced in South Weber. The amount of land upon which the colony was built made self-sufficiency difficult. The number of followers fluctuated between thirty and seventy, and all were poor, if not destitute, upon their arrival. Those who were able not only worked on the colony land but found employment among neighbors or in town. For some reason, Davies made no effort to enlarge the colony holdings, despite the fact that land for homesteading was available all around. As a result, the Daviesites probably never became fully self-sustaining. Contributions were solicited and received from Morrisites in Montana, Nevada, and California. A large share of these funds were used to promote missionary work and to publish tracts. Although certain nonbelievers accused Davies of exploiting his followers to gain personal enrichment, there is little evidence to support this claim.

When Davies first began writing tracts, they were published in San Francisco, but eventually presses were obtained and the Daviesites did their own publishing at Walla Walla. The efficacy of this publishing and other proselytizing efforts was not great. Apparently few, if any, local converts were made, but a few believers were found in various parts of the West—most of whom were already Morrisites. John Livingstone, one of Morris's original apostles, left his post as prophet in Nevada to become Davies' chief executive officer in Walla Walla. As previously noted, John Parson visited the Walla Walla Daviesites in 1872 to satisfy himself about Davies' claims. He was favorably impressed by the visit but soon went his own way and set up his own kingdom in San Francisco on April 7, 1874. Parson baptized a few who had previously been baptized by James Dove. He expected thousands to flock to his kingdom, but his followers never exceeded a score or two. During this period several Morrisites were contending for leadership, but they had little appeal to non-Morrisites. In effect there was a confusing exchange of followers, all defining themselves as Morrisites, but attaching themselves briefly to one leader or another. Some members were baptized three or four times to satisfy the requirements of each successive kingdom.[2]

2 James Dove, *A Few Items in the History of the Morrisites*, pp. 3–5.

Like the other Morrisite schisms, the Daviesites believed in the imminent Second Advent of Christ. However, Davies interpreted that anticipated state in a manner unique from all the others. He took the principle of reincarnation and made it the keystone of his belief system, applying it not only to himself but also to other members of his family. He claimed a distinguished personal identity, insisting that he was Michael the Archangel reincarnate. That is, the spirit of the Archangel inhabited Davies' body and had striven throughout his lifetime to prepare him for his calling. Michael had inhabited several illustrious bodies in ages past, having appeared as Adam, Abraham, and King David. These incarnations were a necessary prelude to the work assigned to Davies. The Bible proclaimed that the Christ was a descendant of the house of David, and when Davies' son, Arthur, was born February 11, 1868, it was revealed that he was none other than the reincarnated Jesus Christ. Davies gave his son the name "Messiah Son of David." When Davies made the announcement eight days after the infant's birth, on the occasion of anointing and naming, the mother feared to take the child back into her arms. Davies reassured her that God had made it her privilege to nurse the infant redeemer. Davies reported that there were thirty-two souls, including children at this place when the child was born, but after that the followers increased to seventy.

This child became known as the Walla Walla Jesus, and his divine identity was taken seriously by Davies' followers. Joseph Morris and several of his would-be successors had expected the Messiah to appear in adult form descending from the clouds of heaven leading a heavenly army. His failure to do so on schedule had been especially troublesome for Morris. But Davies found the near-perfect solution to that dilemma. What could be more natural and defensible than the appearance of the Savior as an infant complete with appropriate earthly father and mother. Furthermore, the child was reported to have developed precociously, showing surprising mental alertness and physical beauty, which delighted parents and proselytes. Even "outsiders were visibly impressed."[3]

On September 28, 1869, another son was born into the Household of Faith. The identity of this child had been revealed to the father and mother prior to its birth. When the time came, Davies anointed it and gave it the name "Our Father," meaning God the Eternal Father of Spirits. Later the child adopted the name of David.

Although the identity ascription of the second child surpassed that of the first, he seems not to have been as well proportioned or precocious and was not as well known outside the community. Nevertheless, both children were accepted by the Daviesites as incarnate members of the Godhead. As

3 Blankenship, *And There Were Men*, p. 89.

such they were central to the movement's ideology and the living symbols of all it stood for.

For more than a decade following the birth of "God the Father," the Daviesite colony continued. Hard work and scant material rewards were reaped by the faithful, but most of them were content in the knowledge that they were inaugurating the Kingdom of God on earth—that they were the chosen founders of the long-awaited millennium. Davies maintained that as father and guardian of deity, neither death nor disaster could enter the colony against his will. This pronouncement comforted his followers for a while, but the time came when it helped set the stage for disaffection and community disintegration.

In 1879 Davies' wife—"the mother of deity"—fell ill and died. A few months later an even greater tragedy occurred. In the winter of 1880 a diphtheria epidemic struck the colony, and to everyone's grief and dismay it infected the "holy" children. On February 15, "God the Father," only ten years old, was taken by the disease. Exactly one week later, his elder brother—"The Walla Walla Jesus"—followed him to the grave.

The shock of this tragedy was too much for the people to bear, and some began almost immediately to openly criticize the prophet. They began to question the ownership of the communal property, and they asked Davies to distribute it among them. Davies did redistribute some of the property, but not all of them were satisfied. In October 1880 three members of the community filed suit asking for compensation for labor performed and for a return of the money they had contributed to their leader. In the trial, held in January 1881, Davies reaffirmed his prophetic calling and his faith in the divinity of his two sons. He admitted he could not understand their premature deaths, but expressed the belief they would once more return to earth to complete their missions.

The court ruled in favor of the plaintiffs, awarding them $3,200 of the community property. Since Davies had no liquid assets, "the sheriff sold at public auction the eighty acres upon which the community had its home, a second tract of land, and a considerable quantity of personal property. The total amounted to just enough to satisfy the judgment . . . and pay [court] costs."[4]

After this legal defeat, Davies moved with some followers and the remainder of his family to a small piece of land he owned on nearby Mill Creek. There on September 1, 1881, he married Cornelia S. Perkins, a schoolteacher he had brought to the colony from San Francisco. In due course she bore Davies a daughter, which he affirmed was his reincarnated previous wife returned to earth for the purpose of completing her interrupted

4 Blankenship, *And There Were Men*, p. 91.

calling. We have no record of his second wife's reaction to this incestuous pronouncement, but Russell Blankenship reported that "the second marriage was the last straw in the breakup of the Daviesites." In any event, Davies eventually abandoned his hopes of maintaining the Kingdom of Heaven at Walla Walla and moved to California. Little more is known about him. James Dove reported in 1892 that Davies was residing in San Francisco, "living on the means that he has gained in some way."[5] Dove seemed to imply that Davies was living on funds obtained from duplicity. However, if those funds came from the disposition of his Walla Walla property, it is unlikely he was living very high. He was probably almost destitute when he forsook Mill Creek.

Today wheat fields cover the old community site, and no physical trace of Davies' Kingdom of God remains. Certainly there is nothing left to suggest the envisioned grandeur of the dwelling place of "God the Father" and his brother "Jesus Christ."

5 James Dove, *A Few Items in the History of the Morrisites*, p. 6.

15 Deer Lodge: The Heavenly City

In February 1868, the Prophet Cainan wrote from Salt Lake City to the Saints in Montana expressing his intention to move there and take up a claim as soon as possible. However, a few months later, probably because he realized that much of his Nevada and California support had diminished, he changed his mind and made preparations to return to his native land to preach the gospel. He departed in January 1869. Along the way he visited here and there with Morrisites, and in Council Bluffs Cainan held a meeting with a group from Iowa and Nebraska. There on January 24 he was sustained by unanimous vote as prophet, seer, and revelator of the Church of Jesus Christ of Saints of the Most High. Soren Peter Guhl, the leader of the Council Bluffs group, was sustained as Cainan's first counselor. Guhl was also set apart to be an apostle and "doctor in theology." Andrew Hendrikson became the clerk and recorder.

Little is known of Guhl, except that he was born in Jyland, Denmark, August 18, 1821, had migrated to America, and had been with Joseph Morris at South Weber. Cainan had appointed him president of the Montana Morrisites sometime after 1865. Whether or not he assumed that office is uncertain, but he was released in February 1868 when William James was appointed to preside there. Although Cainan had called Guhl to a Scandinavian mission in 1865, he experienced numerous delays and had gotten no farther than Council Bluffs when Cainan arrived in 1869. Guhl presided in the Council Bluffs area for about two months, following Cainan's visit in 1869. In April or May he responded to a missionary call to Denmark, and Andrew Hendrikson succeeded him as president. It is evident that Guhl was a trusted follower of Cainan at that time. However, once he got to Denmark he began to develop his own ideas about the leadership of the Morrisites. He, along with a Mr. Laurentzen and a Mr. Poulson, rejected the leadership of Cainan and set up their own church. A few years later Cainan wrote to the Saints in Montana. "Here I am struck with a view of feeling after Guhl, Laurentzen, and Poulson in Denmark who outrageously disagreed with me; that it became wisdom to leave them until more reason overtook them.[1] Apparently Guhl and his compatriots were never overtaken by more reason, for they remained estranged from Cainan.

Andrew Hendrikson (originally Henrikson) was also a native of Jyland, Denmark, born July 29, 1843. He migrated to America about 1861. Like so many of his contemporaries, he left Scandinavia to avoid the military draft and to seek his fortune in America. He arrived in New York and found employment with a farm family in that state. When the family moved, to Council Bluffs, he accompanied them and there came in contact with members of the Morrisite church. He was baptized January 22, 1869.

In January 1869 there were fifteen members in the Omaha congregation and twelve members in Council Bluffs. By October 1871 the names of forty-two persons were listed in the Omaha records and twenty-seven in Council Bluffs. In addition, eight children were recorded in the Omaha record book. Seven of them had been born between September 1869 and November 1870. Two children died in early 1871.[2]

Although the number of Morrisites in the region of Omaha and Council Bluffs was not large, it represented the most cohesive group backing the Prophet Cainan in 1869. From that group came numerous persons who played a significant role in the settlement of the Deer Lodge Valley in Montana.

Headquarters in England

The Prophet Cainan continued on his journey and arrived in England probably in late spring or early summer. On August 17, 1869, he addressed a letter to the Saints in Omaha from Norfolk, England. In it he remarked upon the progress of the work there and intimated that he was grief-stricken to be separated from his wife, Susannah Adelaid Louise Williams, and his children, who had not accompanied him but still lived in Salt Lake City. He asked the Saints to write to them and comfort them in their separation. On January 10, 1870, he wrote to the Saints in Montana, and after telling them of his many trials and vicissitudes, including physical suffering in his journeys and labors, he asked Sister Margaret (Thomas) to write to his family in Salt Lake. Apparently they were not only separated from him but somewhat estranged, for he said: "I seldom hear from my family at Salt Lake, only that in October they were all sick—the seven children and the mother . . . . If you have written and they have not answered, never mind that, do so again."

Four days later he wrote to Brother James and Saints of the Most High in Denmark and Montana. Once more he expressed concern for having been

1 Cainan to the Saints in Montana, 5 September 1871, Loughboro, England, Morrisite Papers, File #1.

2 The Omaha and Council Bluffs records were written in Danish. Translation to English courtesy of Eva Wetzel. Morrisite Papers, File #5.

separated from his family for a year. He said: "I have not been able to send them one temporal assistance and my six children have all been sick together with measles, the mother with her children. This adds anguish to my heart. My mortality must suffer all things to be made perfect. I would invite the Saints in Montana that feel for me and them, to send on to them what is in their power, to comfort my little ones and verily, you do it unto me."[3]

Cainan's letters seldom referred to his family after 1872. Apparently they never reunited and remained estranged. In 1874 he wrote, "Even from my own family came tales [about me] calculated to uproot the faith of many." In 1881 he referred to his physical suffering and loneliness in being separated from friends and family. It appears that his family had little exchange with the Morrisites, although his daughter, Adelaid, taught school in the Deer Lodge Valley in the 1880s.

During his lifetime Cainan governed his church in absentia. He never visited the Deer Lodge Valley, where most of his supporters went to live, although as late as 1879 he said he intended to join them there. In several letters he identified the Deer Lodge Valley as the place where the Second Advent would occur and where the "City of the Great King" would be built. He expected Deer Lodge to be the seat of God's government during the millennium.

It appears that Cainan was too philosophical and impractical to serve as an effective leader. For many years he preferred to dream and speculate about spiritual matters while temporal concerns were ignored. Apparently he existed almost entirely from donations sent by his followers, because requests for financial assistance occurred frequently in his letters. His orientation toward temporal matters is well illustrated in a letter written to Brother James and the Saints in Montana on May 6, 1874. "It is far more genial unto us to write and speak on Celestial principle, or send a Chapter of St. Ann's Hill Records, than to deal with difficulties, for at this late day, the ministers of our Dear Lord in their assemblies, should rise superior to any taint the evil power may send unto them."

The Prophet Cainan was far more literate than his predecessor. In contrast with those of Joseph Morris, his letters are couched in acceptable, though often stilted, English. Obviously Cainan could express himself well through the written word, but frequently his letters are more rhetorical than anything else. He was fluent, but there was little beyond pious phrases and high-sounding admonitions in much of his correspondence. He aspired to creative pronouncements and the development of new doctrines, but for

3 The discrepancy between seven and six children in these two letters is not explained, although there is reason to believe that one of his children died about that time.

the most part he failed to produce anything as cogent as Morris had done. Perhaps this was why his claims to prophethood, initially accepted by many, were eventually discounted. His eloquence at first made him seem strong and purposive, but upon closer examination his words were found to be filled with empty phrases and meaningless cliches. He had a small core of loyal followers, but for many he did not wear well. He seems to have been relatively incapable of formulating concrete goals for his church and people, let alone workable plans and an organization for achieving them. Even when he was asked for advice in solving some pressing problem, his answer was usually couched in such vague and abstract terms that those making inquiry were ultimately faced with finding the solution by themselves.

The St. Ann's Hill Records

One of Cainan's unfinished projects was the translation and publication of a vast store of records he claimed to have recovered from St. Ann's Hill, Surrey County, England, about 1871. These became known as the St. Ann's Hill Records, and he forwarded several chapters of them to the Saints in Montana. On September 5, 1871, he wrote:

> The records from the Hill St. Ann's in the County of Surrey go on to show the vast creations, down to our own earth, how they were brought forth from element, intelligence, force and power—I gave you the 1st Chapter because you asked to be informed. As the work progresses I will forward other portions as you feel prepared to receive it. It is only given me at intervals to translate—it explains the things of God as they existed from the beginning and far exceeds all that the Prophets and Apostles were given to write.

Apparently Cainan wrote at least fifty-three chapters, but only fragments are extant today. What an enormous volume this record would have added to Morrisite literature if only it had been completed and published.

In many respects Cainan was a model of Christian mildness and meekness and clearly illustrates the difficulty if not contradiction of the "meek inheriting the earth." From England he wrote his letters and hoped that mundane problems would solve themselves. Yet, despite his separation from the field of action and his mild philosophical personality, he exerted considerable influence upon his followers—especially those in Montana. All major church leaders were appointed by him, and the church was organized according to his plan.

Mission Presidency of John R. Eardley

In an effort to escape some of the more mundane duties of the church presidency and to allow more time for fulfilling the role of prophet, seer, and revelator, Cainan began writing to John R. Eardley in 1872 trying to persuade him to accept the presidency of the European Mission. Eardley had been one of Cainan's earliest and most faithful supporters, and he had proved himself a competent organizer and businessman. Besides, he still had family ties and business interests in England, which made a trip to Europe somewhat attractive to him.

John Rowley Eardley was born February 23, 1837, to Henry and Mary Rowley Eardley in Derbyshire, England. His family was considered well-to-do, having owned and operated a prosperous pottery and glass factory for two generations. Both his mother and father were active proselytizers for Methodism, often going to various towns to preach in meetings. His grandfather, Reverend Henry Eardley, D.D., had been one of the organizers of the Primitive Methodist church in England. John's mother died when he was two, and he was raised by a stepmother, but the combination of running a business and preaching Methodism continued as a family tradition throughout his youth. John's uncles were also active lay preachers in the Methodist church, but several of them were converted to Mormonism in the 1850s, and so was John. This caused a serious rift in the family, and several of them, including John, emigrated to Utah. John R. Eardley married Sara Jane Jackson, an English convert to Mormonism, on November 7, 1858, and they left for the United States on April 7, 1859. They spent some time in Boston, then traveled by train to Council Bluffs, where a wagon train was fitted out for the rest of the journey to Utah. John served as secretary to the captain of the wagon train, and the Eardley family traveled in relative comfort to Utah, with a nurse along to help Sara Jane care for the children.

Upon arriving in Utah, John was immediately repelled by the practice of polygamy, and he joined the Morrisites shortly after the church was organized in 1861.[4] After the Morrisite War, he moved with his family to Nevada and then to California.

Eardley was not at all anxious to accept a call to the European Mission presidency, but the Prophet Cainan finally prevailed. Eardley sailed for England with his wife and children in early 1873. On April 12, 1873, Eardley was set apart and ordained president of the mission. At that time a blessing was pronounced upon the heads of him and his wife. Cainan told John that he had lived upon the earth shortly after the great flood and that his name was Planoah, the third son of Japheth. He was also told that he would remain on the earth until sixty years of age. Eardley actually lived to age sixty-nine. He died on April 21, 1906, in San Francisco.

---

4 Family Records of Spencer W. Tripp, Butte, Montana. Spencer W. Tripp was the grandson of John R. Eardley.

Sara Eardley was told by Cainan that she had once been Rachael, the daughter of Laban and the mother of Joseph and Benjamin, and that if she would faithfully continue in the work of the Lord she would live to be sixty-five years of age and longer if desired. She died in 1920 at the age of eighty-two.[5]

The Prophet Cainan had great hopes that the appointment of Eardley to the European presidency would greatly enhance the work there. And undoubtedly Eardley tried to bring order and productivity to the European Mission, but to little avail. Within a few years, Eardley returned to the United States, and the European Mission of the Morrisite church languished.

Colonization in Montana

Although Morrisites began arriving in Montana as early as 1863, their leadership was sporadic and uncertain. Of course, William Davies had created considerable divisiveness among the Saints, and his departure for Walla Walla with nearly two-score followers severely depleted the ranks. On February 14, 1868, William M. James was appointed by Cainan to become the leader in Montana. He had been with Joseph Morris at Kington Fort and had been enrolled there in the Morrisite army. After the death of Morris, he moved to Nevada and from there to the Deer Lodge Valley about 1867. Cainan held James in high esteem, considering him to be a "pillar of faith." This support continued to the very end of Cainan's life.

In 1871 a general Morrisite migration to Montana from Iowa and Nebraska began and continued on through 1872. Most of the group traveled by rail to Corinne, Utah, the terminus of the freight line to Montana. There they obtained wagons, draft animals, and supplies and headed for the territory via Soda Springs and the Snake River plain. Some Morrisites from Idaho joined with them, and they traveled together until arriving in the Deer Lodge Valley. Most of them eventually settled between Anaconda and Deer Lodge.

Among these arriving in 1872 were Andrew Hendrikson and Carrie Jensen. Carrie Jensen was fifteen years old when she migrated from Denmark. She first went to live with her aunt in Council Bluffs, and it was there that she met Andrew. She must have been a striking person, for when the wagon train arrived in the valley she immediately caught the eye of a well-established French settler. He asked to speak with her guardian, Mary Jergensen, and upon gaining an audience he offered forty head of cattle for the hand of the fair Miss Jensen. His polite offer was refused.

Shortly after their arrival in the valley, Andrew Hendrikson and Carrie Jensen were married. He was twenty-nine; she was sixteen. They had a long life together and raised a family of ten children.

5 Record of Ordination and Blessing, 12 April 1873, Morrisite Papers, File #1.

Another arrival in 1872 was George Johnson, with his brother Peter. George had emigrated from Denmark about 1870 at the age of fifteen. He went first to Wisconsin, where Peter and a sister were living and from there moved to Council Bluffs. There he met Andrew Hendrikson and other Morrisites and was baptized by Hendrikson on October 23, 1871. Peter Johnson had been baptized two months earlier. The brothers located in Deer Lodge and subsequently became ranching partners on Dempsey Creek, a few miles south of the city. In 1876 George Johnson married Josephine Oleson, whose mother had been killed in the Weber battle. George was twenty; his bride was sixteen. Like the Hendriksons, the Johnsons had ten children. At the age of forty-four, Josephine Johnson contracted measles and was subjected to a popular remedy of the day known as the "cold treatment." This consisted of being given cold baths in an unheated room. In spite of (or because of) the "treatment," pneumonia developed and within a few days she died.

A year after the 1872 migration, William James was called by the Prophet Cainan to fill a mission in Nevada. He had appointed W. P. Thomas and Andrew Hendrikson respectively as his first and second counselors. They were left in charge during his absence. From that time forward Hendrikson was closely associated with the Morrisite leadership in Montana.

In May 1873 W. P. Thomas was called by Cainan to serve on a mission in the Salt Lake area. In the same letter, Andrew Hendrikson was appointed president to serve in the absence of Thomas and James. He also served as recorder. Hendrikson presided until July when Thomas and James returned from their missions. Just prior to Thomas' departure, three teachers had been appointed to visit the Saints in an effort to promote peace, harmony, and spirituality among them. It is evident from the council meeting records of 1873 that considerable disharmony did, in fact, exist among the Montana Morrisites, and a few of them openly questioned Cainan's authority. The record also contains accounts of property line disputes, abuse of cattle by dogs, and other worldly problems. Some of the members began to complain that the visiting teachers were more like spies than promoters of the Lord's work. And the teachers themselves began to find fault with each other and could not agree upon the necessity of visiting the members on a regular basis.

On July 6 the head teacher was removed from his position on the grounds that he was a burden to the other teachers who worked under him, and he was accused of working in apostasy. At the next council meeting William James presided. The visiting teachers reported on a member and his wife who had been invited to appear at that meeting to answer charges of apostasy. They had refused to come. The husband declared that "[he] never would be among this people again, Cainan was wrong altogether a false prophet his Doctrine was wrong . . . [the council could] cut him off together with his wife if [it] wished to do so."

When the husband had been asked how it could be that he now denied Cainan after previously bearing so much testimony to his mission, he replied: "We were asleep but now we are awake you cannot blame a man for what he speak in his sleep. You are asleep yet even all of you but we are glad we have got our eyes open now."[6]

Upon hearing this report, the council voted to cut off the disaffected brother and his wife from the church. Four persons voted against the motion, and W. P. Thomas objected loudly. The record stated that "[he] was . . . desperate making a great noise accusing us for having thieves, Hers and petyjack devels among us giving especial remarks about W. James . . . saying [those just cut off] was better people . . . . The meeting could not be closed in order because of the tomult."

At the next council meeting, held August 3, the case against the errant visiting teacher was considered. When the brethren prepared to take a vote, "W. P. Thomas made a desperate speech pouring out a streem of evil and malice and kept on till he found himself alone in the house."[7]

On September 7 the minutes read:

> This council meeting was appointed to be held in Bro. Daniel Jameses house but owing to the disturbance made by W. P. Thomas in the two former council meetings and the word he had given out that he would come back and make trouble again in this council the Presydency made an arrangement to disappoint disturbers by keeping the meeting in Bro. Rasmussen's house and have the teachers to notify the Brethren privately about the change. W. P. Thomas meat at the old place again angry to find himself disappointed not knowing whare to find the meeting.[8]

In the absence of Thomas, the meeting moved smoothly, and the unfinished business of the last meeting was quickly accomplished. The erstwhile visiting teacher was cut off from the church with only one abstaining vote. After some discussion, it was concluded that W. P. Thomas was unworthy to retain his leadership position, but since he had been appointed first counselor to William James by none other than the Prophet Cainan, he could not be dispatched as readily as the others had been. Consequently, it was decided to report the case about W. P. Thomas to Brother Cainan. In the meantime, the members were to shun him.

The brethren were disturbed by the number of disaffected members, and considerable time was spent discussing the propriety of cutting them off from the church. Apparently, most of the brethren agreed with the

---

6 Council Meeting Records, Saints of the Most High in Deer Lodge Valley, Montana, 20 July 1873, Morrisite Papers, File #6.

7 Council Meeting Records, Morrisite Papers, File #6.

8 Council Meeting Records, Morrisite Papers, File #6.

sentiments of Brother Rasmussen, who remarked upon the "necessity of cutting off transgressions [transgressors] or the whole church would become corrupted and we would not know who ware our Brethren and Sisters or not it is sometimes necessary to cut off a corrupt branch as it is to plant a new tree."[9]

This preoccupation with disaffected members continued throughout the fall and winter, and several more Saints were excommunicated. In January 1874 Andrew Hendrikson and several other Saints disagreed with some new doctrine preached by President William James. James became extremely defensive about it, insisting that as their leader he could teach anything he wished and make binding decisions whether they agreed with him or not. He said:

> wharewith will you disapprove my words or prove my teachings is false you have no right to contradict or dispute my teachings for I receive such things from my guardian angel the holy Spirit who are of higher order than your guardian and reveal unto me hiden doctrines and you have no right to dispute even if you cannot understand or believe it. Then he said if there are any more of you who did not see it as he did . . . make it known by standing up and all arose on their feet except Daniel James and himself. Then he manifested an angry spirit pointed to A. Henrikson with his finger saying don't you know I can move you I have authority to remove you from your place and he toke his hat and left the meeting without to close it although all begged him to stay and close it in the usual order.[10]

This problem was resolved within a few weeks by some concessions being made on both sides, but the seeds of disagreement were sown, and the feeling of unanimity of the brethren was severely strained. The president's authority had been challenged by his second counselor, and by now his first counselor was completely estranged.

Apparently the Prophet Cainan in England had been informed of this and other problems among the Saints in Montana, for he was prompted to write to them on the subject. In a letter dated May 6, 1874, he expressed his dislike at being called upon to settle petty arguments and disagreements. Then he proposed a solution he hoped would be lasting.

> . . . therefore, the voice of the Lord unto me today while writing this Epistle is, to separate into 2 bands, my people on the sides of the North, even in Montana, and let my servant W. James take charge of those who are convenient to him, and my servant A. Hendrikson take charge of those covenient unto him; and there shall be 2 stakes under one head, even my own chosen Servant Cainan . . . . And let my appointment of 2 bands be the

9 Council Meeting Records, Morrisite Papers, File #6.
10 Council Meeting Records, Morrisite Papers, File #6.

> means of healing every rupture and let no opposition be known . . . . Now, if you feel with me, all will rejoice at the solution of a difficulty sometime growing in your midst. And as I understand it, there is to be no division or heartburnings, but 2 Stakes acting cordially with one another.[11]

In the same epistle the prophet called for increased proselytizing; and well he might, for by now the number of members in each group was greatly reduced. The records of Stake No. 1 are missing, but Stake No. 2 listed a baptized membership in 1874 of only twenty-nine. Reliance entirely upon an unpaid lay leadership allowed for operation with a very small budget, but the size of the Morrisite congregations had come very close to falling below what today would be termed the critical mass. Stake No. 2 eventually reached a size of forty-eight members, but virtually all of the new ones were transfers from other Morrisite congregations or were members' children. There is no evidence that proselytizing efforts were ever seriously attempted or effective in recruiting membership in Montana.

Although the exact number of Morrisites in Montana at any given time is unknown, it seems never to have been very large. Their concentration in the Deer Lodge Valley gave the appearance of a sizable group, but it is doubtful that their numbers ever exceeded seventy-five or a hundred.

The division into two stakes not only reduced the efficiency of the total group, it produced some peculiar patterns of participation. This was primarily because the division was based more upon personal preference for a given leader than upon spatial distribution of members. In 1872 a small meetinghouse had been constructed on Lost Creek, and meetings were frequently held in the schoolhouse at Willow Glen. In 1877 a church house was begun on Dempsey Creek at Race Track, about six miles south of Deer Lodge. It was completed and dedicated on August 9, 1879. That small white building, with an inscription above the door reading; "The Lord's House," still stands near the railroad tracks at Dempsey Crossing. It is the last Morrisite edifice in Montana and probably in the world.

In recognition of the need to promote more unity among the Montana Saints, the Prophet Cainan decreed on April 3, 1877, that a more unifying system of governing should be developed. Therefore, he established a pattern for the "Court of the Lord's House" to be held May 10, 1877, and continued each succeeding year. The "court" was charged with the task of taking up all matters related to the state of the church not only in Montana but also throughout the world and was to have representatives from both stakes.

> It shall be called the Court of the Lord's House. It will be the first court held on the continent of America, and to be continued on the 10th of

11 Cainan to the Saints in Montana, 6 May 1874, Morrisite Papers, File #1.

> May in all your generations, and no one shall be exempt from the Court's discussions. It shall be a court of enquiry, of counsel, of business, of help in all matters concerning the Fullness of the Gospel. Each of the Three [members] to be free to speak as he feels and spend all the time in that court in deliberating on the concerns of the whole Church wherever it may be on all the earth, and the voice from this court shall be respected.

In the same letter the prophet gave minute instructions for the pattern of a holy robe to be worn by the court president, William James, and the pattern for a special prayer to be given at the beginning of each court session. The robe was to be made of white linen except for the neckband. "The red silk neckband I here enclose is to come round the neck, and fall in front separately, until reaching the middle of the breast, and there to be joined slightly by the figure of the sun worked in needle work, very neatly, with white silk which I also send."[12]

Minutes of the first court meeting are not extant, but apparently the Court of the Lord's House replaced and expanded the role of the general council meeting, which had been discontinued upon the division into two stakes. During the summer of 1877 it was decided that a court session should be held in the fall as well as spring. Aside from William James, the composition of the court from 1877 to 1881 is unknown.

The Prophet Cainan continued to correspond with the Saints in Montana throughout the 1870s, but his letters lost much of their earlier optimism and became more philosophical and even melancholy. Some letters took the form of defensive apologies, for it was evident that he felt compelled to respond to criticisms and allegations not only from other leadership contenders but even from some of his supporters. Although he seldom directly identified these criticisms, it can be inferred that they centered upon his prophetic calling, leadership ability, financial management, and, in some cases, moral rectitude.

During that period, many of Cainan's letters referred to his associations in England with George Thompson, whom he had set apart as a missionary to that country in 1865. Thompson had responded to that call in 1867. He traveled with his wife, Frances, via Deer Lodge, Helena, and Fort Benton down the Missouri and eventually to England, where his wife died at Liverpool on September 18, 1867. After Cainan arrived in England, he and Thompson were frequent companions and even lived together from time to time. Thompson served as Cainan's first counselor and took over numerous church responsibilities, as Cainan's health began to fail in the early 1880s.

---

12 Cainan to William James, 3 April 1877, 1 Aglaw Place, Shern Hall St., Walthanstow, Essex, England, Morrisite Papers, File #1.

As time went on, Cainan began to realize that he was not going to succeed in uniting the Morrisite movement. In 1875 he named "John Parson, John Livingstone, William Davies, George Dove, and others as traitors who had once admitted to the legal priesthood of Cainan, but fell and attempted a business of their own." In October 1877 he tacitly acknowledged that his dreams of uniting the movement were lost. He proposed to the Saints in Montana that at their next court meeting, to be held November 10, they take formal "action in the case of some traitors to the cause of our merciful God." He named Alexander Dow, William Davies, S. P. Guhl, and James and George Dove.

> All these have taken a leading part and seduced others to oppose and trample upon the Fullness of the Gospel of our Lord Jesus Christ, and trying to set up a system of their own conjuring. For being guilty of this, I propose they all be committed to outer darkness for 1,000 years in which time they will have paid the uttermost cent. All who favor this proposition, use and prove your sanction with both hands uplifted, saying, Amen.[13]

The outcome of the vote was not recorded, but it was probably in accord with Williams' wishes, because the Doves were publicly disclaimed when they visited Montana a few years later.

It is of some interest that despite his claims to prophetic power and the authority to direct the affairs of the church, Cainan respected the power and authority of the court to make binding decisions regarding the spiritual status of Morrisites wherever they were.

On November 10, 1881, the Court of the Lord's House was held at Race Track. Its members were President William James, Bishop Rasmussen, and Andrew Hendrikson, who also served as clerk. At that meeting Hendrikson resigned the clerkship in favor of John R. Eardley, who had recently moved to Montana and established a store at Willow Glen. Eardley had been appointed a court member by the Prophet Cainan. The court records from 1881 to 1890 were kept by him and are still extant. They provide some fascinating insights concerning Morrisite problems and politics during that period. Like the earlier council meetings, the court focused considerable attention upon the state of backsliders and apostates. In general, the period from 1877 to 1890 continued to be marked by instability and factionalism among the Montana Saints. The court, which the Prophet Cainan had hoped to be a source of unity, ultimately resulted in divisiveness.

---

13 Cainan to William James and Andrew Hendrikson and Saints in Montana, 2 October 1877, Morrisite Papers, File #1.

On May 10, 1882, the court was convened, and one of the chief topics centered upon the issue of the two small stakes and the need to reunite them.

> Bro. Rasmussen thought some plan should be adopted to bring together the Saints of the 2 Stakes residing on Warm Springs Creek; but did not clearly see how to bring it about. He did not like to see members of the 1st Stake passing the meeting of the 2nd Stake being held at the same time and vice versa—it had a bad appearance to outsiders. . . . Bro. Hendrikson . . . said that he was willing to accede to any arrangement that could be made to bring about a union . . . .
>
> Bro. Eardley favored the consolidation . . . he thought the sooner a coming together of the two sets of neighbors took place, the better for all concerned.
>
> After further discussion and consideration it was unanimously ordered that an opportunity should be granted the Saints of Stake 2 to join Stake 1 so that all the Saints on Warm Springs Creek could become incorporated under one president, and the matter should be placed before them at the Saints meeting on next Sunday.[14]

Had other things remained equal, this spirit of unity might have resulted in an actual reuniting of the Saints, but fate had already intervened. Unknown to the members of the court, the Prophet Cainan had died on April 25, leaving the following explicit instructions: "Let the organization remain as it is for 12 months after my decease; then let Brother James be placed before the whole Church when assembled at the year's end, and if sustained by uplifted hands, there let him remain, and so on, from year to year."[15]

Unfortunately, the clarity of those instructions was obscured by a letter from George Williams (Cainan) written to "Dear Bro. James" on March 16, 1882. "Be watchful; often engage in secret prayer. *As for wisdom to guide the little band . . . I leave you in charge after my decease* [emphasis added]."

Because of the prophet's death, no action was taken to unify the two stakes. Instead, when the court met on November 10, 1882, the prophet's death was officially noted and his letters of instruction were read. It was decided to retain the present organization and to schedule a meeting for April 25, 1883, at the Lord's House, where the question of William James's presidency would be put to a vote by "a General Assembly of the Whole Church."

On the appointed date the general assembly was held. Thirty-one Saints, including William James, were present. Nineteen voted to sustain James as president. Ten voted against him and one abstained.

---

14 Minutes of the court meeting at Willow Glen Meeting House, 10 May 1882, Warm Springs Creek, Deer Lodge County, Montana, Morrisite Papers, File #7.

15 Cainan to Brethren in Montana, 29 January 1882, Walthanstow, Essex, England, Morrisite Papers, File #1.

> Bro. Henrikson declared Bro. James duly elected President for one year.
>
> Bro. James arose to speak and express his surprise that so many had opposed him. What had he done to them that they should treat him so? And why did those brethren and sisters who had voted against him, come to him with smiling faces and call him brother? He despised such people, and they showed by their actions they were hypocrites.
>
> Bro. Henrikson appealed to the minority to sustain the action of the majority, and called upon each of the opposers to say what they intended to do, upon which each one who cast a negative vote spoke their determination not to abide by the action of the majority—they would not sustain W. M. James as President.
>
> Most of them indulged in bitter accusations against Bros. James, Henrikson, and Eardley claiming this was an individual scheme of theirs.
>
> Bro. Henrikson announced that 30 days grace would be extended to each of the opposers during which time they could apply to their respective Stake Presidents, and certify their willingness to sustain Bro. James as president: otherwise their names would be dropped from the role of membership.
>
> President James announced that he had chosen as his Counsellors: Brother Henrikson to be First and Bro. Eardley to be Second.[16]

There is no evidence in the record that those in opposition to William James's presidency recanted. If they did not, the number of Saints in full fellowship was greatly reduced by their defection.

No record of James's reelection that following year is available, but it may be assumed that he was resustained, for he continued to preside until April 1886. It is evident that William James was not pleased at the prospect of having to stand for reelection each year. On November 10, 1884, he asserted that "his election as President of the Church which took place on April 25, 1883, was for all time, and could not be interfered with by anyone. It was a matter of birthright, and could not be changed until God shall call another Prophet."

The court challenged him on this point, affirming "that Bro. James was no more eligible for the position than other high priests. And that the President shall be chosen on each subsequent 25th of April." At the same meeting it was unanimously ordered that August 9 of each year should be set aside as a special feast day to celebrate the dedication of the Lord's House. Also, February 14 of each year should be set apart to celebrate the birthday of the Lord's servant, Cainan. Those dates were celebrated for many years by the surviving Morrisites—long after their original significance was obscure if not forgotten.

---

16 From Minutes of the General Church Assembly convened at the Lord's House, 25 April 1883, Race Track, Montana, Morrisite Papers, File #7.

The Heavenly City

As noted earlier, James and George Dove visited the Montana Morrisites in the fall of 1885. The court meeting of November 10 noted their presence and passed a resolution to be published in the Deer Lodge *New North West* newspaper "disavowing any connection with those pretenders, so that the people who know of us may not be misled by them." The Montana leadership was especially concerned that the Doves had rejected the mission of the Prophet Cainan and taught that the Kingdom of God would be established at South Weber, Utah, instead of Deer Lodge, Montana. The Montana Morrisites wanted to believe in the words of the prophet given to them on January 6, 1879.

> In that region where you dwell, extending East, West, South and North—in this region will come down the City of the Great King. Before that, many wise men shall find their way there, endowed with intelligence from the Lord to map out and make ready for our dear Lord's coming, with thousands who have toiled and suffered with him here. You are the pioneers. The climate shall be moderated by the earth's 3rd motion southward, without interference with her diurnal and annual motion by which she will be fitted to bring forth all the choice vegetations and floral grandeur she is entitled to yield. No beast of prey may find a place there. All rank and unprofitable growth shall be banished at that day. Neighbor shall meet neighbor in perfect accord, and say—my children are numerous, and everyone sound in body and judgment—and so are mine [yours] . . . . In those days the old men shall not weep, neither shall they depart in sorrow or pain; but angels shall bear them to their resting place. And lights shall be on every hill, and on every dwelling place as the Sun for brightness. And like birds of the air shall men move from place to place, and hold converse with one another. A pure language shall be given from their childhood by which all shall do the will of God on the sides of the North as the angels do in His presence.[17]

A few months later the prophet continued in the same vein: "For the choice place of the earth is handed over to you. Its beauties and riches in part, are yet hidden. But your children will develop it more and more. *For there will be built the City of the Great King* [emphasis added]."[18] The revelations of the Prophet Cainan offered great hope for the future, but the Kingdom of God continually encountered impeding circumstances.

George Thompson Elected President

The minutes of the May 10, 1886, court meeting held in the Lord's House at Race Track reveal some severe problems resulting in a dramatic alteration

17 Cainan to William James, 6 January 1879, Morrisite Papers, File #1.

18 Cainan to William James, Summer 1879, Morrisite Papers, File #1.

in the leadership structure of the Morrisite church. William James failed to appear at the court, and Andrew Hendrikson presided in his absence. Hendrikson declared that Brother James had apostatized and that his place on the court should be filled by someone else. Hendrikson's longtime friend, George Johnson, present by invitation, was appointed to James's position on the court.

> Bro. Hendrikson then offered the following Preamble and Resolution: Whereas, it having come to the knowledge of the Church that President William M. James was assuming to be the sole dictator and revelator of the Church, and under that assumption was promulgating false doctrines in the meetings, and whereas, when arraigned before a General Priesthood meeting of the whole Church which convened at the Lord's House at Race Track on April 18, 1886, he reaffirmed his determination not to be subjected to the examination and criticisms of any council or of the Court appointed for that purpose by revelation through the Lord's Servant Cainan and whereas, he claimed in that Council to be beyond the reach of the combined power and authority of the entire church, and did threaten to cut off and disfellowship all who would not accept him with his claims, and whereas on the following Sunday, April 25, 1886, the General Church Assembly convened at the Lord's House at Race Track for the purpose of electing a President of the Church in Montana and he willfully and purposely neglected to attend said Church Assembly and was in consequence, suspended from the Presidency and was superseded to the election of Bro. George Thompson of London, England, as President of the Church . . . .
>
> Resolved by this court assembled . . . that Bro. Wm. James be suspended from the Presidency of the Church also from the Presidency of the Court and from his membership in said Court, for the Crimes of userpation of authority, and heresy.
>
> Bro. Hendrickson moved to suspend Bro. Wm. M. James from his membership in the Church until he shall make full restitution for his rebellion against the teachings and order of the Church.[19]

At the same meeting, John R. Eardley was appointed president of Stake No. 1 replacing James. Hendrikson noted that eleven members of the church had failed to sustain the election of Thompson as church president, and they were given thirty days to do so or forfeit their membership. In a matter of only three years, support for the presidency of William James had completely reversed itself. Whereas those who had failed to support him previously were cut off, now those who supported him were excommunicated.

Two years later the disagreements either had been resolved or the dissidents had been expelled, for George Thompson was unanimously sustained

19 Minutes of Court Meeting, Lord's House, 10 May 1886, Race Track, Deer Lodge County, Montana, Morrisite Papers, File #7.

at the April 25, 1888, general assembly. The number of voters was not recorded. He was given the same support in 1889 and 1890.

William James remained estranged from the Race Track group, but on May 10, 1890, he was invited to attend the court meeting in the hope of effecting a reconciliation. He attended the meeting but reaffirmed his conviction that he was the rightful president of the church. He reported that a number of members still considered him to be their leader, that he was holding meetings with them, and implied that the Race Track group rather than himself had been cut off from the church. He said, "Bro. Cainan had left him in charge" as he understood it, and there he intended to remain. A reconciliation never occurred, and the Montana Morrisites remained divided.

Although the Montana Morrisites experienced factionalism, bickering, and disagreement about points of doctrine and leadership, they still maintained a basic sense of common identity. The most important common thread was continued loyalty to Joseph Morris and Joseph Smith. This thread was interwoven through the fabric of their lives. In addition, the majority of them were Scandinavian in origin. This common ethnic identity helped even more to foster at least some cooperation and interaction among them. Many of them were unwilling to worship together, but they could and did socialize and work together on a more secular level. At least one observer noting this tendency concluded that "the Morrisites in the Deer Lodge Valley seemed to be more socially than religiously oriented."[20] That statement might have been true in the mid-twentieth century, but at an earlier time it would be more nearly correct to conclude that deep and common religious and ethnic roots provided the primary and fundamental basis for their social relationships. The eventual disintegration of the Morrisite church in Montana did not result from a lack of religious conviction or commitment. On the contrary, individual religious commitment often precluded organizational religious unity.

By the end of the nineteenth century, the Montana Morrisites were caught in a theological trap that perhaps could have been escaped if a strong, capable, charismatic leader had emerged; unfortunately, one did not. The Morrisites, like the Mormons, believed in a strong, centralized, authoritarian leadership structure based upon a charismatic spokesman for God. They were steeped in this ideology, but were forced by default to conduct their affairs largely on a congregational basis. Local and personal differences that might have been readily resolved by a central authority simply could not be handled democratically without producing factionalism. The issue of

20 D. E. Cornelius, "Mormonism in Montana, 1857–1898" (M.A. thesis, University of Montana, 1962).

authoritarian leadership was never resolved. In general, the earlier leaders tried to lead through authoritarian methods, but their source of authority was constantly being challenged. Virtually all of the serious disputes over leadership centered upon issues of authority. Both leaders and followers accepted the assumption that a leader must literally trace his authority directly to God. Unless he claimed prophethood, he must trace it through a prophet, but such tracings were seldom accepted by more than a minority of Morrisites at any given time. Ultimately, this emphasis upon the need for charismatic central authority contributed significantly to the demise of the movement.

George Thompson seems never to have assumed a definitive leadership role, although he did correspond with the Montana Morrisites for several years and gave them words of advice and encouragement. He was a kind and deeply religious man, but like his longtime friend and associate, Cainan, he shrank from attempting to impose his own belief system upon others. Thompson's close association with the Prophet Cainan kept him in the limelight as far as the Montana Morrisites were concerned, and undoubtedly that accounted for his election to the presidency, but there is no evidence that he sought or even desired to assume a general leadership role. The title of president was literally thrust upon him. He was not indifferent to wearing the mantle, but he lacked the enthusiasm and charisma the movement so desperately needed at that time.

Although part of Thompson's motivation for returning to England as a missionary had been his faith in the Prophet Cainan, there was more to it than that. His experiences since leaving England had been largely a series of disappointments, privations, and tragedies, and his wife, Frances, had never been able to adjust to the rigors of pioneer life in the West. They had been married in 1849 in England, had joined the Mormon church and migrated to America in 1853. Their eldest child, Emma, born in 1850, grew to maturity, but all five subsequent children died. One died at sea in 1853, one in St. Louis in 1854, one at Soda Springs in 1865, and another at the same place in 1866. The Thompsons became disillusioned with Mormonism after arriving in Utah and joined the Morrisites in 1861. They assembled with the faithful at Kington Fort and experienced all of the disappointments and privations of those who survived the winter of 1862. Thompson was one of the first to enroll in the Morrisite army, supporting Joseph Morris to the very end. As previously noted, when Morris was killed, Thompson placed himself over the body and requested that the posse shoot him too, because "he had nothing left to live for." One posse member attempted to shoot Thompson, but his gun misfired, and other members of the posse then dragged him away.

After the Morrisite conflict, the Thompsons joined with the Connor wagon train for Soda Springs. It was there that Thompson first met the Prophet Cainan.

As noted earlier, Thompson's wife, Frances, died in Liverpool in September 1867, apparently on the very day they arrived back in England. Their sixth child died two days later. Since his only surviving daughter was still living in Deer Lodge, Thompson returned to England without family, friends, or means.

In 1870, with the approval and urging of Cainan, Thompson married a second time. His wife brought with her a substantial dowry, which assisted him in establishing a mercantile. This he managed until her death about 1890. In 1891 he married Katie Morrell, a semi-invalid, and they soon embarked for America, where they hoped to live happily near his daughter, Emma Thompson Just, who had moved from Deer Lodge to the banks of the Blackfoot River in eastern Idaho.[21] But tragedy was not to be denied. On November 6, 1892, Katie died while giving birth to a premature child, who also died.

Despite Thompson's many tragic experiences, he has been described by his granddaughter, Agnes Just Reid, as a calm and contented man who was more interested in comforting others than in being comforted. Yet these problems, plus his need to make a living, did take their spiritual toll. Thompson was unable to provide the dynamic leadership the Morrisites so badly needed.

The Montana records do not mention Thompson after 1890, but it is likely that he continued to serve as their nominal leader in absentia, even after returning to the United States. On June 4, 1894, while riding with his sister near Ririe, Idaho, his horse bolted and ran away. He and his sister were both thrown from the cart and against a bridge abutment, killing them both. Thus, a life filled with personal tragedy ended in the same vein.

Without a strong charismatic leader and a vital organization, the Morrisite church continued to decline. Proselytizing, always haphazard and faltering, ceased entirely. The children of the original converts began to lose interest, and no provision was made to prepare them for active participation or leadership. It is unclear whether another general president of the Morrisite church was elected after the death of George Thompson, but in all probability he was the last.

Andrew Hendrikson served as president of the Montana Morrisites from 1886 until his death on July 3, 1921. He was succeeded by George Johnson, who had been his friend and associate for over fifty years. Johnson presided at the Lord's House until shortly before his death at the age of ninety-eight, April 29, 1954.

Contrary to all other Morrisite leaders, Hendrikson and Johnson had never been affiliated with the Mormon church. Hence, they were less

21 Agnes Just Reid, *Letters of Long Ago,* Tanner Trust Fund edition (Salt Lake City, Utah: University of Utah Library, 1973).

oriented toward Mormon doctrine, authority structure, and leadership patterns than their predecessors. They revered the name of Joseph Morris, but they had never known him and were selective in preaching his doctrines. Neither of them was actively interested in promoting the principal of reincarnation, and they never developed the strong antipathy towards the Mormons that was so characteristic of those who had participated in the Weber battle. Both of them believed in the Second Advent, but they were not obsessed with its immediacy. For all practical purposes, long before Johnson's death, the millenarian fire that had consumed Morris and his immediate disciples burned out.

After the influence of William James declined and John Eardley left Montana about 1900, Morrisite styles of leadership and sources of doctrine became more and more eclectic. In later years George Johnson was more humanistic than fundamentalistic, and he evidenced kindly tolerance toward all creeds. His preaching came to resemble liberal Protestantism much more than conservative Mormonism.

As time went by, options to the Morrisite church became more appealing and acceptable to many members, especially as its sectlike qualities diminished. The Reorganized Church of Jesus Christ of Latter Day Saints began active proselytizing in Montana in 1868. Except for polygamy, the reorganized church taught most of the basic principles of Mormonism. Thus, it was attractive enough to gain numerous converts from the more conservative Morrisites. More liberal Morrisites began to be attracted toward conventional Protestant denominations. By the 1940s the active Morrisite membership had declined to less than a dozen.

As the last Morrisite leader, George Johnson was deeply respected and revered by those who knew him. At his funeral it was said that he was "strong, fearless, tender, sympathetic; incapable of meanness; blazing against all kinds of wrong, upholding the right; his heart and mind deep and wide as the ocean, simple and transparent as a child's; keen for the truth of God." His eulogy ended with a poem he had written himself.

Death is a beautiful transition—passing over into
  the spiritual world called paradise.

All evil, sickness, and sorrow is banished there.
  Perfect Health, peace and harmony prevail with all.

There father, mother, brother and sister meet again—
  Then all sorrows will be turned into joy.

With the death of George Johnson, the Morrisite church also came to an end. The Lord's House was boarded up, as it remains today. The bitter winds sweeping through the valley remind us that, contrary to Cainan's prophecy, the winter climate was not moderated, and in summer the dusty streets of Deer Lodge contrast sharply with his vision of the beautiful City of the Great King. Yet, as Cainan predicted, lights on the hills and dwelling places shine at night as the sun for brightness, and men do move from place to place like birds of the air. Perhaps only secular features of Cainan's prophecies have been fulfilled, and even these may be coincidental. But descendants of the Morrisites still inhabit much of western Montana, and many of them are firmly convinced that their forbears did indeed find a paradise on earth.

16 The Deer Lodge Jesus

Although the Morrisite Movement actually ended with the death of George Johnson in 1954, the Deer Lodge prophecy of George Williams (Cainan), surfaced again several decades after Johnson's death and a century after Williams' demise. In 1979, an obscure messianic sect headquartered in Missoula, Montana, made a startling announcement. The sect's name was Baha'is Under the Provisions of the Covenant. Its leader was a local chiropractor named Leland Jensen, affectionately known as Doc. Using scriptural and circumstantial proofs, Jensen claimed that he was the returned Jesus Christ, and he predicted that nuclear bombs would be dropped on the United States precisely as 5:55 P.M. Mountain Daylight Time on April 29, 1980. He induced his followers (some 150) to build bomb shelters, and more than a dozen were constructed in the Missoula area.

When Jensen's initial prediction was not fulfilled, he announced a new date and time for the attack—May 7, 1980 at 6:11 A.M., explaining that the delay had occurred in order that the world might have an opportunity to hear the warning of their savior and be saved. After May 7 passed without incident, Jensen proposed that the bombs would fall on May 22 or 23, but by that time many of his followers did not even bother to hide in their shelters.

These failed prophecies greatly lowered the morale of Jensen's followers, and several members defected, especially in outlying locations, and proselytizing virtually ceased.[1]

Jensen's Background

Before moving to Montana, Doc Jensen had been a well-known Baha'i teacher who had been expelled from the world Baha'i Faith in 1960 because of aligning himself with a dissident leader named Mason Remey, who taught that a great flood would inundate much of the central and eastern portions of the United States. This belief led Jensen to move to the Missoula Valley,

1 Balch, Robert W., Gwenn Farnsworth, and Sue Watkins, "When the Bombs Drop: Reactions to Disconfirmed Prophecy in a Millenial Sect," *Sociological Perspectives* 26, no. 2 (April 1983), pp. 137–58.

some three thousand feet above sea level, where he expected to escape the flood waters. (Ironically, the Missoula Valley had several times been buried under hundreds of feet of ice-age water some fourteen thousand years ago when Lake Missoula covered the entire Clark Fork drainage with a volume half that of Lake Michigan. It would have been nearly one thousand feet deep where Jensen's house stood.)[2]

The central and eastern states flood never occurred, and perhaps that prophecy failure was another factor besides a 1963 doctrinal dispute in leading Jensen to entirely quit teaching. According to Balch et al., in 1969 Jensen was convicted of performing a "lewd and lascivious act" on a fifteen-year-old patient, and despite his claims of a frame up, he was sentenced to twenty years in the Montana State Penitentiary.[3] Not long after Jensen began serving his sentence, an angel visited him in his cell, he later claimed, and told him of his spiritual identity.

Recognizing the remarkable congruence between events in his own life and certain biblical prophecies, Jensen proclaimed in 1971 that he was Joshua, the exalted priest prophesied in Zechariah. Jensen announced that Joshua was the returned Jesus who would establish the kingdom after the atomic holocaust. Like Joseph Morris and George Williams, Jensen claimed to have numerous other biblical identities. In particular, Morris and Jensen each claimed to be the Seventh Angel, which became part of the title of Doc Jensen's short monograph published in 1994.

Once the angel had alerted Jensen to his sacred calling, he began to carefully study various ancient records in addition to the Bible, including Baha'i teachings, pyramidology, the Quran, and Buddhist writings. In trying to tie all of these together, he concluded that all of the evidence led to an inescapable conclusion: a nuclear attack was imminent. Strangely enough, he believed that the war would begin in 1980 when the superpowers became enmeshed in conflict over Mideastern oil. Although no nuclear weapons were used, the first Gulf War, in 1990, and the second Iraq conflict, which began in 2003, fit well his emphasis upon control of oil and weapons of mass destruction as underlying causes of conflict, but his prediction turned out to be one and two decades ahead of actual events. Jensen further believed that after four waves of destruction, the world would be free of evil, and the remainder of mankind would accept the Baha'i Faith, bringing peace and harmony for the next thousand years. He announced this would happen by the year 2000.

Not long after the angel's visit to Jensen's prison cell, he began to hold evening meetings with his fellow inmates. Although many prisoners thought

---

2 *Missoulian*, August 26, 2004.

3 Balch et al., "When the Bombs Drop,"pp. 140–41.

he was a crackpot, others were attracted to his apocalyptic message and became devoted followers. It appears that about twenty to thirty inmates regularly attended his meetings, and some of them became effective proselytizers in their own right. Jensen was paroled in 1973 and immediately began proselytizing outside the prison—especially in Missoula, where he gained a sizable following.[4]

One of Jensen's central beliefs was that the Montana State Prison in Deer Lodge was actually Ezekiel's Temple as described in the Bible. It was on a trip to the prison that the leaders of Jensen's sect were introduced to the prophecies of George Williams, via this book, *Joseph Morris and the Saga of the Morrisites*. In it they found an account of George Williams's January 6, 1879, prophecy identifying Deer Lodge, Montana, as the place where the Second Advent of Jesus would occur and where the City of the Great King would be built at a future time. The Baha'i leaders and members seized upon Williams's prophecy as full confirmation of the high calling of Dr. Jensen and a validation of his own prophetic powers.

Although *The Saga of the Morrisites* was first published in 1981 and hence could have been available earlier to the Baha'i group, they assert that they were first introduced to the Morrisites and George Williams in 1990 on the occasion of their trip to Deer Lodge for the purpose of measuring the Montana State Prison to see if its dimensions corresponded to those of Ezekiel's Temple. They reported, "To our amazement in God's perfection, all the prophesied dates found in both the Bible and the Great Pyramid of Giza were also found inculcated in the stone masonry of the prison." Their guide told them of the book about the Morrisites, who anticipated that the Second Advent would take place in Deer Lodge.

> We were elated and said, "the prophecy is fulfilled right here in this prison." None of us, not even Dr. Leland Jensen, who fulfills the prophecy for the return of Jesus, had ever heard of the Morrisites before. His proclamation made on April 29, 1971, was based purely on the fulfillment of Biblical prophecy in Zechariah 3 and other places, which pinpoint the return of Jesus, the High Priest . . . in this Old Montana State Prison which is the "stone with seven eyes" [Zechariah 3:9] that Jesus II, the High Priest is to have before him. Therefore, a completely independent source, not associated with the Baha'i Faith prophesied of his coming to Deer Lodge in the prison, the seven-towered Temple of Ezekiel.[5]

On March 21, 1991, Neal Chase, one of Jensen's chief lieutenants, issued a press release that announced: "The Return of Jesus has appointed a quorum of seven out of his 12 apostles to form the Second International Baha'i

4 Balch et al., "When the Bombs Drop,"pp.141–43.

5 Dr. Leland Jensen, *The Seventh Angel Sounded.* Acme Press, 1994. p.40.

Council. This is the preliminary step toward the establishment of a World Government, called New World Order of Baha'u'llah which is the Kingdom of God on earth." The press release went on to give the group's brief official Baha'i version of the significance of the Morrisite migration to Deer Lodge.

> The appointment of the Second IBC (International Baha'i Council) is an epic-making event that parallels the announcement of the return of Jesus in Ezekiel's Temple in Deer Lodge. This event was heralded by the migration of the Morrisites to Deer Lodge, Montana under the direction of the Mormon prophet, Geoge Williams, as John the Baptist heralded Jesus on his first coming. In April of 1863, about the same time Baha'u'llah made his proclamation in Baghdad, Iraq the Morrisites came to Deer Lodge by the instruction of George Williams to 'prepare the way of the Lord,' the second coming of Jesus whose mission is to establish the New World Order . . .[6]

According to Balch et al, between 1979 and 1995, Doc Jensen and Neal Chase made twenty specific eschatological predictions. Of these the first two were made by Jensen and anticipated worldwide catastrophes. The previously noted first prophecy gained considerable media attention. The second prediction surfaced in 1985, when Jensen pronounced that Halley's Comet would fall into the earth's orbit in 1986, break up, and crash into the earth with devastating effect, creating physical, social, and political upheaval that would culminate in the Battle of Armageddon. The failure of these two prophecies caused some dismay and disaffection of members, but Jensen and Chase continued in their belief that they were doing God's will.

During the 1990s, the making of predictions was taken over by Neal Chase, with the approval of Doc Jensen. During that decade, Chase produced eighteen predictions pertaining to small-scale disasters that would cumulatively lead to the Apocalypse. These included upheavals from comets, asteroids, and meteors, but most pertained to nuclear attacks upon New York City by Middle Eastern terrorists. Although none of these predictions unfolded precisely as given, Chase asserted that all had been essentially fulfilled. On the other hand, Balch et al. conclude that none of the twenty predictions actually occurred.[7]

In 1990, Chase wrote a monograph called *Ezekiel's Temple in Montana.* It went into considerable detail about the connection between the Morrisites and the mission of Leland Jensen, "Jesus II." However, it contains numerous errors regarding dates and intentions of the Morrisites who settled in

6 Baha'i Press Release. March 21, 1991.

7 Balch, Robert, John Domitrovich, Barbara Mahnke, and Vanessa Morrison, "Fifteen Years of Failed Prophecy," in Robbins, Thomas and Susan J. Palmer, eds., *Millennium, Messiahs, and Mayham* (New York and London: Routledge Press,1997), pp. 73–90.

the Deer Lodge Valley. It also attributes much more prophetic ability to George Williams than he actually possessed. Equating Ezekiel's Temple with the Montana State Prison also requires a considerable stretch of the imagination. Certainly, the assertion that the gathering of surviving Morrisites held August 9, 1969, at the Lord's House (the first full day of Jensen's imprisonment in Deer Lodge) was intended to anticipate the Second Advent has no substantive proof. The Morrisites celebrated two special holidays—February 14, the anniversary of George William's birth, and August 9, the anniversary of the dedication of the Lord's House in 1879. Both were designated as feast days. They were more social than religious occasions. By 1969, there was little, if any, interest in the imminent Second Advent on the part of the few surviving Morrisites. By then, all were second or third generation followers of Morris. They were far removed from the prophecies of George Williams or Joseph Morris.

Leland "Doc" Jensen died on August 6, 1996. Neal Chase then assumed the leadership of that Baha'i sect, but it continued to decline. Eventually, Chase moved to Colorado and little, if anything, remains of the movement founded by Jensen in the Deer Lodge Prison.

Although the Missoula-based Baha'i group was relatively small and seemingly obscure, several of Neil Chase's apocalyptic new releases gained national attention. *Harper's Magazine* devoted 1½ pages to reproducing six of his releases, dating from August 4, 1993, to October 9, 1994. All of the releases dealt with recent or future catastrophes in New York City. The reproductions appeared under the heading, "The End Is Nearish."[8]

8 *Harper's Magazine,* February 1995, pp. 22–24.

Conclusion In Retrospect

The preceding chapters have been an effort to accurately present the colorful saga of the Morrisites, but as so often happens in historic matters, a number of important questions still remain unanswered. The real complexity of the situation is belied by the simplistic answers given earlier by partisan observers who either tried to dismiss the Morrisites as deluded banditti fully deserving the justice meted out to them or saw them as innocent victims of religious persecution. The Morrisite drama was played on a stage constructed of social, cultural, political, religious, and geographic components—components far more diverse and colorful than the simple black and white backdrop painted in earlier times. Whether the outcome of the drama was as inevitable as it might appear, the fact remains that a real tragedy occurred at Kington Fort, which resulted ultimately in the disintegration of a thriving religious movement and the shattering of millennial dreams.

The seven-score years since Joseph Morris recorded his first revelation have taken with them all those who knew him personally and all of their children. With them also have gone many of the firsthand accounts that might have given answers to many questions now unanswerable. But, fortunately, they also took with them most of the bitterness and hatred infecting participants on all sides, whether Mormon, Morrisite, or Gentile. Perhaps now that more than a century and a half has passed, we may look more dispassionately at the Morrisite experience and hopefully see with less partisan eyes the lessons it has to offer.

The Morrisites at Kington Fort were the epitome of pathos—suffering indescribably for an ideology and a way of life that were ultimately untenable. That such suffering contained a large measure of nobility can hardly be denied, yet the obvious message that fanaticism breeds serious consequences is not to be denied either.

What if Morris Had Survived?

Although this question is moot, it is nonetheless intriguing. What would have happened to the Morrisites if Joseph Morris had not been killed during the surrender proceedings at Kington Fort, but instead had been convicted and then pardoned, as was the case for most of his militant followers. Put another way, was Morris's death the key to Morrisite disintegration, or would the movement have declined anyway? On this point, we can only speculate, but our speculation need not be based entirely upon pure guesswork or wishful thinking. The Morrisite experience was unique in many respects, but not entirely so. Scores of other millennial sects have followed a prophet who foretold the Second Coming or some other miraculous event with no more accuracy than Joseph Morris. Their followers often suffered grave hardships and bitter disappointments, but the majority seem to have remained faithful, at least for a time. On the other hand, some followers defected at the very first sign of prophecy failure. Nevertheless, one thing seems clear. Although millennial movements are remarkably resilient, they can seldom withstand a long series of built-up expectations based upon specific predictions followed by a series of disappointments when these predictions fail. After a while, the people lose both interest and faith, and the movement declines. In order for a prophet to retain his credibility and his following, he must provide an acceptable explanation for the apparent prophecy failures and then begin making more general and abstract predictions less susceptible to specific disconfirmation. There is some evidence that Joseph Morris was beginning to learn this lesson in the winter of 1862 when he refused to set any more specific dates for the deliverance of his people, but by June he had reverted to his earlier pattern of making highly specific predictions of miraculous events. In any case, the Morrisite conquest by the posse was so clearly out of line with the central thrust of Morris's prophecies that he would have been hard put to find a suitable explanation if he had lived. It was much easier for his followers to revere him as a "crucified" martyr than it would have been to accept his explanations in the flesh. It is even quite possible that he might have become a scapegoat once the enormity of the consequences of his unfulfilled prophecies was fully understood. After all, several faithful followers lost their lives as a result of his prophetic resistance to the posse, while others were frightfully wounded. All this was contrary to Morris's assurance that none would be harmed. In death it was said of him that his mission upon the earth was actually symbolic and a foreshadowing of that which was to come. This explanation made it possible for other prophets such as Cainan and Davies to emerge and attract a following of his disciples, but it might have been much harder for Morris to have retained the prophetic role himself.

Actually, the issue of Morrisite continuity had both practical and ideological components. At the time of Morris's death the entire colony was destitute and had been for several months. The need for decisive practical solutions to physical want and deprivation would have been a matter of absolute necessity whether Morris had survived or not. It seems doubtful whether Morris could have successfully dealt with that problem considering his long personal history of financial mismanagement and economic dependence. Perhaps his counselors, Cook and Banks, could have helped resolve that issue if allowed more autonomy, but, as noted previously, Morris had successfully brought both of them to bay when they had exercised too much autonomy a few months earlier.

In any case, Morris would have had to completely revise his orientation not only toward the procurement of necessities but also toward the conditions expected to accompany the Second Advent. The late Dale Morgan once declared: "But what is perhaps ultimately most fascinating is the fact that the Morris schism may be seen as a Mormon microcosm. The parallels with Joseph Smith are many and exact, the surrounding culture viewing him as a fanatic or worse, his adherents as lawless banditti, etc. But in this instance the surrounding culture was the Mormon culture itself.[1]

If Dale Morgan was correct, clues to the survival of the Morrisite movement might be found in examining the parallel experiences of the Mormons. And to some extent that has already been done in regard to their leadership and proselytizing. Nevertheless, in one respect Joseph Morris and his successors were very much unlike Joseph Smith and Brigham Young. Both Smith and Young believed that a great many temporal preparations must be made before Christ would return to earth. At the very least these included the establishment of a kingdom of the faithful, the building of a Holy City, and the construction within that city of a magnificent temple that would be His abode. On the other hand, Morris taught that Christ's appearance would be contingent only upon the establishment of a kingdom of the faithful and the performance of certain holy rituals. He preached that the faithful would inherit the houses, lands, and substance of the unjust. In effect, his people would inherit the fruits of the labors of others, and the Holy City and temple would be built after Christ had commenced His reign. This underlying philosophy that "the Lord will provide" pervades Morris's writings from his earliest correspondence with Brigham Young to his very last revelation. For example, on May 6 Morris was told by revelation:

> You need not fret about the poverty of these people, for I will provide for them myself. I will continue to open a way for them, so that they will have sufficient food until I deliver an abundance of everything into their hands . . . . Therefore, rest yourself contented and trust in me, and I will supply the needs of my people unto the end. I am the Lord.[2]

1 Personal correspondence with Larry J. Halford, 24 April 1970.

2 Morris, *The Spirit Prevails,* p.541.

Just ten days before the posse appeared, a revelation continued in the same vein: "And now, behold, I say unto you—you need not trouble yourself about the destitute condition of these people. They shall not want for bread; for when they are apparently out of flour, I will open a way for them to obtain more, until I place all the means in this Territory in the hands of my faithful people."[3] Because of this he could never consider long-range solutions to meeting the physical needs of himself or his people. At best he consented to temporary trips into the mountains for fuel, to exchanges of livestock for wheat, to last-minute trips to the mill for flour, and to living in tents, wagon boxes, and dugouts. All of these things were seen as temporary inconveniences until such time as the Savior would appear bringing bounty to His people as a reward for their spiritual steadfastness.

Because of Morris's basically passive approach to meeting the needs of his people, there is reason to believe he was rapidly approaching a management crisis. Every religious movement faces three fundamental challenges that must be satisfactorily resolved. The first is attraction of potential converts, and Morris succeeded there admirably. The second is making of converts, and again Morris must receive high marks. But in regard to the third challenge—postconversion management—Morris was standing on very shaky ground, and the prospects for improvement were not good. Morris had promised too much for too long, and his credibility was approaching its limits, war or no war. In all probability, the Morrisite movement would have declined more rapidly with Joseph Morris alive than with him dead. Three brief prototypical historical examples of abortive millennial movements might serve to illustrate some possible alternative outcomes of the Morrisite movement. These are: the Millerites, the Ghost Dance of the Pai Indians, and the Sun Dance of the Comanches.

In the early 1840s, William Miller preached to a large following of American Protestants that the Second Advent would occur between March 21, 1843, and March 21, 1844. The earlier date became the one originally focused upon, but when Christ failed to appear, attention focused upon the latter months of 1843. By early 1844 the March date was the center of attention, but it came and went without incident. The Millerites, several thousand strong, had experienced several great hopes and disappointments, but they refused to give up their faith. Finally, they focused all of their faith and energy upon the date of October 22, 1844. However, when that time came and the Savior failed to appear, the cumulative disappointment was too great. The movement collapsed almost immediately.[4]

---

3 Morris, *The Spirit Prevails*, p. 598.

4 Leon Festinger, Henry Riecken, and Stanley Schacter, *When Prophecy Fails*, paperback edition (New York: Harper and Row, 1964), pp. 12–23.

In 1889 the Pai Indians of northwestern Arizona embraced a messianic movement known as the Ghost Dance, which was believed to have the power to drive out the white man, restore their earlier way of life, and bring the dead back to life. This movement flourished at first but began to decline by early 1891 because all the dancing had failed to achieve the expected outcome. Then a medicine man named Pay-sui-ya determined to put the Ghost Dance to the supreme test. He organized a dance to resuscitate a tribal member who had just died. The dance was joined with enthusiasm by a large number of followers, but when the corpse began to decompose, their faith left them, the entire movement soon broke up, and Pay-sui-ya was branded as an imposter.[5]

In the summer of 1874 a large band of Comanche Indians invited their Kiowa friends to attend a Sun Dance to try to decide what to do about the depredations of white buffalo hunters who were literally destroying all of the buffalo in their area. Soon they were joined by some northern Cheyennes and Arapahos who were also angry with the white hunters. Isatai, a medicine man possessing great magic, assured them that if they would attack the white hunters, his magic would protect them from their bullets. Under the leadership of Quanah Parker, some seven hundred warriors attacked the hunters' headquarters at Adobe Wells. The hunters opened up on the Indians with long-range, telescopic-sighted buffalo rifles before they could get close enough to do harm with their own short-range weapons. In a few minutes fifteen Indians were dead and many more were severely wounded. They returned to their camp, where they took out their frustration and rage upon the hapless medicine man. He was severely beaten and probably would have been killed if Quanah Parker had not intervened.[6]

And, of course, the decline of Doc Jensen's more recent Baha'i movement after numerous failed prophesies illustrates the toll that high expectations followed by great disappointments may take.

The above examples do not, of course, prove what would have happened to the Morrisite movement if Joseph Morris had survived the Morrisite War. Nevertheless, his prophecies by that time had so frequently failed (and with such devastating consequences) that the prospects of his continuing to successfully perform the prophetic role were anything but bright.

Why Did So Many Remain Faithful for So Long a Time?

Given their great privations, physical sufferings, external harassments, and exposure to numerous prophecy failures, how could so many of Morris's

5 See Henry F. Dobyns and Robert C. Euler, *The Ghost Dance of 1889 among the Pai Indians of Northwestern Arizona* (Prescott, Arizona: Prescott College Press, 1967), pp. 30–31.

6 Brown, *Bury My Heart at Wounded Knee, pp.* 254–56.

followers have remained faithful for so long? This intriguing question deserves more than passing attention, for it has implications not only for the Morrisite movement but also for other prophetic movements with great demands and great expectations. In any case, the number of defectors during 1861 and early 1862, and even in the face of the armed posse, seems to have been only a tiny fraction of those who remained faithful to the very end. How could this be?

Perhaps a more meaningful answer can be found if this question is rephrased. There is substantial evidence that a great majority of the Morrisites remained with Morris until his death, but we have relatively little direct information about the state of their faith at any given time. Perhaps the real question is: why did so many remain at Kington Fort instead of departing? This question allows for much more latitude in dealing with Morrisite motivations than if we assume that remaining with a group is necessarily direct evidence of faith in its ideology and leadership. Perhaps there are considerations in conjunction with, or other than, faith that allow people to join and remain with groups. Let us explore some of these in regard to the Morrisites. But in doing so we need not and should not make the assumption that large numbers of Morrisites were lacking in faith. In all probability, as individuals they experienced fluctuations in faith and commitment. Perhaps at times they were in every sense "true believers." At other times they may have been skeptics. Yet most of them remained at Kington Fort until removed by force of arms.

First of all, we must remember that the Morrisite enclave was hundreds of miles from any substantial non-Mormon settlement and was surrounded by people seen as hostile by the Morrisites. To have departed probably would have required that defectors seek assistance from those they feared as enemies. The Mormons might have welcomed defectors with open arms, but that would have seemed quite unlikely to many Morrisites. After all, they had all once been Mormons, and many of them were excommunicated apostates. They knew it and so did the Mormons.

Second, virtually all of the Morrisites were destitute of horses, oxen, wagons, food, and other supplies. Having consecrated their possessions to the church, they no longer had any means of escape other than on foot. Those few who tried to reappropriate their consecrated possessions and depart had been imprisoned. The message was clear. Departure was a risky business.

Third, an armed guard surrounded the Morrisite enclave. The Morrisites claimed this guard was to protect them from depredations from the Mormons. The Mormons claimed the guard was established to prevent the escape of dissidents. In all likelihood the guard served both functions. It might well have discouraged some external harassment, but it certainly would have made the departure of defectors more problematic.

Fourth, a large proportion of the Morrisites were recently emigrated Scandinavians who spoke little or no English. Thus they were faced with all of the above impediments plus the inability to communicate effectively. This would have seemed like a formidable obstacle if they had contemplated seeking help on the outside.

Fifth, the Morrisites regularly participated in ceremonies, testimony meetings, demonstrations of commitment, and other displays of solidarity when the collective pressure to conform was intense. To have repudiated those experiences would have been difficult, if not truly dangerous.

Sixth, although Morris made numerous unfulfilled predictions, he also made some that were remarkably accurate. Furthermore, he usually produced reasonable explanations whenever a prediction went awry. Given the tendency of believers (or those who want to believe) to focus upon successes and to overlook or reinterpret failures, it is not surprising that Morris retained a large following for a considerable length of time.

In short, many Morrisite experiences reinforced their faith or commitment, and these were complemented by a wide variety of structural conditions making defection difficult, if not impossible.

What of Morris's Personality?

One of the most persistent questions emerging from the story of the Morrisites focuses directly upon the personality of Joseph Morris. There are those who believed he was more than a religious fanatic—that he was "weak minded" or even insane. Apparently both Brigham Young and Joseph's brother, George, regarded him in that light, and even some disciples such as Emma Thompson Just eventually came to question his mental balance. Others, of course, thought he was anything but crazy.

From a modern standpoint, Morris would undoubtedly be judged psychologically disturbed, but it would seem more fair and much more appropriate to judge him within his own social-historical context rather than by ours. Morris lived in a time and place where speaking to God and receiving messages from Him were highly honored and respectable. Furthermore, Morris's prophetic role was closely patterned after that of his predecessor, Joseph Smith. In form, and even to a great extent in substance, most of what he did was well within the religious norms of the Mormons and not without precedent in other nineteenth-century sects. That he was an extremist cannot be doubted, but most prophets have been considered so.

Although Morris may have been mistaken about the source of the mental impressions, which he claimed were revelations, he seems never to have lost complete touch with reality. His revelations were remarkably logical and consistent, given the nature of the premises upon which they were based, and on many occasions he was troubled by the fact that certain revelations apparently had not been fulfilled literally. For example, on the last day of his life Morris was obviously perplexed by the rapidly moving events and the fact that the posse had been able to approach so near without causing the intervention of the Hosts of Heaven in support of the Morrisites. He realized that to fulfill all of the promises he had received by revelation the posse would have to be destroyed by miraculous assistance and above all that he could not surrender and be consistent with those revelations.

During most of his tenure as prophet, Joseph Morris longed to see Jesus Christ with his own eyes as Joseph Smith had claimed to have done, but this wish was never granted. Within his last revelation he was promised: "I have not shown myself unto you in a plain, visible and satisfactory manner up to this time; but I cannot hide my face from you many more hours. I shall have to unveil myself to you and this people in the course of a few hours."[7] Perhaps the failure to see Christ was his great disappointment, for he often referred to it in his writings. He had a keen imagination, but there was some limit to what it allowed him to do. That he was naive and misguided can hardly be doubted, but that can be said for a great many people who have lived quite successfully without psychiatric care or the stigma of institutionalization. As a prophet and mystic, Joseph Morris performed the role remarkably well, at least up to a point, but as an executive and practical political leader, he failed tragically. However, even in this regard he was wise enough to appoint spokesmen and executives with no small ability. The main problem was that he was too sure of his calling as prophet, seer, and revelator to allow his immediate subordinates sufficient autonomy.

Perhaps the most disquieting thing about the personality of Joseph Morris was his tendency to become more and more defensive and more and more fanatic as pressure from the outside increased and defectors began to depart. This, of course, is a common reaction to such crises, but in Morris's case it began to take on truly sinister overtones. Morris made it clear that the three prisoners eventually would be put to death. He frequently stated that apostates must die, and he planned to subject all of his people, except children under fourteen years and adults seventy or over, to a supreme test of loyalty a few days after the great foreshadowing. Those who failed the test were to be immediately killed by the Morrisite army, or by the Hosts of Heaven if the army failed to do its duty. Joseph Morris seems to have had an aversion to personal involvement with violence, but his rhetoric was frightening, and if such a test of loyalty had actually taken place, who can be sure that some zealot in the militia might not have "done his duty"?[8]

7 Morris, *The Spirit Prevails,* p. 630.
8 Morris, *The Spirit Prevails,* p. 570.

What of the Role of Brigham Young?

Another question which emerges from the Morrisite story is the role played in it by Brigham Young. Was he the aloof bystander who allowed things to develop in their own natural course (as his supporters have generally argued), or did he take an active part in helping to shape events so that the Morrisite threat could be stopped before it got completely out of hand? Since little direct evidence has been found to implicate Brigham Young, there seems little value in too much speculation. However, some value might be derived from rephrasing the question. Perhaps it would be more fruitful to ask: was it in Brigham Young's nature to stand aloof from any event in Utah which posed a threat to his leadership or to his conceptions of the welfare of the Mormon church? The answer to that question is, of course, an unequivocal no. Brigham Young was concerned, and he sought tirelessly to promote his own interests as well as those of the church. The real questions then are: (1) how serious a threat did Brigham Young see in the Morrisites, and (2) what steps could be taken if he thought the threat serious?

Evidently as early as February 1861 he saw some threat even from the small, early inroads made by Joseph Morris, for he dispatched two apostles to investigate. Clearly he would not tolerate disloyalty, for he took immediate steps to cut off Morris and all of his followers. Of course, once excommunicated, there were no more direct ecclesiastical sanctions that could be exacted upon them. So what more could be done?

First, there is persuasive evidence that after mid-1861 the Morrisites were subjected to more or less continual harassment and considerable inconvenience by many of their Mormon neighbors and by several Mormon public officials. Was this simply the natural result of two groups competing for the same territory, or was it part of a broader plan designed by Mormon leaders to force the Morrisites from Utah? This is hard to answer, but two things seem reasonably sure: Brigham Young could hardly ignore the harassment taking place since several of the Mormons involved were close to him—most especially Lot Smith, sheriff of Davis County, well-known guerrilla fighter and at times Young's personal bodyguard. Second, Young could have stopped the harassment, but he definitely took no steps to do so. In fact, he apparently encouraged it by forbidding the Mormons to grind wheat or engage in certain kinds of barter with the Morrisites. Of course, it might be said of the Morrisite affair, as has been said of the Mountain Meadows Massacre, that the mischief was entirely the result of excited local extremists who were out of touch with the church's General Authorities. Although this is a tenable hypothesis in the Mountain Meadows affair, it hardly squares with the circumstances surrounding the Morrisites. In the first place, there simply was no time for intervention at Mountain Meadows. The entire affair transpired within a very few days. And the distance was too great to be covered in less than about three days and nights under the best of circumstances. The most recent authoritative and comprehensive study of the Mountain Meadows Massacre has convincingly concluded that Brigham Young could not have been directly involved. The message from Young, insisting that the immigrant train should not be meddled with, reached local Church leaders two days after the immigrants had been massacred.[9] The harassment of the Morrisites, however, persisted for nearly a full year. Furthermore, the events at South Weber unfolded only a day's ride from Salt Lake City, and, of course, much of the legal proceedings originated in that city itself. Brigham Young might possibly have decided to mostly neglect the Morrisite question, but such neglect would have been anything but benign.

What other avenues might Brigham Young have had for dealing with the Morrisites? After all, he no longer held any official political position in Utah. Certainly he had several avenues if he wished to make use of them. First, Judge John F. Kinney was not only a friend of the Mormons, he was a personal friend and confidant of Brigham Young. The content of his letters to Young, especially after mid-1863, makes this perfectly clear. By then Kinney was not only Utah's representative to Congress, he was actively promoting church interests. On his journey from Utah to Washington, D.C., he regularly and in considerable detail reported to Young about possible settlement sites and other church-related interests in the Midwest.[10] Why Kinney should do this when so many capable Mormons were available is something of a mystery, but it does demonstrate that Young and Kinney were anything but strangers. Clearly, Young had the ear of Judge Kinney. Whether he used it against the Morrisites is a matter of conjecture. Second, Frank Fuller, the acting governor, was a Mormon. Presumably, Young could have brought pressure to bear upon him if he had so wished.

Third, by 1862 Robert T. Burton had served the church for many years and had been prominent for a long time in the Nauvoo Legion. The fact that Burton continued to be prominent in the church and in local politics long after the Morrisite War suggests that his actions against the Morrisites were not disapproved of by Mormons generally nor by Young himself. By coincidence or otherwise, Burton was not forced to stand trial for the murder of a Morrisite until after the death of Brigham Young. Certainly Young and Burton were well acquainted, and there can be no doubt of Burton's loyalty to him. Young could have exerted great pressure on Burton as far as the Morrisites were concerned. Whether or not he did has yet to be demonstrated.

---

9 Walker, Turley, and Leonard, *Massacre At Mountain Meadows*, pp. 225 – 26

10 Brigham Young Correspondence, Archives, Historical Department, Church of Jesus Christ of Latter-day Saints, Salt Lake City, Utah.

Indeed, Robert T. Burton was about as close to Brigham Young as any church leader. He had even served for a time a Young's bodyguard. He held many church and civic positions and was a firm believer in polygamy—having three wives, and twenty-seven children. His service for thirty-two years as a member of the Presiding Bishopric placed him in a position of great responsibility for the material welfare of the church. And it is notable that Burton was one of the church leaders present, along with family members, when Brigham Young died. Robert Burton's biographer said of him: "While his life was an example of kindness, unselfishness and fatherly love, he was remembered after his death for his courage in *fighting the enemies of the Church* [emphasis added], his role as a builder of the state, and his service as a Bishop, missionary, and member of the Presiding Bishopric."[11]

The role of Brigham Young in the Morrisite affair has, of course, a direct bearing upon another related question. The Morrisites claimed from the beginning that their problems with the law and with their neighbors were foisted upon them by the Mormons, who were interested primarily in religious retribution. The Mormons, on the other hand, maintained that their only quarrel with the Morrisites was their unwillingness to abide by the law and to be good neighbors. Governor Harding, Colonel Connor, and a good many others agreed with the Morrisites, but the charges and counter charges hardly settled the issue of whether the Morrisite War was fought primarily over legal issues or religious issues. Again, the answer to this question requires some speculation. However, the question might also be more productive if turned around. Perhaps a more meaningful question to ask: what would the outcome of imprisoning the three Morrisite defectors have been if a more normal state of affairs had characterized the Utah territorial government at that time? Specifically, we might ask: would the territorial chief executive have called out such a formidable posse if he had been a Gentile, especially if he had been Stephen S. Harding? If a posse had been formed, would it have been so enthusiastic about the hasty use of cannon and long-range rifles if it had been composed of non-Mormons, especially if it had been made up of California volunteers under the command of Colonel Connor? What would the nature have been of the exchange between the posse and Morrisites if the posse had been commanded by U.S. Marshal Henry W. Lawrence rather than Deputy Marshal Robert T. Burton? And finally, could the Morrisite War have occurred at all ten months earlier or ten months later? The reader may wish to answer these questions, but great caution should be exercised in doing so, for the fate of the Morrisites most assuredly hung in the delicate balance of power found in Utah in 1862.

11 Janet Burton Seegmiller. *Be Kind to the Poor: The Life Story of Robert Taylor Burton* (Robert Taylor Burton Family Organization, Inc., 1988). pp. 327 & 421.

Personal Observations

Although I have been unable to find conclusive, documentary evidence of Brigham Young's involvement in the Morrisite affair, I have concluded, after some four decades of examining what scant evidence there is and after serious contemplation, that Brigham Young must have taken more of an active interest in the proceedings than the extant records reveal. I am inclined to believe Judge Kinney when he asserted that he took no action against the Morrisites without Young's assent. I also conclude that Robert Burton believed it was his duty to take whatever measures were necessary to reduce the perceived threats of Morris and Banks—threats not only to the law but to the Mormon Church as well. The sudden absence of U.S. Marshal Henry W. Lawrence, which placed command of the posse in Burton's hands, might well be explained by motives other than Lawrence's personal desire for a vacation. It does appear that Lawrence was more reluctant to take extreme measures than Burton.

Furthermore, Brigham Young's inflammatory remarks about the surviving Morrisites, given in the Salt Lake Bowery, June 29, 1862 (quoted later in this chapter), made it clear that the Morrisites were unwelcome—that Utah Territory was no place for them. The termination of the Morrisite War probably did not occur exactly as either Morrisites or Mormons expected, but it certainly had the effect of dispelling whatever threats the Mormon leaders saw, whether real or imagined.

Political Implications of the Morrisite Affair

Another general question concerning the Morrisite affair is: what was its significance, if any, in the broader picture of western history, especially in Utah's perennial bid for self-determination through statehood and for closer ties with the United States? This question has many ramifications, but perhaps we can confine ourselves to a few salient points.

The issue of polygamy has for many years been considered a prime deterrent to Utah's struggle for statehood. There can be no doubt that the Mormon practice of plural marriage was a key issue. And in the popular mind at times it may have been the only issue. Nevertheless, in many respects polygamy was probably more a symbol of the basic struggle between the authority of the federal government and the theocracy of the Mormons than a political issue in and of itself. In any case, the Morrisites were considered by most observers to be against plural marriage and in that respect on the "right" side of morality. From that perspective it was also reasonable to assume that the Mormons would do everything possible to suppress a second antipolygamy movement just as they had successfully dealt with the Gladdonites.

Of course, what most observers failed to realize was that Joseph Morris's opposition to plural marriage was qualified, not absolute. He did not approve of it as it was then practiced by the Mormons, but he did see it as a proper form of marriage within the appropriate context. Several of his followers were polygamists, including the worthy Bishop Cook, his first counselor. Nevertheless, the Morrisites had the image of being against polygamy and hence worthy of persecution from Brigham Young. In that respect they had the sympathy of many observers who abhorred the practice.[12]

But perhaps the biggest political issue in the Morrisite affair was how evenhanded the Mormons might be in dealing with apostates or Gentiles in Utah. The primary fear of the federal government seems to have been that the Mormons would allow religious law to take precedence over civil or criminal law whenever push came to shove. There can be no doubt that in the period before the Morrisite affair much federal policy toward the Mormons was predicated upon this fear. Whether justified or not, the "invasion" of Johnston's Army was for the purpose of reasserting federal control over Utah. And the concomitant discharge of Brigham Young as governor was clear evidence of that policy. Of course, the appointment of Gentile and often anti-Mormon judges was more of the same. At the same time, the Mountain Meadows affair of 1857 was seen as evidence that the Mormons would resort to any measures required to maintain their way of life. The Mountain Meadows affair had transpired while the Mormons were in political control of Utah, and it looked bad no matter who was directly responsible. Furthermore, the failure of the Mormons to take any corrective action against the perpetrators was not encouraging.

The Civil War, of course, focused the attention of the federal government upon vital matters closer to home, but the supposed duplicity of the Mormons was not forgotten. As soon as possible the government arranged for Colonel Connor to head a force of California volunteers to place the Mormons once more under federal surveillance and control.

Connor was a no-nonsense commander who came to Utah with the prime purpose of keeping the Mormons under control and contained if not loyal to the Union. If the federal government had really trusted the Mormons, there would have been no need for Connor's force at all, since many recruits and experienced officers were already available in the Nauvoo Legion.

Of course, by the time Colonel Connor and his force arrived in Utah in November 1862, the Morrisite War was over. Connor conferred at that time with Governor Harding, and they seem to have agreed perfectly upon three

12 It is of interest to note that Joseph Morris believed that Jesus Christ had only one companion (wife) in heaven, while God the Father had one hundred and forty-four thousand. Hence His need for many mansions. Morris, *The Spirit Prevails*, pp. 517, 610–12.

issues. One, the Morrisite War had been primarily a case of Mormon religious retribution. Two, the Mormons were basically disloyal and hoped for the defeat of the Union. And, three, a fort should be built overlooking Salt Lake City so there could be no question of federal military control.

After the Morrisite trial in the spring of 1863, Connor fully supported Harding's pardoning of those convicted and did everything possible to aid and support the Morrisites who needed assistance. Of course, Governor Harding ceased to be of much consequence in Utah politics after June 1863, but Connor rose to fame as an Indian fighter and mining promoter whose opinion carried weight for many years.

The actual role of the L.D.S. church in the Morrisite affair has been a matter of controversy, and little direct evidence linking the church or Brigham Young with it has been found. Judge Kinney claimed that he did not issue the writs until Young approved the action, but Young claimed to have remained aloof from the proceedings.

Nevertheless, with the exception of Kinney, all of the principles in the affair were Mormons. Acting Governor Fuller called out the posse, Robert T. Burton and his lieutenants were Mormons, and so were all of the posse members. Even those accused of harassment prior to the conflict (the most notable being Lot Smith) were Mormons. This, of course, supplied ample circumstantial evidence for those wishing to implicate the L.D.S. church. Whether justified or not, the Morrisite affair conjured up the image of a Mormon-Morrisite battle, with the Mormons coming off as the villains.

Furthermore, although not extensive, there is more than circumstantial evidence that Brigham Young held the defeated Morrisites in contempt and intended to punish them. For example, John Eardley declared: "Brigham Young, in the Tabernacle, shortly afterwards [after the battle] reminded the people that the Morrisites were now scattered among them and counseled them to have no dealings with them and not allow them to live in their houses. On every hand they met with disfavor and were told to leave the Territory."[13]

An even more telling indictment is recorded in the diary of Charles Lowell Walker, a faithful Mormon, whose father joined the Morrisites. On Sunday, June 29, 1862, just two weeks after the Weber battle, Walker wrote: "Went up to the Bowery. Got there rather late. Br Brigham Spoke on the principle of apostacy. Spoke of the clan that had been led by Morris and Banks. Showed their folly and wickedness; forbid any of the Elders of Israel to baptize any of them at their Peril. Said let them alone and let them wait a thousand years and then see what chance they will be for them. Forbid

13 Eardley, *Gems of Inspiration*, p. 31.

them coming into the congregation of the Saints. Said he would Kick them out if they came nigh him."[14]

This statement alone from Brigham Young would have given ample reason for many Mormons to shun the Morrisites both spiritually and temporally. Certainly the message was remarkably similar to the one he delivered to the Gladdonites a decade earlier.

When Governor Harding came to Utah, he sensed a feeling of disdain not only for himself but for the Union in general. This may or may not have been true, but he believed it and so did Colonel Connor. At worst, Harding and Connor saw a form of treason in the apparent indifference of the Mormons to the Civil War and in the convening of the ghost government of Deseret, which had elected Brigham Young to the office of governor in March 1863. At best they saw these things as marks of disrespect for the Union and for its local appointed officials. By the same token, the two men saw the Morrisite affair as a clear case of religious persecution at worst, and at best as the height of vulgar pettiness when juxtaposed against the life and death struggle of the Union government. Furthermore, they were well aware of the Mountain Meadows Massacre, which had occurred so recently, and they drew parallels between it and the Morrisite War. Perhaps in this regard the Morrisite War assumed greater significance than would appear at first glance. Whether justified or not, the Morrisite War was seen as the culmination of a series of incidents and events which seemed to demonstrate that the Mormons still required policing and imposed government. In short, the Morrisite affair was taken as clear evidence that the Mormons were not yet ready for self-government. It appeared that they were still unable to clearly distinguish between church and state and hence were unworthy of statehood.

If the Morrisite War had not occurred, would Utah still have been denied full self-government and statehood for more than thirty years? Perhaps so, but one thing is clear. The Morrisite War did nothing to enhance the popular image of the Mormon church and people. If those Mormons who participated in the Morrisite affair had shown more compassion and tolerance for those they considered duped, misguided, and even weak-minded, they would have demonstrated in a most convincing way that they were dedicated not only to evenhanded justice but to mercy as well. But they chose to exact the full letter of the law and thereby missed a prime opportunity to "let their light shine" before the Gentiles. Had they made the other choice they would have lost nothing religiously. And politically, they may have gained a great deal.

14. A. Karl Larson and Katherine Miles Larson, editors, *Diary of Charles Lowell Walker*, 2 vols. (Logan: Utah State University Pres, 1980), 1:232

Conclusion

Had Joseph Morris been allowed his preference in 1861, he would not have organized a church distinct from the one headed by Brigham Young, for he was first and foremost a Mormon, as were his followers. Despite the development of certain unique items of metaphysics and his premillennial orientation, Morris was almost as devoted to the memory of Joseph Smith as Young himself, and Morris's primary aspiration was to complete Smith's interrupted work by ushering in the Kingdom of God on earth. Morris and his followers were involved in tragedy, yet they were not in and of themselves completely tragic figures. Their ideology was optimistic, transcending, and dedicated to human perfectability. Great sacrifices were required, but even greater rewards were expected. Like their Brighamite counterparts, the Morrisites were willing to endure incredible hardships for the sake of a brighter future, and they never doubted that they were God's chosen people or that America was the promised land.

Like Mormons generally, they could identify with their leaders' strengths but could also overlook (or ignore) their weaknesses, at least as long as God seemed to be in command. This made it possible for them to exert heroic efforts and to sometimes succeed where success seemed hardly possible. And, of course, they sometimes failed where failure could have been avoided if aspirations had been more consistent with reality.

Like the Mormons, the Morrisites regarded heaven and all its inhabitants in anthropomorphic terms, and they expected to dwell eternally in a tangible kingdom in the presence of a tangible God. This expectation forged a concrete link between the events and circumstances of this life and the life hereafter, making each day a real and meaningful unit of eternity and giving rewards and punishments greater immediate relevance than is usual for more traditional Christendom. In other words, this life was seen as part and parcel of eternity. Consequently, death was not seen so much as an ending of this life as it was a continuation of that existence preceding this life, an existence which needed enrichment and vitalization through life upon the earth. Because of this, the death of Joseph Morris, while traumatic, was not completely devastating. Like Joseph Smith, Morris was seen as a martyr, and his work, now sanctified by his own blood, could be continued by someone else. Unfortunately, no Brigham Young was poised in the wings to carry on that work effectively.

Since the Morrisites saw each day as an integral part of eternity, they felt much more beholden to religious law than to civil law. Like the Mormons, they regarded civil law as a more or less temporary measure to be used only until the higher law could be made operative. Morris's insistence upon the superordinate position of religious law was, of course, the key to the confrontation with the posse, and he held out even unto death.

The Morrisites tried to do on a small scale what the Mormons had tried to do in larger terms. They brought their people together in a tight enclave, where indoctrination could be enhanced, where fellowship could be fostered, where control could be made more effective, and where external threats could be blunted, if not nullified. They made their religion not just a way of life, but life itself, with escape nearly impossible.

Since their entire system was based upon the conviction that Joseph Morris was a personal representative and spokesman for God, a centralized authority structure and unquestioning obedience were mandatory. At least in part, because of Brigham Young's considerable executive ability, the same model of leadership had proved to be highly effective for the Mormons. But because Morris and most of his would-be successors were deficient in that ability, that model had proved disastrous at Kington's Fort and contributed ultimately to the movement's demise. In any case, the Mormons had succeeded by recognizing that the material needs of a people must be met, but that divine Providence seldom precedes human effort—"that God helps them who help themselves." The Mormons had also learned that the demands of human governments must sometimes be obeyed, that discretion is sometimes the better part of valor. On the other hand, the Morrisites under Morris rejected these principles, but after his death perhaps most of his disciples emphasized them at the expense of more spiritual concerns.

On December 31, 1861, Joseph Morris had declared that "Christ will come tomorrow morning." Christ did not come, but the expectation of His imminent return was retained for several decades. The Doves expected Him to descend upon South Weber, Utah. Cainan prepared his followers for the Second Advent in Deer Lodge, Montana. William Davies brought forth two sons in Walla Walla, Washington, who were heralded as gods incarnate. Eventually, of course, the Morrisites ceased to look for Christ's imminent return and focused their attention upon more worldly pursuits. Their search for the millennium had ended, and in a few more decades their organization also came to an end.

No doubt it would have surprised the Morrisites to learn that a century after Cainan's death, another millennial group would seize upon his "City of the Great King" prophecy to bolster its claim that Jesus had made his appearance in Deer Lodge. Surely it would have surprised them even more to learn that Jesus was locked in a cell in the old Montana State Prison and that the prison was really the Temple of Ezekiel, as foretold by the holy scriptures. They might have been somewhat skeptical.

Perhaps the great irony for the followers of Morris, Williams, Dove, Davies, and Jensen is that they were all seeking and anticipating a time when there would be a thousand years of peace on the earth. Despite their hopes, dreams, and efforts and those of an untold number of similar groups, the world seems farther from achieving peace today than ever before.

At Dempsey Crossing, just south of Deer Lodge, the last edifice of the Morrisites stands silent and alone. In faded letters above its door is the simple inscription, "The Lord's House." It rests upon the very spot where Christ was once expected to make His Second Advent. It is a humble building, hardly fitting for a king and certainly as unimpressive as any sanctuary could be. It seems truly incongruous that such a modest structure could ever have been intended as the site of so grand and glorious an event. Yet there it stands in all its modesty, even ugliness, redeemed only by the recognition that beauty is, after all, a relative matter. No doubt it was the best that those pioneers could do. And perhaps they felt it did not compare too badly with the traditional site of His first appearance—a primitive stable in an obscure village called Bethlehem.

Bibliography

I Unpublished Materials

Bryant, Seth L. "Reviving the Millennial Kingdom: Mormons, Morrisites, and Massacre," Annual Meeting, John Whitmer Historical Association, Voree, Wisconsin,2008.

Chase, Neal. Press Release. 21 March 1991.

Missoula, Montana. Copies of Originals in Possession of C. LeRoy Anderson. Morrisite Papers, Files 1–7.

Rogers, Eric Paul, "The Morrisites and the Sociology of Religious Schism," Annual Meeting, John Whitmer Historical Association, Independence, Missouri, 2006.

Salt Lake City, Utah. Church of Jesus Christ of Latter-day Saints. Historical Department. Archives. Brigham Young Correspondence.

Salt Lake City, Utah. Church of Jesus Christ of Latter-day Saints. Historical Department. Archives. Niels Anderson to Joseph F. Smith, 3 March 1903.

Salt Lake City, Utah. Church of Jesus Christ of Latter-day Saints. Historical Department. Archives. Mark H. Forscutt Manuscript. "Sketch of Joseph Morris."

Salt Lake City, Utah. Church of Jesus Christ of Latter-day Saints. Historical Department. Archives. Journal History of the Church of Jesus Christ of Latter-day Saints, 1830–1872.

Salt Lake City, Utah. Church of Jesus Christ of Latter-day Saints. Historical Department. Archives. "A Short Sketch of the Genealogy and History of George Morris."

Salt Lake City, Utah. Church of Jesus Christ of Latter-day Saints. Historical Department. Archives. Journal of Wilford Woodruff.

Salt Lake City, Utah. University of Utah. Special Collections. Diary of Hans Olsen Magleby.

Salt Lake City, Utah. University of Utah. Special Collections. Journal of John L. Blyth, 1858–1863.

Salt Lake City, Utah. University of Utah. Special Collections. Pioneer Journal of Jacob Miller.

Washington, D.C. National Archives. General Records of the Department of Justice. Record Group 60. Chronological Files, Utah, Box 683. Sumner Howard, U.S. District Attorney, to Charles Devens, Attorney-General, 28 July 1877.

II Published Materials

Anderson, C. LeRoy. "The Scattered Morrisites." *Montana, the Magazine of Western History* 26 (October 1976) .

———, and Halford, Larry J. "The Mormons and the Morrisite War." *Montana, the Magazine of Western History* 24 (Winter 1974) .

Anderson, Nels. *Desert Saints: The Mormon Frontier in Utah.* Chicago: University of Chicago Press, 1942.

Anderson, Peter H. "The Wound that Never Healed." *Frontier Times* (July 1965).

Ardent. John. *Over the Wall of Oppression.* Self-published, 1995.

Arrington, Leonard J.; Fox, Feramorz Y.; and May, Dean L. *Building the City of God: Community and Cooperation among the Mormons.* Salt Lake City, Utah: Deseret Book Company, 1976.

Articles of Faith. San Francisco: Committee of the Firstborn, 1887.

Balch, Robert W., Gwenn Farnsworth, and Sue Watkins. "When the Bombs Drop: Reactions to Disconfirmed Prophecy in a Millennial Sect." *Sociological Perspectives.* 26, No. 2 (April 1983).

Balch, Robert W., John Domitrovich, Barbara Mahnke, Vanessa Morrison, "Fifteen Years of Failed Prophecy." In Thomas Robbins and Susan J. Palmer, editors. *Millennium, Messiahs, and Mayhem.* New York and London: Routledge Press, 1997.

Bancroft, Hubert Howe. *History of Utah 1540–1886.* Vol. 26. San Francisco: History Company, Publishers, 1890.

Banks, John. "A Document History of the Morrisites in Utah." B.A. thesis, University of Utah, 1909.

Barnard, Lula; Bybee, Faundy; and Walker, Lola. *Tosoiba.* Soda Springs, Idaho: Daughters of Utah Pioneers, 1958.

Bear, John L. "The Autobiography of John L. Bear." *Journal of History.* Lamoni, Iowa, 1911–12.

Beck, Martha. *Leaving the Saints.* New York: Crown Publishers, 2005.

Bigler, David L. *Forgotten Kingdom, The Mormon Theocracy in the American West.* Logan, Utah: Utah State University Press, 1988.

Blankenship, Russell. *And There Were Men.* New York: Alfred A. Knopf, 1942.

Bliss, Sylvester. *Memoirs of William Miller.* 1853. Reprint, New York: AMS Press, Inc., 1971.

Bringhurst, Newell G. and John C. Hamer, eds. *Scattering of the Saints Schism Within Mormonism.* Independence, Missouri: John Whitmer Book, 2007.

Brooklyn Eagle. 6 February, 1863.

Brodie, Fawn M. *No man knows my history: The Life of Joseph Smith.* 2d ed., rev. and enl. New York: Alfred A. Knopf, 1971.

Brooks, Juanita. *John Doyle Lee: Zealot, Pioneer Builder, Scapegoat.* Glendale, California: Arthur H. Clark Company, 1961.

Brown, Dee. *Bury My Heart at Wounded Knee.* Paperback ed. New York: Bantam Books, 1972.

Chase, Neal. *Ezekiel's Temple in Montana.* Self-published, 1990.

Cornelius, D. E. "Mormonism in Montana, 1857–1898." M.A. thesis, University of Montana, 1962.

Dobyns, Henry F., and Euler, Robert C. *The Ghost Dance of 1889 among the Pai Indians of Northwestern Arizona.* Prescott, Arizona: Prescott College Press, 1967.

The Doctrine and Covenants of the Church of Jesus Christ of Latter-day Saints. rev. ed. Salt Lake City, Utah: Church of Jesus Christ of Latter-day Saints, 1921.

Dove, George S., and Dove, James. *A Voice from the West.* San Francisco: Church of the Firstborn, 1879.

Dove, James. *A Few Items in the History of the Morrisites.* San Francisco: Church of the Firstborn, 1892.

Eardley, John R. *Gems of Inspiration: A Collection of Sublime Thoughts by Modern Prophets.* San Francisco: Joseph A. Dove, Printer, 1899.

Eliade, Mircea. "Paradise and Utopia." *Utopias and Utopian Thought.* Boston: Beacon Press, 1967.

Festinger, Leon; Riecken, Henry; and Schacter, Stanley. *When Prophecy Fails.* Paperback ed. New York: Harper and Row, 1964.

Fisher, Vardis. *The Children of God.* New York: Vanguard Press, 1939.

Foster, Lawrence. *Religions and Sexuality: The Shakers, the Mormons and the Oneida Community.* Urbana, Illinois: University of Illinois Press, 1984.

Halford, Larry J. "Mormons and Morrisites: A Study in the Sociology of Conflict." Ph.D. dissertation, University of Montana, 1972.

Harper's Magazine. New York: Harper's Magazine Foundation, February, 1995.

Hickman, Bill. *Brigham's Destroying Angel: Life Confessions and Startling Disclosures.* Salt Lake City: Shepard Book Company, 1904.

Holley, Val. "Slouching Toward Slaterville; Joseph Morris's Wide Swath in Weber County." *Utah Historical Quarterly,* July, 2008.

Holzapfel, Richard N. "The Flight of the Doves From Utah Mormonism to California Mormonism: The Saga of James and George Dove." In Launius, Roger D., and Linda Thatcher, eds. *Differing Visions, Dissenters In Mormon History.* Urbana and Chicago: University of Illinois Press, 1994.

Howard, G. M. "Men, Motives, and Misunderstandings: A New Look at the Morrisite War of 1862." *Utah Historical Quarterly* 44 (Spring 1976).

Jensen, Leland. *The Seventh Angel Sounded.* The Acme Press, Missoula, Montana, 1994.

Jenson, Andrew. *Latter-day Saint Biographical Encyclopedia.* 4 vols. Salt Lake City, Utah: Andrew Jenson History Company, 1901–36.

Krakauer, Jon. *Under the Banner of Heaven: A Story of Violent Faith.* New York: Doubleday, 2003.

Larson, A. Karl, and Larson, Katharine Miles, eds. *Diary of Charles Lowell Walker.* 2 vols. Logan, Utah State University Press, 1980.

Lee, John D. *Mormonism Unveiled: The Life and Confession of John D. Lee, Including the Life of Brigham Young.* 1877; Albuquerque: Fierra Blanca, 2001.

McKiernan, F. Mark. *The Voice of One Crying in the Wilderness*: Sidney Rigdon, Religious Reformer, 1793–1876. Lawrence, Kansas: Coronado Press, 1971.

Montana, the Magazine of Western History 25 (Winter 1975).

Morgan, Dale L., III. "A Bibliography of the Church of the Dispersion." *Western Humanities Review* 7 (Summer 1953).

Morris, Joseph. *The Spirit Prevails: Containing the Revelations, Articles, and Letters Written by Joseph Morris.* San Francisco: George S. Dove and Company, 1886.

Orwell, George. *Nineteen Eighty-Four.* New York: Harcourt, Brace and Company, Inc., 1949.

Pitzer, Donald E. *America's Communal Utopias.* Chapel Hill: The University of North Carolina Press, 1997.

Quinn, D. Michael. "To Whom Shall We Go, Historical Patterns of Restoration Believers With Serious Doubts." *Sunstone*, May, 2005.

Reid, Agnes Just. *Letters of Long Ago.* Tanner Trust Fund ed. Salt Lake City, Utah: University of Utah Library, 1973.

Roberts, Brigham H. *A Comprehensive History of the Church of Jesus Christ of Latter-day Saints.* 6 vols. Salt Lake City, Utah: Church Deseret News Press, 1930.

Rogers, Eric P. "Mark Hill Forscutt: Mormon Missionary, Morrisite Apostle, RLDS Minister." *John Whitmer Association Journal* 21 (2001): 61–90.

San Francisco Chronicle. 19 June 1892.

Seegmiller, Janet Burton. *Be Kind to the Poor: The Life History of Robert Taylor Burton.* Robert Taylor Burton Family Organization, Inc. 1988.

Smith, Joseph Fielding. *Essentials in Church History.* 13th ed. Salt Lake City, Utah: Deseret News Press, 1953.

Smith, Timothy L. *Revivalism and Social Reform: American Protestantism on the Eve of the Civil War.* New York: Harper and Row, 1965.

Soda Springs Sun, 11 June 1931.

Stenhouse, T. B. H. *Rocky Mountain Saints.* London: n.p., 1872.

Talmage, James E. Articles of Faith. Salt Lake City, Utah: Church of Jesus Christ of Latter-day Saints, 1956.

Thompson, Charles B. *The Laws and Covenants of Israel Written to Ephraim from Jehovah, the Mighty God of Jacob. Also Ephraim and Baneemy's Proclamations.* Preparation, Iowa: Zion's Presbytery, 1857.

Tuveson, Ernest Lee. *Redeemer Nation: The Idea of America's Millennial Role.* Chicago: University of Chicago Press, 1974.

Walker, Ronald, Richard E. Turley, and Glen M. Leonard. *Massacre At Mountain Meadows.* New York: Oxford University Press, 2008.

Young, Brigham, et al. *Journal of Discourses.* 26 vols. (London: Church of Jesus Christ of Latter-day Saints, 1853–86),

Young, Richard W. "The Morrisite War." *The Contributor* 11 (June 1890).

Index

About the Author

C. LeRoy Anderson is professor emeritus of the University of Montana, where he taught for thirty-three years. He also held professorial positions at Willamette University and the University of Arizona. He served as a faculty exchange fellow at Sophia University and Toyo University in Tokyo, Japan. He received his doctorate of sociology from the Ohio State University in 1962. At the University of Montana he served several terms as chair of the Sociology Department and several years as chair of the Asian Studies program.

Professor Anderson's research interests have ranged from the sociology of the family to American social movements and millenarian sects and the consequences of prophecy failure. In collaboration with his wife, Joanne R. Anderson, and Professor Yunosuke Ohkura of Toyo University, he edited and contributed to *No Longer Silent: World-wide Memories of the Children of World War II*, published in English and Japanese.

This edition of the story of the Morrisites is the result of more than four decades of study and research. Although the surname Anderson appears among the Morrisites, the author of this work is not related by blood or marriage to anyone within that movement. His interest in the Morrisites is purely scholarly.